All GROWN up

NURTURING RELATIONSHIPS
WITH ADULT CHILDREN

Celia Dodd

GREEN TREE
LONDON · OXFORD · NEW YORK · NEW DELHI · SYDNEY

GREEN TREE
Bloomsbury Publishing Plc
50 Bedford Square, London, WC1B 3DP, UK
29 Earlsfort Terrace, Dublin 2, Ireland

BLOOMSBURY, GREEN TREE and the Green Tree logo are trademarks
of Bloomsbury Publishing Plc

First published in Great Britain 2022

A catalogue record for this book is available from the British Library

Library of Congress Cataloguing-in-Publication data has been applied for

ISBN: TPB: 978-1-4729-8076-2; ePub: 978-1-4729-8077-9; ePDF: 978-1-4729-8078-6

2 4 6 8 10 9 7 5 3 1

Typeset in Adobe Garamond Pro by Deanta Global Publishing Services, Chennai, India
Printed and bound in Great Britain by CPI Group (UK) Ltd, Croydon CR0 4YY

To find out more about our authors and books visit www.bloomsbury.com
and sign up for our newsletters

For Paul, Adam and Alice

Contents

Introduction

The relationship between parents and their adult children is one of the most important in their lives and lasts far longer than the 20-odd years that it took them to grow up. It has a huge impact on well-being and how parents feel about themselves yet it gets remarkably little attention. The impression is that once children are grown up, the parents' job is done and the relationship becomes less significant. We know that this is nonsense, but parents are still left feeling horribly uncertain about the future when their children first leave home. From then on there's an assumption that the relationship will carry on – or not – of its own accord, without requiring much attention or effort from either side, and that advice or discussion is no longer needed.

Yet if popular drama is anything to go by, we're obsessed by relationships with adult children, whether it's *EastEnders* or *The Archers* or *King Lear* – not forgetting real people like the Kardashians and the Royal Family. It's an indication that people are looking for clues and reference points when negotiating relationships with their own adult children. That's borne out by the parents who share their experiences in this book. One mother whose son is in his forties summed it up perfectly: 'It wasn't the empty nest that was a problem for me, it was what came next in my relationship with my son that continues to be the challenge. Like any relationship, it changes all the time and it goes through definite stages. The empty nest itself goes through stages, it's fluctuating and progressive. But then marriage or partnership is a very different stage and when your child has children that is another very different stage. For me they were bigger transitions than the empty nest.'

There are times when parents feel at sea. Many parents I spoke to found the relationship puzzling and demanding. Parents' great love for their adult children is mixed with irritation, anxiety and all kinds of other emotions. One mother said, 'My son visited last night, nothing I can put my finger on, but I feel I have been run over today.' That rang a lot of bells with people I spoke to. An encounter with an adult child can be uplifting and life-enhancing, but it can also leave parents feeling undermined or even bruised, without quite knowing why. A child's raised eyebrow at a comment you've made, or a dismissive remark – theirs or yours – can leave you brooding for days.

These are complicated, delicate relationships, yet there's little acknowledgement that they require empathy, effort and skill, just as they did when children were growing up. Much more has been written about *being* an adult child than being the parent of one. Guidance on parenting adult children is largely restricted to major problems and dysfunction. If your adult child is estranged or stealing cash from your wallet, you can probably find a book to help, but there's little discussion of the everyday dilemmas and difficulties all parents face with their adult kids. That's why I wanted to write a book about the continuing connection as it ebbs and flows throughout our parallel lives and to focus attention not only on the crises and calamities (see Chapters 6 and 7), but also on the ordinary problems and anxieties that keep us awake at night.

Because no matter how old your child is, you will always be their mum or dad. And the old saying 'You're only as happy as your least happy child' remains true, whatever your child's age. With the increase in life expectancy, parents and children are now likely to share more time on the planet than ever before in human history: five or six decades has become run-of-the-mill. This is a big demographic change: it's estimated that one in four children born in 1900 had lost at least one parent by the age of 15, compared to one in 200 in the 1970s. These days, people like my 94-year-old mother-in-law, whose children are 67, 65 and 59, are not uncommon. Many parents of adult children now are also adult children themselves, yet it feels odd to refer to a retired 67-year-old – or indeed a 27-year-old – as a child or even an 'adult child'. It's a contradiction in terms and harks back to a phase of life when dependence was strictly one way.

Parents now often say they feel closer to their adult children than they did to their own parents. Marc Szydlik, Professor of Sociology at Zurich University, points to demographic changes, like increased life expectancy, that have both strengthened individual relationships between parents and adult children and added new layers of complexity. He believes that the trend towards smaller or single-child families has heightened the importance of parent-adult child relationships. Currently about 50 per cent of families in the UK have one child, and although official statistics don't take account of families who plan to have more children (or where older children have left home), the figures do indicate a trend towards smaller and single-child families. With fewer siblings and cousins, parents' attention and resources are more concentrated.

Meanwhile, economic pressures and instability in the job market force many young adults to stay connected to their parents. That's not necessarily the bad thing it's often made out to be. The boomerang generation not only fly the nest later, they may well spend most of their twenties moving in and out of home. They take longer to settle into a career and their own version of family life, with or without children, as the trend towards delaying marriage and having babies continues. These trends don't just have a big impact on the relationship during the emerging adult phase, but in the years to come too. Parents now are involved with their adult children in many different ways throughout their lives. Yet at the same time they're fit, healthy and keen to pursue their own separate interests.

So, it's not surprising that many parents feel ambivalent. After all, the relationship hinges on this central conundrum: how do you treat someone who was once utterly dependent on you like an independent adult? Many parents discover that they don't lose their primeval protectiveness, even with middle-aged offspring, yet at the same time they have to let go and allow children to make their own mistakes. Their role is to hover in the background, ready to provide a safety net, because adult children, whatever their age, still need support from time to time. Many parents have mixed feelings: they agonise about whether it's the right thing to do and feel torn about compromises to their own independence. Ambivalence also stems from the heady mix of conflict and love that characterises relationships with adult children. It is horribly uncomfortable when children make choices and express opinions that go against what parents hold dear, but there's not much you can do about it. The cards are stacked in the younger generation's favour: they don't have to do what you say, or have anything to do with you if they don't want to.

The phrase 'second-phase parenting' has been coined by academics to get away from the notion that a parent's job is done when children reach adulthood and acknowledges the important place that the bond occupies throughout people's lives. It allows us to see the relationship in a new light, as a lifelong connection that doesn't gutter like a candle when kids leave home, but continues to grow, change and develop. It also calls into question the assumption that independence and adulthood are synonymous. To some extent this reassessment has been prompted by the difficult economic circumstances that now shape young people's lives. Different cultural norms also influence our thinking, thanks partly to the rise in intercultural and interfaith marriage. In some cultures it's the norm for young adults to receive continuing support from their parents, just as adult children expect to look after their parents in old age. As a result, definitions of adulthood are slowly changing: teenagers are no longer expected to grow up overnight. Instead, the journey to adulthood is seen as a slower, developmental process that can take years, and hiccups along the way are to be expected. We increasingly buy into research that suggests that adult children can spread their wings more confidently, and be more independent, with the right kind of support – both emotional and practical – from their parents. It's less likely to be seen as failure if young adults live with their parents.

But this book is not only about emerging adults or the boomerang generation who live at home, although there are chapters devoted to both. It's also about the need for parents to take a long view of a relationship that will hopefully stay strong and keep evolving for many years and that makes big demands but also brings untold rewards. Adult children enrich their parents' lives in so many ways. They open windows into areas of life we would otherwise be unlikely to encounter; they introduce us to new worlds and fresh perspectives.

That's as long as parents stay flexible, open to change and willing to keep learning. Because nothing stays the same: events in the child's life make ripples and waves in their parents' lives, and vice versa. Again, it was the parents who shared their experiences in this book who brought this home to me. When I sent their quotes for approval some 18 months after we first spoke, many of them said how dramatically things had changed. Adult children who had seemed lost turned a corner, others fell in love, got sick, had babies, found a place of their own, went into therapy. The changes in parents' lives have an influence too: they downsize, divorce, find a new partner, retire. 'What's fascinating is that there's just no certainty,' says Renate, whose three children are in their twenties and thirties. 'When children are little it's an act of faith being a parent, you've no idea how it's going to turn out. I always thought that one day we would all arrive at a place and think, Oh, that's how it works out, but in fact we're still working it out.'

The Lifelong Connection

Being a parent of adult children feels so different from parenting younger kids that I'm not sure it should even be called 'parenting'. To me, it sounds too hands-on, too one-sided for a relationship that is more or less equal. 'Second-phase parenting', coined by academics, is something of a mouthful, but it hits the nail on the head. With parents now sharing as many as 70 years of the lifespan with their children, they need to take the long view. The relationship has to be recalibrated as it keeps evolving and moves in and out of different phases. Dr Myrna Gower, a family therapist and Honorary Research Fellow at Royal Holloway, University of London, says, 'There are several stages in parenting adult children: parenting emerging adult children; parenting middle-aged children and parenting older children. Parenting emerging adults is very different from parenting middle-aged children. My children are now in their forties and I can't relate to them in the way I did when they were in their twenties. It's a completely different phase of parenting. And it is determined by the age of the children, not by the parent's age.'

Dr Gower's view is that the idea of the empty nest can be misleading and often fails to represent the extent of the important contact between parents and adult children that continues throughout most of our lives. Perhaps it's not surprising that I disagree, having written a whole book on the empty nest! The parents who have told me about the huge impact it has had on their lives would also disagree. But Dr Gower makes an important point when she says that the empty nest is unhelpful because it carries a misplaced sense of a break in the relationship. The transition is framed as an ending, when in fact it's a change of gear, albeit a very dramatic one. She says, 'If there is no ongoing expectation that connectedness between adult children and their parents is a valued element of successful adults, how do we ever evolve together?'

Everyone agrees that things get more complicated when kids are adults. Helen, who has two daughters in their early twenties, told me, 'When you're facing the empty nest that is obviously the focus of your mind but little do you realise what the path ahead is going to require of you in terms of flexibility and adapting.' Kids can be distant one day, demanding the next. They say and do hurtful things. There's more at stake, because they can vote with their feet by choosing not to see you. The balance of power has shifted. From her research Dr Gower adds, 'Parents clearly reported that this relationship is principally based on the terms laid down by adult children. As parents we recognise this phenomenon (albeit with ongoing discomfort), as we renegotiate our expectations of children as they mature, carefully mindful of how much we value this attachment. We get a great deal out of this relationship. It feeds us in so many respects. It's rich, they're amazing, they keep us engaged, they keep us in touch with the world.'

That's one of the nicest surprises for parents who had expected the connection to weaken or even fizzle out when their child first left home. Most of the time being a parent of an adult child is really great. It's difficult and demanding, you still worry – sometimes you worry a lot – but when you stop being responsible for another person's daily care and safety, you can relax into a more equal relationship. In many ways having adult children is even better than what's gone before. OK, it might not be better than building sandcastles with a toddler, but it's certainly nicer than agonising about a teenager. Lucy, whose son and daughter are in their late twenties and both live at home, says, 'I think it's infinitely preferable to have adult kids than adolescents. In our case they're independent, they manage for themselves. And they care about us. They're very generous to us, very curious about us, very supportive. It's so much nicer because you don't get so tangled up with them. There's no emotional drag going on, or so much worry, or irritation – well, obviously there is occasional irritation and I'm sure that's mutual!' What's so special is that the toddler and the teenager are still present in your adult child and the way you were together back in the day continually shapes your relationship now. Celeste Ng's description of a mother looking at her nearly adult child in her bestselling novel *Little Fires Everywhere* is so apt: 'layered in her face was the baby she'd been and the child she'd become and the adult she would grow up to be, and you saw them all simultaneously, like a 3-D image.'

THE NEW CLOSENESS BETWEEN PARENTS AND CHILDREN

There's also a new closeness between the generations. A cynic might say it's just because young adults need their parents' financial backing in a way they didn't in the past. Clearly that has had an impact. But most of the adult children I spoke to value the continuing connection with their parents highly. They're proactive about seeing them because they enjoy their company, not out of duty or because they want something. Meanwhile, the balance of support is constantly shifting. Adult children give their parents good advice and support as well as vice versa and it's possible to have grown-up conversations about all kinds of things. You can't be friends with a teenager, but you can be friends with an adult child – although there will always be an extra dimension. Theresa, a single mother of four children in their twenties and thirties, says, 'I used to only be a parent. Now I can be friends with the children much more than before. You can't be friends until you've done the parent bit for a long time. It's lovely to have got to that stage.'

Marc Szydlik, Professor of Sociology at Zurich University, points to the demographic changes that lie behind this new closeness and the growing importance of intergenerational relationships within individual families. Increased longevity is part of it, while the trend towards smaller families, with fewer siblings and cousins, has heightened the significance of parent-child relationships. Professor Szydlik's research, published in 2016, found evidence of increased family solidarity all over Europe. And contrary to all the hype about intergenerational spats between 'snowflakes' – over-sensitive millennials – and baby boomers – the supposedly well-off, selfish, post-war generation of parents – only 5 per cent of the families he studied spoke of frequent conflict. It seems that these dismissive stereotypes don't hold much water within individual families.

Steve, who has a married daughter in her early thirties, two grandchildren and a son in his late twenties, says, 'I really like the relationship I've got with both my kids now; it's great watching them grow as adults. I like the fact that we're having much more adult conversations. It's less of a parent-child relationship and more equal; the fierce protectiveness I felt for them when they were young has diminished. I learn a lot from them both. Last week Sean and I were sitting in the garden talking about life and work and marriage, and I thought, you've got a wisdom way beyond your years. He's very laid-back in a way that I sometimes haven't been. It makes me think I could take a leaf out of his book, and just relax a bit more into stuff. I didn't have that kind of relationship with my dad; we weren't open with each other, and he certainly never hugged me. But I think that's just the way society was in the 1950s.'

This openness to keep changing and learning – not least from our kids – is important. It's a mistake to get stuck in the past, with ideas about what children used to be like and how the relationship used to be. The classic is when a mother says, 'I've made your favourite – gazpacho,' and her son says, 'What are you talking about? I hate gazpacho!' Parents need to keep up with the changes in their children's lives, interests and tastes, and alert to the subtle shifts in the dynamics between them. The family therapist Judith Lask says, 'The best relationships have a developmental trend to them. They adapt as the needs of the relationship and the needs of the family or circumstances change. If you get stuck in a particular relationship it can be difficult. My grandmother had ten children, eight of them boys. Right up until she was in her eighties and they were in their fifties and sixties she treated them as if they were children, and they acted as if they were children. In consequence they did not all give her the help and support she needed in her older age.' Equally, children need to be open to the way their parents keep changing. It's part of growing up to accept parents, warts and all, and make allowances for difficult circumstances. Rather than jumping to the kind of unforgiving judgements teenagers often make, children's views in adulthood tend to be softer and more nuanced.

PARENTS' INFLUENCE DIMINISHES

Key to the evolving relationship is accepting that your influence as a parent is waning. It's a process that started in childhood and gained momentum in adolescence, but it still takes some getting used to. Friends, partners and the prevailing zeitgeist all jostle with parents for influence on an individual's values, ambitions, career, political views, where they live, what they eat, how they spend their spare time. Upbringing is only one part of the jigsaw, although hopefully it provides the same kind of reliable growth medium as humus-rich compost, its nourishment ingrained at the roots.

Parents are often taken aback when their adult children behave in ways that don't chime with values they hold dear. They can make parents feel past it and irrelevant. You can't tell adult children what to do any more, although most parents find subtler ways to express their disapproval. An adult child's stance has more solidity than transient teenage rebellion. One father described how, when his son was 19 or 20 and they argued about conspiracy theories or capitalism, they both still came away feeling that ultimately, Dad knew best. That is no longer the case now that the son is in his thirties.

It's particularly disconcerting when this first happens. The best parents can do is respect their children's ideas and preferences, otherwise the danger is that communication shuts down. However, they don't have to agree. Helen says, 'My daughter is becoming a different person. She's very passionate about the different causes she espouses – currently veganism. So something new has become very important to the child that as a parent you've had no input into. Whereas in a way, when they're younger, you facilitate their interests.'

It's equally upsetting when they disapprove of you, whether it's how much you drink or your views on trans rights or your love life. Again, this isn't the same as teen outrage. It's a weightier assertion of a different viewpoint from someone who is very much their own person. You might notice it more when they're in their twenties, but it's just as likely when kids are middle-aged. Children have an unerring sense of knowing how to push their parents' buttons: even a jokey or throwaway remark cuts to the quick. Of course, it works both ways. Throughout your lives you continue to have a huge emotional impact on each other. What you do, say and think of each other matters more than you expect. Dr Myrna Gower explains, 'We don't want to disagree with our adult children; we want them to think like we do. Yet we don't always like what they do and what they say: who they partner with, how they spend their money, the colour they paint their houses, how they parent… it just goes on! And when *they* disapprove of *us*, it's so painful, it's agony – even the littlest thing is painful. There is this ambivalence between us and our kids that makes the relationship very difficult for us as parents. That's why it's so important to normalise this ambivalence.'

It was a real lightbulb moment when first Dr Gower and then one of the mothers I interviewed brought up this notion of ambivalence: the complicated mixture of feelings parents often have about their adult children, and the sense of feeling torn in different directions. It makes so much sense to me. You want to help if they ask, but at the same time you want to get on with your own life; you want to let go but the connection exerts a powerful pull. You want to treat your son like an adult, but on some level he will always be the baby whose nappy you used to change. Renate, who has a son and two daughters in their twenties and thirties, says, 'I feel more ambivalent as my children become more independent and in charge of their own lives. If they have the same expectations of me that they had when they were more dependent I feel a very strong resistance. One example is if they phone and don't check that it's a good time for me to talk. But the ambivalence is not just around them, it's about what I want too.'

Research suggests that the closer the relationship, the greater the feelings of ambivalence. And since mothers tend to be closer to their children, they often feel more ambivalent than fathers. Similarly, daughters often feel more ambivalent than sons, who are more likely to simply keep their distance if they have negative feelings. Ambivalent feelings often come to the fore during transitions that affect both parent and child, such as marriage and leaving home. And it seems that mothers feel more ambivalent towards adult children who haven't yet established independent lives.

STAGES AND MILESTONES OF ADULTHOOD

I. The transition to adulthood

The transition to adulthood is a joint enterprise between parents and their children that gains momentum in the years before they leave home, when they are teenagers or even younger. Parents facilitate self-sufficiency in all kinds of everyday ways, by encouraging their children to cook, or ride a bike to school, or learn to drive, or open a bank account. They can nurture emotional resilience by helping their children to understand that it's normal to feel out of sync and a bit sad during transitions, such as changing jobs or moving house or leaving home, and encouraging them to talk about how they feel. Growing up in a family where people are honest when they've had a bad day, rather than either pretending everything's lovely or being a drama queen, is a good grounding. Dr Ruth Caleb, an expert in young people's mental health and well-being, has this advice: 'By being authentic about their own feelings parents encourage children to be authentic about theirs. They need to know that it's a strength, not a weakness, to ask for help. It's also critical that they are able to enjoy their own company, by finding a hobby or pastime they enjoy doing alone; so many young people find their own company challenging and seek the constant company of friends, often online, rather than enjoying their personal interests.'

All the time parents are there, hovering on the sidelines in case their teenager needs help. As children gradually need less support and become more self-sufficient in different areas of life, so parents' confidence in their abilities grows. More subtly, parents are also adjusting to their own changing role in relation to their child and learning to step back. Dr Myrna Gower explains, 'In the teenage years the relationship with the child begins to transition into something different and requires adjustments to our parenting. Similarly our parenting in relationship with emerging adult children does not happen one day after the other. This stage of parenting happens over a long period of time. The rather old-fashioned empty nest idea is that you parent your children like children over whom you've got all this influence, then they leave home and it's gone. The absurdity of this idea is in our lived evidence that it rarely happens that way. There is huge preparation as we move from the dependence of childhood towards adolescence and then towards emerging adulthood. It is rehearsed way before children leave home, and it most certainly doesn't happen overnight. It is developmental, so that there is a way in which emerging adults begin to get more confidence in how they manage themselves and the evolving and important ongoing connectedness to their parents.'

2. Emerging adulthood (ages 18–29)

When emerging adulthood (see also Chapter 2) was first identified as a distinct phase 20-odd years ago by the American psychologist Jeffrey Arnett, it was thought to end at around the age of 25. He now recognises that it can take up the whole of people's twenties. This is an acknowledgement that this stage is rarely smooth, but is increasingly peppered by hiccups and obstacles. The growing acceptance that it's perfectly usual to stumble or change direction is a big step forward. It allows parents to offer support if it's needed without either parent or child feeling like a failure.

Emerging adulthood has three phases: leaving home for the first time, the years after university or training and moving back home. These are explored in greater detail in Chapters 2 and 5.

• Leaving home for the first time

When a child leaves home for the first time at 18 or 19, whether it's to go to work or university or on a gap year, it's not uncommon for parents to feel their child is still their baby and that they're not ready for them to leave. In fact, of course, they've been growing into adults, with or without their parents' help, for years. By the first visit home they're already aware that their child is different, more grown-up. Phoebe, who is now 25, remembers, 'My dad always said that every time I came home from university, I was different. He noticed something I wasn't aware of.' Liam, also 25, felt it strongly himself: 'Every time I came home from university, I felt I was changing more and more. I came back a different person.'

At the same time that parents are getting used to seeing their children in a more adult light, they have to adjust to their own new role – and their new identity – as parents of adult children. At times it feels like an emotional rollercoaster: things go quiet for ages and then suddenly kids need help. When you're least expecting it, a phone call comes out of the blue about some disaster, such as a lost passport or a broken boiler. It's all part of the process, according to Dr Myrna Gower: 'You've got to get used to bailing your children out by being there when they call for help and often having to grit your teeth when they think and do things with which you may not agree. That is the beginnings of recognising your evolving relationship with your emerging adult children.'

- The years after university or training

A wise headteacher once compared the transition to working life to whitewater rafting and it's so true. The escalator ride from school to university is so straightforward that it's almost like being on automatic pilot: if pupils are bright and put in the hours, they'll jump the hurdles and achieve their goals. But everything changes in the years after graduation. For current generations of young adults this phase is characterised by uncertainty and turbulence, and it brings all kinds of challenges for young people and their parents. The straightforward bargains of reward for effort disappear; a good degree doesn't guarantee a foot on the career ladder. The gig economy (where organisations rely more on freelancers and independent workers than permanent staff) has brought flexibility, and in some ways that's welcome, but short-term contracts make the working world less stable and jobs insecure. There are fewer financial safety nets if people get sick or can't get work. It's hardly surprising that this is the time when many young people struggle, now more than ever before, and that parents' support is often needed.

- Living with parents

Living at home with parents (see also Chapter 5) has become the new normal for young adults and research indicates that the trend is here to stay. According to a recent study by Loughborough University, the number of young single adults who have either never left home, or who have moved back in with their parents, has grown by a third over the past decade to a staggering two-thirds of single 20–34-year-olds in the UK. Some spend the best part of a decade of their young adulthood living at home.

Yet some young adults – and their parents – still see this as a bit of a failure. After the heady freedoms of the student bubble it can feel like coming back to earth with a thud. Some kids like it, some lump it and of course that has a lot to do with how well they get on with their parents and where their parents live. And it's undeniable that living at home can restrict young people's choices, and that can be a real disadvantage.

Meanwhile, many parents feel something's not quite right if their kids haven't been successfully launched, and that they haven't 'let go' in the way they feel parents are supposed to. That's partly because, rightly or wrongly, parents often feel kids aren't fully adult if they are still living at home. The belief persists that independence happens overnight and that there are certain milestones young adults ought to achieve by a certain age. It's a bit like when they were babies and there's so much anxiety and comparing notes about where your little one is on developmental centiles. In fact, it comes down to individual circumstances and personalities and that's why comparisons with peers are so unhelpful. A different approach, which views independence as the gradual process it really is, allows parents to celebrate positive progress with their kids and avoid seeing everything through a lens of failure.

The period when adult kids move in and out of the family home may last several years. Even when they seem to be settled, they may come back if they're unemployed, or having the builders in, or they've split up with their partner. Parents understandably feel ambivalent – they want to be supportive, they'd feel churlish if they said no, they love their adult children's company, but they would also like to move on in their own lives. They feel they've gone beyond making compromises to accommodate their children's needs. Several studies have shown a significant decline in parents' well-being when their adult children move back home. But ultimately it has to be said that most parents find that living with adult kids, whatever their age, brings huge rewards too. Mixed feelings are par for the course.

3. Late twenties/early thirties: settling down

For some people everything falls into place in their early twenties, only to unravel further down the line. Dissatisfaction often creeps in when the euphoria of getting that first job and holding it down begins to wear off. As people move up the career ladder excitement gives way to the question: is this really how I want to spend the rest of my life? In the late twenties and early thirties it's not unusual to look for a change of direction, which may involve retraining or perhaps a period of unemployment. If that's the case, parental support is a boon.

If children have been living at home, it's often a bit of a relief when they leave for good, even if you enjoyed their company. Now both your lives can move on and your relationship has a better chance of changing direction. One mother said it felt 'developmentally appropriate'. Within weeks of her 28-year-old son moving out, Angie noticed a big difference and a new equality: 'Every time he rings, he sounds older. At first the calls were what do I do about council tax and how do you make carbonara. Now he asks much more about us, what we've been up to and how we are. My husband's sister-in-law died a few months ago and he was concerned about how his dad was feeling in a way he just wouldn't have been in the past.'

Increasingly, parents give their children financial help with rent or to get a foot on the housing ladder. In 2020, nearly one in four property purchases relied on help from the bank of Mum and Dad, an increase from nearly one in five during the previous year, according to a survey by Legal & General. Parents also help with the stressful legal admin of buying a place, as well as the whole palaver of moving: helping to put up shelves and letting the Virgin Media engineer in.

There is huge satisfaction in seeing your child settle into a place that feels like their home. Yet there is finality too in knowing that this time they really have left for good and from now on, this is how life is going to be. It sets the final seal on the end of an era, and that's sad for parents even though they share their child's excitement and optimism. There is also something poignant about your child creating their own version of home – which may be very different from yours – and knowing that's where their emotional future is invested. That's surely why parents press furniture and kitchen equipment on to their departing child: it feels like a symbolic connection.

It goes with a new rhythm in the relationship. There's a feeling that life is moving into a calmer rhythm generally. Paying rent or a mortgage is a sobering experience, quite literally. That doesn't stop parents worrying. And their support is still needed, but less often. Adult children find other sources of support: from partners, siblings, friends. Sensible parents know when to back off when they're not needed, even if they're hovering in the wings. Paul, whose three daughters are 34, 32 and 29, says, 'Financially they're totally self-sufficient. I'm very proud to say they earn more than I do. People don't get it but to me, I've succeeded as a father if my daughters drive brand-new cars while I drive a beat-up one. And they are much more likely to go to each other for advice than come to us. They know that they've only got to ask and we'll be there.'

4. The first long-term relationship or marriage

When your child embarks on their first serious relationship – whether they get married or not – it's a major milestone in both your lives that has a profound impact on the way you get on (see also Chapter 10). That's true whether you like the new person or fear that your child is making a big mistake. Either way, it's likely to give rise to mixed emotions: you're happy that they've found someone who loves them, but sad that the emotional landscape of your relationship has changed and concerned about the implications of such a big step, both for them and for you. Parents often feel that something has been lost and that's borne out by studies indicating that relationships with parents become less intense with less contact and less financial, emotional and practical support.

In many cultures marriage is seen as a marker of adulthood. It's an indication of the sense of emotional letting go that many parents feel, almost like handing on the baton of care to the child's partner.

5. When children become parents

What's fascinating about the birth of a baby – quite apart from the baby itself – is the way it changes your relationship with your child (see also Chapter 11). For a start there's the sheer mind-boggling awesomeness of the fact that your baby has had a baby. It's such an everyday event and yet totally miraculous to the individual family. As the legendary Rolling Stone Keith Richards once put it: 'When you see offspring of offspring, something else hits home.'

A baby brings a family together, as siblings become doting aunts and uncles. It draws adult children closer to their parents and gives them a new appreciation of what it means to be a parent. That's usual in the early days at least, but as babies grow into children, so does the potential for tension. There are so many areas of possible disagreement – routines, breast or bottle, childcare – and of course it makes a massive difference whether it's your son's baby or your daughter's. Once your child has their own separate family unit, parents have to work out what their role is in relation to it. Many parents I spoke to singled this out as the biggest and most challenging change in their relationship with their adult child.

6. The balance keeps shifting: children support their parents

Adult children can be supportive, as long as parents can concede that they no longer know best (see also Chapter 7). They are a good sounding board about all sorts of things. One successful novelist I interviewed always sends her son her first drafts because she values his judgement more than anyone else's. Some kids know a lot about something particular, like cars or tech or travelling in the Far East. Others are just wise, calm, sensible and objective. Adult children who have been through tough times themselves can offer invaluable emotional support. When Tania's mother had a massive row with her sister, Tania was there for her and their roles were reversed: 'I probably became the parent over it a bit,' she says. 'I was quite forthright, going on about how I had dealt with a toxic relationship myself. I wonder if sometimes she wished I would quieten down about it! But what it did do was enable us to talk and that didn't happen during our childhood.' The new closeness Tania talks about seems common; there's something about accepting an adult child's help that takes things on to a deeper level. The intensity may pass, but the impact on the relationship is lasting.

In many cultures parent-child relationships are based on a greater mutual expectation of support than is usual in the West. In traditional Chinese families, for example, children take their duty to support and assist their parents very seriously, just as parents' duty is to rear and educate their children. In many countries it's much more common for elderly parents to live with their adult children than it is in the UK, but even in Britain the support adult children give parents increases as the years go on, until the balance finally tips in old age: a prospect that most of us see as unwelcome.

One of the unnerving repercussions of the COVID-19 pandemic has been the way it transformed adult kids' attitudes to their parents overnight. Suddenly they were as concerned about our health and well-being as we have always been about theirs. Many parents – myself included! – found this sudden role reversal disconcerting: people in their sixties got ticked off for drinking in gardens with friends, or banned from going to the shops. One mother who lives alone says, 'I don't like the idea of being looked after. I'm the one who looks after people.' When the first UK lockdown was imminent, she decided against moving in with her boyfriend because she wanted to be on hand for her children and grandchildren, and he lives two hours' drive away. She was taken aback when the kids said she should leave: 'I'm the mum, I wanted to look after them if anything happened but suddenly I was no longer in that role. They're the ones in the caring role and it was clear that it was easier for them if I left. It's a big change in the relationship and I found it quite upsetting.'

WHAT INFLUENCES YOUR RELATIONSHIP WITH YOUR ADULT CHILD?

Over the years the relationship with adult children naturally ebbs and flows. External circumstances, like where you live and how busy you are, draw you closer or apart from each other. People move away from their parents for all kinds of reasons. An adult child falls in love with someone who lives at the opposite end of the country, or gets a job on the other side of the world. Some kids actively want to put physical distance between themselves and their families, particularly when they're first establishing a separate life. Moving into a different cultural context adds a new dimension and complexity to the relationship with parents.

There are many other things that form a complex web of influences. Some are firmly in the past but continue to shape the present, such as the way you brought your child up and how you interacted with each other when they were teenagers, the number of children in the family, the things you wish you'd done differently. When your child is an adult, each change you both go through in your parallel personal development resonates across the relationship. Underpinning it all are your own experiences of being an adult child.

Your child's upbringing

The quality of the attachment between parent and adult child has its roots in childhood. The influential psychologist John Bowlby believed that the emotional bonds between child and caregiver have an impact throughout life. The more secure you both feel, the more independent you can be, because you both know that although the connection will go through changes, deep down it is solid and cannot be threatened by distance or other relationships. Family therapist Judith Lask says, 'Attachment is always at the heart of relationships with adult children. Generally the more secure the attachment, the better things go from all sides.'

We all aim to raise adults who feel secure, but circumstances can get in the way. Steve's wife left the family when his daughter was 12 (she is now 31). Steve says, 'I would like to think I've been a rock in both my kids' lives, a constant. But not long ago, Samantha and I were having a chat and she said, "If your mum leaves you, then anybody can leave you." And I said, "Let's have a reality check here. *I* haven't left you, and there is only one way I'm ever going to leave you and that's when I stop breathing." It's trying to instil the mindset that there are people who will be with you forever.'

Most parents angst about what they got wrong when their children were younger and play down the positive grounding they've given them. They beat themselves up for not playing with them more, or being distracted by work or personal problems. Yet the incidents that stick out in parents' minds may not be the same as the childhood grievances their adult children hold on to: *you made me have my hair cut like a pixie, you sent me to the wrong school, you always preferred Sarah*. Some children keep things to themselves and find their voice as adults.

No one can change the past, but acknowledging and trying to understand what went awry is a step forward. As a consultant family therapist and Director of the London Intercultural Couples Centre at the Child and Family Practice, Dr Reenee Singh helps adult families deal with childhood experiences that continue to cause problems. She finds that the impetus for change usually comes from adult children, often after they've been in therapy on their own. It's painful for parents too. She says, 'There must be something so hard about hearing your adult child's pain and feeling blamed and criticised; it doesn't help that adult children can say things in such biting and attacking ways. Parents can feel hurt and indignant when children complain about their own experiences, because they feel they were just doing their best, often in difficult circumstances. When parents are struggling with our own issues, whether they're with our partners or our own parents, we get so caught up that often we don't have the bandwidth to attend to our children's emotional experiences. Often parents don't have a clue about what their child went through, partly because the child hasn't been able to talk to them about it.

'As a therapist I've learnt how important it is simply to make that space for the adult child to say, "It was really awful for me when you did or said..." Parents really need to slow down and listen. At the same time the parent needs to be affirmed for the fact that they were doing their best in a difficult situation, and that it's not their fault.'

When parents have lost their own parents they become more aware of the importance of clearing the air; regret at the things that didn't get said or done often runs deep. It was during a month-long Buddhist retreat that it struck Steve that he wanted to be sure his son and daughter did not harbour any misunderstandings from childhood, particularly about his divorce from their mother. The time felt right: as adults, they would have a better understanding of life's complexities: 'As you get older, you realise just how important your influence is when the children are very young, and how it can affect them when they're adults. I've become more aware of things I might have done or said that could be misinterpreted by a child – the sort of throwaway remarks I still remember from my own childhood. I wanted to apologise if there was anything I had said, and explain that I didn't mean to cause offence or hurt.

'When I was at the monastery, the thought came to me that you should never leave anything unsaid with your kids. When I got back, I talked to each of them separately. I told them that if they'd been hurt by anything that I had ever said or done, or if they had any questions about the divorce, they should ask me. So that they didn't just interpret things but got my version as well, because that might help them understand what was going on in my head at the time.

'Something deeply personal did come out – completely out of the blue – that happened 20 years ago. It was something my ex-wife said I had done that I hadn't. I was able to say, actually it wasn't this way, and you've got to understand that at the time feelings were running high. Whether that resonates with them, I don't know. But at least by just opening up that dialogue there's no room for doubt.'

Changes in both your lives now

Changes in adult children's lives clearly have a big impact on their parents, but it works both ways. Significant events and transitions that both parent and child go through ripple across the relationship. People marry or move to another country or join Extinction Rebellion or take up a new religion or get sick. And while we tend to think it's adult children's lives that keep changing, parents' lives can change just as much. People are living longer, healthier lives, they've still got plenty of energy to take up new challenges. This stage offers rich opportunities to explore a different side of life.

When their children leave home it's very common for parents to find different kinds of work, new interests, new relationships. Volunteering gives a whole new perspective. Since Brenda retired, she has volunteered for her local mental health trust and that's made her question her own thinking about mental illness. This in turn led to a new understanding with her son and her daughter-in-law, who opened up about her own mental health issues in a way that she would not have done in the past: 'I didn't know until recently that Allison has had several spells of therapy. I don't think she or my son would have shared it with me if I hadn't been with the mental health trust, because they would have thought I'd be judgemental – and I probably would have been. For the same reason I don't think they would have included me when their son needed extra help because he may be borderline autistic.'

The crises and turning points that puncture both your lives often bring families closer: illness, infertility, redundancy, stress at work, divorce, retirement, bereavement. You connect emotionally in a more intense way as you support each other. You speak more frequently and communicate at a deeper level. The intensity may pass, but the impact on the relationship endures. Both sides learn from the experience and develop greater resilience. Adult children can be a big help when parents are having problems, as well as the other way round. Their understanding of their parents, and the situations they face, grows. They're less prone to demonise or worship them; many young people say they first felt like adults when their eyes were opened to their parents' flaws and mistakes. As they wrestle with the complexities of their own lives, they come to view their parents' behaviour in a kinder light. For example, a 22-year-old who refuses to speak to his father after a messy divorce might be more empathetic in his thirties and forties.

The turning points of middle age and beyond, such as the empty nest, retirement, the menopause and the death of elderly parents, naturally prompt people to question their priorities in life and search for new meaning. They are increasingly open to try new practices, like meditation or yoga, that change their outlook on life. It's no longer considered too late for therapy or counselling, whatever your age. Above all, there's a growing recognition that people never stop developing or learning. Renate says, 'More and more, I feel that if your nature is to keep growing and challenging and looking at yourself, and if you're awake to what your issues are, that process never really stops. You never reach a point where you feel your child is cooked and you're cooked.'

In his fifties Renate's husband had three years of therapy that had a profound impact on his relationship with their three adult children. Renate remembers, 'When the kids were young, I was much more aware of their emotional life than Martyn and they talked to me more. But now Martyn has very consciously made it clear that he's available to them, and that's partly because he's had therapy, so he's in a different space. Now they're just as likely to call him as me.'

Your own experiences of being an adult child

We can learn a lot from our own experiences of being adult children, both now, if our parents are still alive, and in the past: they're a natural reference point.

Having adult children has made me think about how I treated my widowed mother when I was the age they are now: 29, 34 and 36. It's a bit sobering, to be honest, and I know that a lot of my friends feel the same. I didn't think about her feelings as much as I expect my three to consider mine; I just took her good humour as a given. When I first left home I rarely got in touch and inevitably made choices that gave her grief or made her anxious. When I spoke to Dr Myrna Gower for this book, she made me reflect further on the version of my young adulthood I had always told myself: that I left home without a second glance because my parents expected me to be totally independent. On reflection, that's rubbish! They didn't pressurise me to separate and they would have been happy to support me. Sadly, my mum died 15 years ago, so I can't ask how things were for her.

If your parents are still alive, you can keep gaining fresh insights from your relationship with them that illuminate your relationship with your own children now. It's one advantage of being part of the generation sandwiched between adult children on one side and our own parents on the other. Renate, whose parents are in their eighties, while she is in her sixties and her kids are in their twenties and thirties, says, 'Being around my parents as an adult myself over the past 40 years, as well as seeing aspects of my parents in my children, has helped me understand the challenges I've had with my son and daughters, as well as the challenges I've had with my parents. That then also informs how I am with my adult children.'

People often say they don't want to repeat the mistakes their parents made and that's as true with adult children as when they're growing up. But it's not just about mistakes. It is equally helpful to notice patterns of behaviour and the ambivalence you often feel: you love your kids, but sometimes they drive you bonkers (and vice versa, of course!). Family therapist Dr Myrna Gower believes it is vital for parents to reflect on their own experiences as adult children: 'When you think of yourself as an adult child, and all the compromises you have made, it will immediately put you in touch with the fact that it's not all about parents' compromises. This is an important relationship that is constantly building and makes new demands on both parents and adult children.

'It's very sad when parents die young and you hear their adult children, who are parents themselves, say they missed out this part of family life and find it very hard to reflect on how to best parent their emerging adult children. Maybe you could say that sometimes that gives them a freedom to design their own family scripts, rather than those of us who have overarching narratives to live by or to edit. However, in my practice, where parents have no guidelines from their own experience about how to be a parent of adults, they acknowledge being at sea and they tend to resort to earlier styles of instructive interaction with their children, leading to lots of conflict.'

2

Emerging Adulthood

This chapter focuses on twenty-somethings who are trying to find their place in the world, whether or not they go to university. It's surely significant that this age group now has its own label. 'Emerging Adulthood' is now recognised as a distinct stage in people's lives; there is even an international academic organisation devoted to its study called the Society for the Study of Emerging Adulthood (SSEA). Teenagers are no longer expected to spring from dependent adolescence into fully fledged independent adulthood overnight; these days, it's generally accepted that it's a gradual process between the ages of 18 and 29. It goes without saying that it is a gradual process for parents too. Ideally, they're an unobtrusive background presence, ready to step in if support is needed.

The threshold between graduating and getting a foothold in the world of work, and taking on adult responsibilities, lasts far longer than it did for previous generations. It's generally put down to the job market, property prices and rising interest on student loans, but there are other factors. Some kids just take longer than others to work out what they want to do with their lives. There are often hiccups and glitches along the way. Living at home has become more acceptable: one recent study found that 71 per cent of people in their early twenties live at home. Besides, being adult no longer has the cachet it once had: youth is what we all aspire to now. The increase in life expectancy means that time is on the side of young adults, while fertility treatment has had an influence too. It's become common to delay starting a family until the late thirties or forties, with the average age for first-time mothers 28.9 in 2019, according to the Office for National Statistics (ONS) – five years older than in 1970, when it was 23.7.

Parents are unsure what to make of the long and winding road to independence because it's so different to what they did themselves. As a result, they often give mixed messages. Some adopt a sympathetic but slightly patronising 'poor you' attitude, while others dismiss their kids' generation as a bunch of self-indulgent snowflakes. They veer between acknowledging how tough it is for young people now and saying 'When I was your age…' It's not hard to imagine how irritating that must be, but it is hard not to say it! While personal experience is a natural reference point, experts agree that it's better to try to put yourself in your child's shoes, by being curious about what it's like to be twenty-something now, not 30 years ago.

If parents want to be genuinely supportive they need to understand just how different life is for young adults today. This involves thinking about what independence and being adult mean, and whether they are as synonymous as we generally assume. Is a 28-year-old who lives at home an adult? Lucy, quoted later in this chapter, clearly thinks so. Is a 30-year-old who gets a loan from his parents to retrain or buy a car an adult? Again, the answer is probably yes. It seems that independence might not be such a reliable marker of adulthood after all.

Dr Myrna Gower, who researches relationships between adult children and their parents, believes that parents could be less anxious about independence, or what they see as the apparent lack of it, and refocus instead on how to build the important connectedness with adult children as they go forward in their own lives. One mother in Dr Gower's research describes her twenty-something children as 'not so dependent' rather than 'independent'. That seems like a better way to frame what is a gradual, developmental process, not a one-off event. Parents' attitudes and behaviour are directly involved too.

That doesn't mean independence shouldn't be a goal: parents rightly feel they've done their job if they've raised kids who are self-sufficient, and kids want it just as much. But it's not all-or-nothing: parents and children remain dependent on each other in changing ways throughout their lives. And it certainly doesn't happen overnight. Dr Gower says, 'We need to emphasise new narratives of connectedness and challenge traditional views of the family life cycle. The idea of second-phase parenting, and that it's different, is very important. When asked, everyone seems to know about the continuing and important influence of parents, yet most of us do not subscribe to a narrative that we are still "allowed to" be parented or parent our adult children. We all think, that's it then, when kids turn whatever age we think adult is. I'm proposing something different. If when our children are leaving home we could be thinking that we are simply entering the next phase of our lives in relationship with them, we would have a whole different preparation and perspective. At the moment all we have to look forward to is the empty nest. But if we know we are moving into the next phase of our relationship with our children, we have other things to look forward to and to work at together.'

MARKERS OF ADULTHOOD

For previous generations there were clear markers that perpetuated the idea that adulthood happened overnight: 21st birthday cards had Babycham bubbles and the key to the door, and were swiftly followed by marriage, babies and jobs for life. Some women in this book went straight from their parents' home to married life and motherhood in their early twenties, with no threshold years in between. Far fewer young people were able to go to university, so it was more common to leap straight from school into a job for life. There are still concrete markers: legally, UK adulthood starts at 18, when teenagers can vote or get married without parental permission. Younger teenagers can drive, join the army and make decisions about medical treatment, but generally definitions of adulthood have become more fluid. As Dr Reenee Singh points out, 'The whole idea of what it means to be an adult, and what your responsibilities towards your parents are, are quite different in different cultures.'

When I asked people across the generations what being an adult meant, everyone came up with a different answer. People in their twenties and thirties talked about moving out of their parents' home, a sense of personal responsibility, marriage, having a baby. Liam, 25, said it was when he first became aware that his parents had flaws and made mistakes. Gurpreet, 27, says, 'Having to sort things out for yourself when they go wrong – like when the boiler breaks down or the loo gets blocked. That's what being an adult is.'

Parents' views of adulthood are more subjective: they're a lot to do with how capable they think their child is. Dr Gower says, 'When people ask me when a child becomes an adult, I always say that the answer lies in the relationship between the parent and the child and how they define themselves.' For me it boils down to the thought that if I died tomorrow my kids would all cope perfectly well without me. They've passed their driving tests and have dug themselves out of all manner of holes. Finding a long-term partner and having children of their own take adulthood on to the next level (see Chapters 10 and 11). Lucy, whose son is 29 and lives at home, says, 'I don't worry about Duncan at all now. That's a sign that he has made the transition. He's grown up and I have grown up too in my relationship to him – even though he still lives with us.' Theresa felt her sons were grown up when they became financially independent and settled down with their girlfriends. She says, 'Just the other day I was thinking that Alfie hasn't asked to borrow any money for a very long time. Having their own place, and having to pay their own bills, makes kids grow up because they can't spend all their money on drinking and having fun. And when they've got someone who loves them as much as you love them – that's when you feel they are totally independent. It's very different to when I was their age. I thought I became an adult when I had my first child at 24 – I'd lived at home until I got married at 23. Looking back, I don't think I ever felt really independent until I was 40 and got divorced. That's when I felt I grew up.'

There is often a lightbulb moment that jolts parents into seeing their child in a new, adult light rather than as a grown-up teenager. Parents naturally cling to old ideas and anxieties about their kids, and assumptions about what they can and can't do, until something happens that brings home how much they've moved on. Often it's prompted by seeing your child as other people see them. Steve remembers, 'There have been two major moments, one in each of my kids' lives, where I've thought, they're going to be fine. With my daughter, it hit me like a sledgehammer. She runs a panto group for local children and about four years ago I was watching a performance from the sidelines. What suddenly struck me was the laughter coming from the audience – adults as well as children were genuinely laughing out loud. And I thought, all this is down to my daughter, and what a skill to write comedy for kids that chimes with adults as well. For all those years they're your little girl or boy and then… it just made me think, if that's the sort of thing she can do, what have I got to worry about?'

HOW ADULT CHILDREN SEE EMERGING ADULTHOOD

The twenties can be tough, but they can also be an exciting, fluid time of life, full of possibilities and exploration. Before the responsibilities of mortgages and families kick in, and with no teachers or parents to tell them what to do, young adults are free to focus on finding out who they are and what they want to do in life. They can travel, live with different partners, explore their sexuality, experiment with different ways of living. There's a sense that anything is possible. Such uncertainty can feel exciting, unsettling or terrifying. And when things stall, or obstacles get in the way, it's deeply frustrating.

These days, the obstacles for young adults are piling up. Rents are high; few young people can afford to buy a place unless the bank of Mum and Dad can stump up a deposit. Employment has changed radically in recent years. The gig economy allows people to move around more easily, but short-term contracts and freelancing add to the general sense of insecurity and instability. COVID-19 has added to the economic uncertainty that young adults have faced since the 2008/9 global financial crisis. The signs are that COVID-19 will not only take its toll on current career prospects, but continue to have a long-term impact. In May 2021 people aged 18-24 were two and a half times more likely to be out of work than older people, according to the Resolution Foundation, an independent think-tank focused on the living standards of households on low and middle incomes. It doesn't help that casual work, once a reliable source of income and experience en route to a career job, has become much harder to come by.

If it takes too long to get a foot in the right niche, young people understandably panic that life is passing them by and that is a horrible feeling. Social media doesn't help if it creates the illusion that everyone else has made it with good salaries and fabulous lifestyles. It's a blow to discover that a first-class degree doesn't guarantee a foot on the ladder and that bosses can be difficult and unfair. It can be hard to hold on to idealism and optimism in the face of the compromises demanded by work. Yet compromise is not always bad. According to research at Michigan State University in 2019, inflated self-worth and sensitivity to criticism declines when people start working, because they're forced to accept negative feedback and adjust their behaviour to working in a team. It goes hand in hand with building one of life's most useful skills: resilience.

Liam's experience since graduating two years ago has been challenging but not unusual. When he finished his degree in product design at Manchester, he decided to stay in the city and rent a shared house. Looking back, he thinks it was a naive mistake. When we spoke, Liam was 25, looking for his second career job and trying to break the 'experience conundrum': employers want experience but you can't get experience without a job. He says, 'This has been a very difficult transition, both emotionally and financially, so it's definitely been good to have my parents to support me – having that safety blanket behind me. When I left university, I got myself into a bit of a bad situation because I had to pay rent but didn't have a job. It was very difficult and a bit scary. I was expecting it to be easier to get a job. I felt I'd put the effort into uni and done well and although I didn't think I would walk into a job exactly, I definitely thought I would be able to find something. That's why it really took me by surprise that I couldn't find *anything*. That first job is the most difficult step, because you're applying yourself to something you feel quite inadequate about. It suddenly felt like real life, whereas at uni you have the safety net of a student loan.'

CHALLENGES FOR PARENTS

For parents, the post-university years can be equally demanding, not least because they've been looking forward to taking their feet off the gas. They want to help, but they're not sure how, or whether help might actually be counterproductive. Steve says, 'The worst bit is when you can see your child is going to make a mistake. You've been there before, you've done it yourself, you know what's going to happen and you've just got to grit your teeth and allow it to happen. I find that hard, because Sam is someone who treads on landmines. Sometimes they're just there, sometimes she manages to plant them and forget where she's put them.'

University is a halfway house between adolescence and adulthood that allows both parent and child to adjust to changing levels of dependency. Graduation from university is on another level: it feels permanent, the beginning of the rest of both your lives. Liam's mum Corinne says, 'I found it really difficult when Liam decided to stay in Manchester – much harder than him going to university in the first place. Then I knew he would be coming back in the holidays, whereas from now on it will only be for a few days rather than a few weeks.

'The reality when graduates come out of university is very different from the one they were promised before they applied. It was difficult for Liam and it was hard that we weren't near him. All his friends had left, he was living in a crappy house, he never had any money but found the whole process of signing on extremely stressful because he suffers from social anxiety. That triggered really painful eczema. We were trying to fund him as much as we could. But it wasn't only the lack of money – he's not very materialistic. I think he really missed the daily stimulation of a job and home and being near friends you can trust, not just acquaintances.'

Rather than settling into what for previous generations was the stability of the next phase, parents and adult children find themselves in yet another halfway house. Parents often assume that their job would be done by now; they weren't expecting to keep supporting adult kids, either financially or emotionally. They worry whether it's normal that their kids aren't yet fully independent; comparisons with their peers' children often just make it worse. They know it takes some people longer than others to find their feet but they can't help wondering whether that's just because it's tough out there, or whether their child lacks gumption. Are they being too picky about work or where they live? Should they be more realistic and lower their sights? If they're still loving living like a student, should you push them out of it?

EMOTIONAL SUPPORT: 'I'M NOT A CHILD, MUM!'

Parents are torn. They know it's pointless to try to exert control in a way that might have worked with younger kids. It's no longer possible to offer guidance in the way you might have done in the past, yet it's agonising to stand back, because the connection still exerts a powerful pull and the protective instinct doesn't go away. Kids are understandably touchy if they think parents are interfering: 'I'm not a child, Mum!' is the indignant cry of middle-aged children and young adults alike. Adult children get defensive if parents broach the subject of work or ask about their love life and often clam up if things aren't going too well. While they're happy to accept support when they ask for it and with some things – money, obviously – they definitely don't want it in other areas of their lives.

Many parents, like Renate, have learnt to wait to be asked. When her younger daughter, who's 26, was living on her own in a new city during the first COVID-19 lockdown, she confided in her mum about how isolated she felt at times. Renate said she'd leave her phone by her bed so her daughter could call at any time if she felt anxious: 'Twice Mia called me at 3 a.m., really panicking. I ended up talking to her for about an hour and a half and she felt much better. But there are other areas of her life she definitely wouldn't want me to be involved with. You accept their invitations, you don't ask or look for them. It's the same with my other children, who are older. Often if I make a suggestion or a comment there's a sort of chill from them. They give you a look like "I'm an adult, I make my own decisions". I've thought, OK, that means back off. So I do back off!'

Some parents drop hints or leave articles about jobs and leaflets about courses lying around. If a child shows the slightest interest in a course or a career, they throw themselves into researching it and try to broach the subject casually. Theresa's daughter was so resistant to suggestions that Theresa took her away for the weekend in the hope that relaxing time together would make it easier to talk about her future. That didn't work, so she felt she had no choice but to write her a letter: 'In the end it felt like the only way she would listen to what I was trying to say, because before it was like I was criticising her. If I ever said anything about work she would just get really defensive. When I suggested teaching, although she had already thought about it herself, she went off on one about how we didn't value her job. She's actually very clever and works incredibly hard but she has never fulfilled her potential. I felt if I didn't say anything, I would never forgive myself for not trying.'

Even if kids ask for advice they don't always accept it gracefully. I've heard endless tales of parents who've been asked to help with a CV or a job application and ended up having an irritable row. That's not surprising since, on the whole, kids would rather manage without their parents' help and feel frustrated that they have to ask. And parents' suggestions, however well-meaning, often come across as more critical than they're intended to be. It's equally likely that their advice is a bit wide of the mark because they don't know as much as they think they do about the jobs in question, or what employers are looking for. But if their suggestions don't go down well, parents naturally wonder why they bothered.

Then there are those intense phone calls that come out of the blue and demand your immediate full attention – this is something many parents of twenty-somethings complain about. It's extra irritating if kids automatically assume you've got nothing better to do than have a heavy chat; they haven't yet learnt to check whether it's a good time. These conversations leave parents feeling ambivalent:

emotionally drained and anxious, but at the same time grateful that their child still comes to them for support. Helen's experience rings a lot of bells: 'It was Saturday evening and I was looking forward to a nice FaceTime chat with my daughter. My husband was watching the rugby, we were having a nice relaxing time. But then it was "Oh, Mum, what am I going to do with my life?" She wanted to work out whether to throw herself into music auditions for conservatoires. I'm afraid I let my guard down and I just said, "Oh no". I just thought, not another intense, demanding conversation. So that became a bit of an argument, and my daughter got cross and rang off in a huff because I wasn't in the correct mode. I didn't know that that mode would be required! When I talk to friends it brings forth similar stories about phone calls out of the blue.'

It's not that parents don't want to help – of course we do. In an urgent crisis you drop everything immediately. And it's not that we don't want our kids to come to us whenever they need advice or support – that's still a parent's job. The difficulty stems from timing and expectations. Weeks go by when things seem to be going well – you tend not to hear about the good things – and then suddenly you're required to be on red alert. I often think that at this stage parenting is like being a lifeguard because most of the time you're not needed – you're ignored, even – but then when the call comes, you're expected to switch instantly and be totally on it. Whatever mood you were in before the call is shattered.

The other difficulty is that it can be hard to read what your child really wants from you. They're not necessarily looking for concrete advice or offers of help. Kids often just need to vent their feelings about an infuriating boss or a failed job application or an argument with a housemate. That can take some getting used to and it's particularly frustrating for people who like coming up with solutions. Parents need to listen attentively rather than jump in, ask open questions and be sensitive, non-judgemental and thoughtful in their responses. That's a big ask, but it keeps the connection alive and growing. The right kind of support helps kids build resilience.

Infuriatingly for parents, it's often easier for their children to accept advice when it comes from someone else. It's obvious why: advice from a friend or relative is less likely to make them feel they're still being treated like children, because it comes without history or emotional baggage. It's similar with step-parents, if they have a good rapport. Theresa, who described earlier how defensive her daughter became when she tried to talk to her about work, told me with a wry smile how the same daughter happily considered similar career suggestions when they came from her stepmother. Professor Lisa Doodson, a psychologist and expert on stepfamilies, says, 'Because the step-parent doesn't have that biological tie they can be a little removed. It doesn't mean they don't care. They can be more realistic, the voice of reason, whereas the parent says *but he's my baby*. One of the positives of stepfamilies is that children have this other adult in their life to make sure they're OK, to guide them. And because the step-parent isn't biased, they will be more honest. If you get on with your stepchild in a real way, it's a fantastic gift for both of you.'

Fathers and mothers, whether step-parents or biological parents, often have very different ideas about how much support they should offer adult children. A report for Sainsbury's Bank in 2016 found that fathers expected to be able to cut the purse strings when their son or daughter was 27, three years earlier than mothers, who thought children would reach financial independence at 30. It can cause friction unless parents keep talking through their differences and are open to compromise. Professor Doodson advises, 'In biological families as well as stepfamilies there is always one parent who is more liberal and one who is more disciplinarian. One parent might be a bit harsh, whereas the other wants to give as much as they can. It's about finding a happy medium somewhere in between, by trying to understand the other parent's perspective.'

MONEY

These days, most emerging adults need financial help at some point and the most likely source is the bank of Mum and Dad, which is much less scary than a high-interest loan. Parents generally help if they can, even if it means cutting corners in their own lives: either directly, with gifts, loans or paying for stuff; or indirectly, by offering board and lodging to kids who live at home.

Money is also responsible for one of the biggest shifts in adult family life over the past 20-odd years: the dramatic increase in adult children who live at home. It has rapidly become the new reality. Statistics on this vary wildly, but Loughborough University's large-scale 2020 study estimates that the numbers increased by a third over the previous decade. Dr Reenee Singh, Director of the London Intercultural Couples Centre, explains, 'Finances determine how families are structured. That's partly why in the Western world the whole notion of adult families is changing, because there isn't enough money for young people to move out, so they don't have a choice. Meanwhile, in a lot of Asian families it's traditionally adult sons who carry on the family business. The idea of freedom and autonomy is quite different if you're also bound up financially.'

Giving money encourages independence

It sounds counterintuitive, but one of the chief motives for giving money is to encourage independence. You would think that doling out cash would have the opposite effect, but it makes perfect sense when it comes to helping with funding training or study, driving lessons or even with the cost of a car. A few years ago, Nisha's daughter was living at home with her young baby and doing odd jobs. She remembers, 'I suggested that, rather than giving me a contribution, she put all the money she earned into saving for a car and driving lessons. That enabled her to make a huge life change, which has really benefited her. Living at home rather than paying rent allowed her to save money and be more independent.'

Yet parents inevitably have mixed feelings, according to groundbreaking research on intergenerational gift-giving at Birmingham University. It found that although many parents wanted to contribute to adult children's independence by providing help if they could afford it, they had reservations about making their lives too easy. Giving money also seemed to go against an important principle that parents wanted to pass on to their kids, that people should work hard to achieve their goals. But fundamentally, helping adult children out was seen by all social classes as simply what families should do.

Parents are surely right to worry that if their child relies on bailouts it could prevent them taking responsibility. If your son loses his phone (again), and he depends on it for work, should you help him buy a new one? If your daughter wants to do a BA in clowning, should you fund it? It's a fine line between providing a safety net and being overindulgent, which won't do anyone any favours. Steve paid his daughter's rent for a few months when she left her husband, but with a proviso. 'I will help both my kids out if I feel it's necessary, but sometimes what's needed is tough love,' he says. 'My daughter is a money pit, and at times I've had to say to her, I'm not going to work at the hospital just to pay your debts off. You are going to have to learn how to deal with this. I wasn't very good at that at first. It can be really tough not to give your child money when you think she's in trouble. But if I do, I feel she's never going to learn.'

Giving involves a range of emotions

What's confusing for both parents and their children is that money gets mixed up with love and all kinds of other emotions. Professor Karen Rowlingson, co-author of the Birmingham University research, writes that for the parents in her study, the decision to give money was not purely rational or logical, 'but one in which a huge range of emotions were experienced, from affection and love, happiness and hope, to pride, guilt and anxiety.' Being generous is an easy way to make your child like you; it creates a bond. If parents feel guilty about something they've done or failed to do, giving money can make them feel better. One father I know says writing a cheque makes him feel that he's still needed, something he really misses since his two daughters left home. But parents need to reflect on their reasons for giving, what they're getting out of it, and how that might affect the relationship.

As Steve says, it's really tough not to help if your child is struggling. Allowing them to sort out their own financial difficulties can make you more anxious than you would be if you bailed them out. The same goes when safety is at stake: parents often fork out for car repairs or for a taxi home late at night because they can't bear the anxiety. There are so many other grey areas: Corinne says, 'It takes an effort not to step in and help. My younger son's travelling round Australia and I found out he's in debt to the gym. I'm worried that if the debt goes to court it won't help his credit profile but at the same time I think it's his mess and if I phone up and sort it out that won't help.' I know parents who pay for their child to have a cleaner, stump up for their children's parking fines and have a date in their diary when their kids' house insurance is due.

It's almost impossible to give money with no strings attached or an element of control. Most parents want to feel that their hard-earned cash is being used wisely, especially if they are making sacrifices themselves. But there's a fine line between reassurance and wanting too much control. There may be a reluctance to let go and allow the child to make their own choices, and that's not particularly good for the relationship. Most kids would much rather be self-sufficient and in a position to pay their own way.

The idea of a snowflake generation who fritter their money away on lattes and takeaways adds to the confusion, but there is a real gulf between baby boomers and their adult children when it comes to attitudes to earning, spending and saving. I was brought up in the 1950s and 1960s with a piggy bank and savings stamps with portraits of the young Prince Charles and Princess Anne. When the UK's first credit card was launched by Barclaycard in 1966, I remember it being greeted with some suspicion. In those days buying a sandwich was regarded as a criminal waste of money.

Nisha sums up how a lot of parents feel: 'Perhaps I've got a grumpy old woman attitude but I think some young adults have a nicer lifestyle than we did. You can't have foreign travel, craft beer, nice clothes, go out every night *and* save for a deposit on a flat. Something's got to give and with us it was deciding not to go out or buy new clothes or have holidays until we were established and could afford it. Young people complain that it was all right for my generation, but it wasn't. You had to work hard and prove yourself. We worked overtime to save for a deposit on our first place.'

3

Parents Need Independence Too

'The best gift you can give to your child is to be happy yourself, rather than trying to make your child happy.' Haemin Sunim's wise words have stayed with me since I first came across an interview with the Buddhist monk and spiritual leader a few years ago. There is so much thought given to adult children's independence that it's easy to forget that the other side of the coin is important too. Adult children can only be fully independent if their parents are.

For Steve, a single parent, finding his own new direction was bound up with his son and daughter forging theirs. He says, 'When I retired, I went to volunteer in Nepal, and I said to the kids, you've got your lives but equally I've got mine. I'm there for you but there are things that you're going to have to sort out for yourselves. I have always been determined to put my family first, no matter what. When my wife left, I made sure there was as little change as possible for the children: same house, same schools, even the same car. But now that they're 27 and 31 I naturally tend to be less involved with their lives. It's less of a parent-child relationship and more equal.'

Having a life and a rounded sense of self that expands beyond the family, while remaining anchored firmly in it, allows the relationship with the adult child to move forward. But it's not just about the relationship with the kids: independence is equally important for parents' own well-being. It contributes to self-confidence and self-respect, allowing you to look ahead positively, to seize the challenges of the next stage of your life, and the continuing connection with the children, rather than looking back wistfully to the way things were.

It automatically becomes easier for parents to focus on themselves when their kids no longer need looking after and financial responsibilities wane. People have more autonomy, more control over their own lives when they don't have to compromise around children's schedules and demands or mould their interests to children's likes and dislikes. Parents who have devoted years to child-rearing, however happily, welcome an opportunity to pursue their own passions more wholeheartedly. Renate says, 'I feel I gave a lot to the kids when they were growing up and now I want to give myself the chance to do all the things I want to focus on.'

At this stage in our lives there is an added impetus to make the most of precious time and that's even true for parents who are spring chickens when their kids reach adulthood. Perhaps that's why many parents say they feel more adventurous as they get older: they travel to wild places they would never have considered with a family, they start up new ventures, they try internet dating. They care less about what people think – they can see wrong turns and blind alleys as experiments rather than mistakes. Yet parents will always be parents, first and foremost; putting children first is in their DNA. They still factor their children into their plans, although it rarely works the other way round! Dr Myrna Gower, whose research focuses on second-phase parenting across the lifespan, quotes an interesting study by the Institute for Social and Economic Research that indicates that when parents move house, they take into account and try to move near where their adult children are. But when adult children move, where their parents live does not present as a primary driver when choosing location. She sees it as an indication of how the relationship seems heavily driven by adult children's needs.

Parents today are increasingly involved in their adult children's lives in all kinds of ways. They want to be on hand if adult children need them, even if it involves making sacrifices in their own lives. Often children's needs are unpredictable: one minute everything's trucking along merrily, the next the sky's fallen in. I've come across many parents, like Brenda in Chapter 6 and Tania's parents in Chapter 7, who threw up their own dearly held ambitions because they wanted to help a child get through a difficult phase or an unforeseen crisis, such as a divorce. Equally, a parent might decide to give up their own plans if a child reaches out to re-establish a connection after a period of little or no contact.

So parents face yet another juggling act between being involved in their children's lives and pursuing their own path, and at times the two seem incompatible. Children often have strong views about their parents' choices, whether it's a new partner or a trip to the Hindu Kush. They may disapprove or feel put out if they've taken it for granted that parents will always be on hand. They might feel disconcerted by what feels like a role reversal, because they're used to being the ones who do the adventurous stuff.

Yet parents are just as likely to hold themselves back with too many 'What ifs?': What if they have children? What if something bad happens at home when I'm trekking round South America? If I take this promotion, will there be enough time for the grandchildren? If I downsize, where will the kids stay when they visit? There are times when it's sensible to think round corners – it's a skill that parents hone to a fine art when their kids are growing up. But you can think round too many corners – I do, anyway. Adult children can be the perfect excuse to stay in your comfort zone. They join the other self-limiting excuses that prevent people from finding new fulfilment and purpose at this stage in life.

Sometimes compromise is required. The trick is to work out when, by dissecting any reservations in a realistic light. For example, if there was an emergency at home while you were travelling, you would probably be able to get back pretty quickly. On the other hand, if moving to an idyllic location made it harder for the kids to visit, that could have a serious impact on your well-being. The journalist and writer Sophie Radice's mother, Penelope, seems to have got the balance right. She became an intrepid traveller in her seventies, an ambition unfulfilled when she was busy teaching and bringing up her family. Her daughter wrote in *The Observer* in 2010, 'She knows we are proud of her, and not resentful of her time away because when she is home she is such an attentive mother and grandparent.'

INDEPENDENCE DOES NOT MEAN A LACK OF CONNECTION

Independence should not be confused with selfishness or a lack of connection or care. It doesn't make the relationship more distant or less supportive – quite the opposite. Mutual independence makes things more equal. The quote from Haemin Sunim at the start of this chapter is inspiring. He added, 'Focusing less on [your adult child], and more on yourself, your partner and the people around you, will bring benefits to your child.' If you've both got your own lives then there's always something new to talk about; the conversation doesn't get stuck on what the other kids are up to or well-worn family stories from the past.

Jane, who has always been fiercely independent, remembers a conversation with her son when he was in his mid-twenties and had been living abroad for four years: 'He said, "Mum, when I was 14, I really wished I had a mother like other boys, who made cakes and all that kind of thing. But now I think it's great to have a mother like you, because I can talk to you about all my experiences. Most of my friends can't." On another occasion he said, "My friends love their mothers but they don't respect them." I found that really poignant.'

It is even possible to be independent when you live near each other, or under the same roof, as the growing numbers of families who opt for multigenerational living are discovering. That may sound counterintuitive and it only works if both sides observe boundaries and give each other space to lead separate lives. It's not only parents who have to respect adult children's autonomy; adult children need to respect their parents' independence too. This works well in Lucy's family: her son and daughter are in their late twenties and both live at home.

'I certainly don't think having the children living at home hampers my lifestyle and creativity at all,' she says. 'I work all the time and I'm writing all the time. The kids lead their own lives and we rarely see them; they're like cats who come and go. They're independent, they manage for themselves, they're very curious about us, very supportive. We don't have a lot of family meals but when we do it's always very animated and lively, and there's a lot of talk about what we're all doing and about films and plays and thoughts and podcasts. And that's nice. If they were morbidly dependent on us – or we were dependent on them – it would be a completely different story.'

NEEDY PARENTS: 'I DON'T WANT TO BE A BURDEN'

I hate the phrase 'Get a life', but when parents put pressure on their kids to visit more often it's usually because there's something missing in their own lives. Adult children feel free to get on with their lives if they know their parents are getting on with theirs and not hanging on their next visit or feeling lonely without them. The family therapist Judith Lask says, 'Life doesn't end when you stop being a hands-on mother or father, there are other things to explore, and as a parent that's your issue. If it becomes your child's issue, if they have to be looking after you in an emotional sense, things are a bit unbalanced.' So while all parents say they would hate to be a burden on their children, it's important to acknowledge that this isn't merely a vague possibility when powers begin to fail in the far distant future, but something to guard against now.

There are many different and subtle ways that parents can be needy or dependent, even when they're still full of vim and vigour. This is something Steve has become increasingly wary of as he approaches a significant birthday: 'I'm 60 in July. I've started to look at myself and think, in the next 20 years I don't want to be someone the kids get sick of, or feel "Oh God, we've got to go and visit Dad". Everyone says they don't want to be a burden on their kids but I really don't want them feeling they've got to come round and look after me. I want them to live their own lives. It goes with the strong sense I have that I should try to maintain "dad distance" and that there are areas of their lives that as a parent I can't access and that it would be a mistake to try. For example, when my son plays a gig I always try to go and watch the band, and I make a point of having a quick pint with them afterwards. But then I resist the temptation to outstay my welcome and clear off home, because I recognise that this is his time, just as it was mine when I was a young man in the eighties.'

Sometimes parent and child rely too much on each other for emotional as well as practical support. I once read about a man in his late twenties whose anxious mother still treated him like a child; she even looked after his financial affairs and when he came home for a visit and went out with friends she insisted on giving him a lift home. She clearly needed to let go, but then he needed to assert himself too. Sometimes the situation is temporary if, for example, the adult child feels responsible for making things better after a parent's divorce. But it can become a habit and if people become co-dependent, it can be hard to break out of. Judith Lask says, 'In that sort of situation the child is stuck in a relationship in which they're looking after their parent, but it also fulfils a big need in themselves. And the parent is over-reliant on the relationship with their child for their own satisfaction and well-being. Because they are both fairly reliant on the situation, it keeps it going.'

HOW TO BE INDEPENDENT WHILE STAYING CONNECTED

So how can parents develop a life and interests beyond the family while continuing to nurture the connection with their children? The experts' view is that we should have been doing this since our kids were born, but the reality is that most people are too busy and preoccupied to think much about their own needs. It's far more common for parents to lose sight of dearly held dreams and ambitions. And when the kids grow up, their sense of self and purpose gets a bit shaky.

This used to be a particular issue for women, but fathers feel it too, especially when children first leave home. It can be almost impossible to get your head round the idea of having your own independent life. When my kids first left it was certainly the last thing on my mind; I just wanted the old era back. It's this initial transitional phase that presents the biggest challenges, but also the richest opportunities for growth. Some parents struggle more than others.

Paul, who describes himself as a typical East End bloke, became clinically depressed when his youngest daughter left home and he had to take long periods off work. He remembers, 'Suddenly it was as if the girls didn't need me. They had their own lives, their own partners. It's hard to put into words, but basically, I felt I had no purpose. I didn't feel needed any more. I didn't really know who I was.' His wife Toni felt the same: 'I couldn't imagine being without the girls. I wanted them to be young again. That first Christmas Eve when we were on our own was horrible. It's like all that's gone – everything's changed.'

But in time even parents who struggle with the empty nest, like Paul and Toni, come to see its positive side. Fears that the connection will weaken turn out to be unfounded; indeed, parents generally get on better with their children as both sides pursue parallel existences and flex their independent muscles.

The gap left by a child gradually turns into a space full of potential for parents to explore a side of themselves beyond parenting and discover new meaning in their lives. Paul found a totally new mission in life that saved him from depression. Although he and Toni knew nothing about dogs, a random internet search gave them the idea of taking in rescue dogs who had been brutally treated. Paul says, 'Sheba, Shane and Sky have given us a whole new life. Thanks to them, the girls have got their lives and we've got ours. They're a huge commitment. In a way they're like your kids, and that helps a lot; they have reinstated my role as a father. They've made me much more able to talk about my emotions; they've made me a better person. I'm more patient, more forgiving, more caring. We've made an amazing circle of like-minded friends through them, and through volunteering for the dog rescue.'

ADJUSTING TO A NEW IDENTITY AS A PARENT OF ADULT CHILDREN

Being a parent of grown-up kids changes how you feel about yourself. One minute you're a yummy/slummy mummy, the next you're mother of the bride. It's not just an age thing, although of course that comes into it. Sometimes I find it hard to get my head round the fact that next year my children will all be in their thirties. It doesn't just make me wonder where the time went, but where does that leave me? It doesn't feel like a great image. The absence of kids' energy in daily life alters how parents look and feel about themselves – and how they appear to the rest of the world. The everyday props and habits of parenthood can no longer be relied on to define you, both to yourself and others; perhaps that's one reason why people over 50 talk about feeling invisible. Other characteristics of this stage of life help shape our shifting identity: approaching the end of your career or retiring, having ageing parents and dying friends, feeling that you're moving towards the end of the race while your kids are right in the thick of it. Your mirror face is a disconcerting reminder of how your mother or father looked at the same stage.

Confronting this shift of identity, as Renate did when her son first left home, is an important first step. She remembers, 'I had to let go of the boy my son had been, and the mother I had been to that little boy. It felt like a rite of passage I had to go through.' It helps to embrace a new equilibrium between the different elements that combine to define you. You'll always be mum or dad, but it's possible to breathe new life into other aspects of your identity that could do with more attention and expansion. The image that springs to mind is of a life-coaching wheel, divided into different segments, including career, leisure, personal/spiritual growth, friends and family, partner. The ideal is to achieve balance.

There is now time and space to attend to the fabulous Japanese concept of *ikigai*, which roughly translates as 'a reason for being', by staying curious, open-minded, finding new interests and developing relationships with other people. It is a never-ending exploration that keeps changing course, but it might need a gentle push when adult children first leave home.

Relationships with people outside the family are key. Old friends and colleagues provide all-important continuity; they're a reminder that your personality has many facets beyond your identity as a mother or father. It's both grounding and reassuring to spend time with people who knew you before you had children. There can be a new connection with childless friends. New people – random acquaintances as well as proper friends – contribute to well-being and a developing sense of self. I think it's advisable not to talk about your adult children too much, whether or not friends have children. You're the only one who's interested, unless your son's getting divorced or your daughter's just been arrested – everyone loves hearing about adult children messing up! If you can't resist whipping out the photos, it could be a sign that you need other things in your life.

Work might be part of it too. Now that life no longer centres on child-rearing, parents can, if they choose, give more time and energy to their work; it's also the perfect opportunity to retrain or change tack to something they really love. Nisha, a writer and textile artist, whose daughter and her baby were living with her when we spoke, says, 'I love having the kids around but I'm not dependent on them. I'm equally happy on my own. When my daughter moves back to Portugal in a few months I'm not going to be sitting here thinking I've got nobody to talk to. I'll be writing and I get plenty of human contact through teaching and friends. As a single person I can be adaptable in a way I couldn't be if I was married.'

Parents who took a career break to bring up their children, or who are retired, have to be more proactive when looking for new meaning and purpose. Judith Lask explains, 'Once the parenting role goes you're not quite sure who you are and if you don't have a profession or a big interest that defines you it's a really difficult stage. That's less common for women now, but some women would be really happy if they could stay as a mother of younger children all their life. That's when they blossomed. They were good at it and they were important to their children. It can be hard adjusting to something different. It's natural to feel "Who am I? Am I important to anybody?"'

In retirement, Steve has worked hard on exploring new directions in life. He's tried different jobs, both paid and as a volunteer, and if they don't turn out to be as fulfilling as he hoped, he uses the experience as an opportunity to learn more about himself and his needs. Steve has done three volunteering stints in Nepal, where again, he learnt from his mistakes. He explains what inspired him to go: 'It's a big world out there and I wanted to do something completely different. So one day I just jumped on a plane. I was testing myself to see whether I could leave the kids and home and do something that was completely beyond anything I had ever done before. It felt really good to know that I could do it and that I would be all right.'

It helps that Steve practises meditation and goes on regular Buddhist retreats, sometimes even silent ones. That might sound a bit hardcore but it's one way to stand back from the mental clutter of mundane daily concerns and get to the heart of what really matters. There are endless other ways to free up the mind, from yoga retreats to activity holidays that give the brain a rest and allow creative rumination. It doesn't really matter what the activity is, as long as it's enjoyable, creates flow and sets the mind free to wander. It could be anything: walking, sketching, surfing, patchwork. And of course, it's also good to find a meditative activity to do at home: again, anything goes, as long it doesn't feel like a chore: gardening, knitting, DIY, pond maintenance, even ironing.

BEING A COUPLE WITH GROWN-UP CHILDREN

Life as a couple with grown-up children looks and feels very different from life as a double act of two hands-on parents. The joint daily enterprise of caring creates a strong bond and without it, the relationship sails into uncharted waters. There is a lot more hanging on the marriage; it becomes the main source of happiness and satisfaction. Some couples can't survive without the glue of family life; 'silver' divorce is increasingly common after children leave home (more in Chapter 7). For those who choose to stay together, there are huge challenges too.

'The relationship won't stay the same, that you can be sure of,' says Elizabeth Hamlin, a psychoanalytic psychotherapist at Tavistock Relationships, a charity with an international reputation for its services for couples. 'It's a fluid process, and at times, that can be disconcerting: sometimes you're more distant, sometimes closer.' Each person is adjusting not only individually to his or her own changing identity, but also to their partner's. They have to find new ways to relate to each other as partners first, parents second. After years of conversations that pivoted around family life there's an urgent need to find new stuff to talk about.

Marriages that stand the test of time develop resilience over the years and that gives both partners the flexibility to adapt yet again to a different future. Judith Lask says, 'The best couple relationships adapt as the needs of the relationship, and the needs of the family or circumstances, change. So when a couple first has children they can adapt to allow more space for them and different ways of maintaining intimacy as a couple. Then when the children leave they can find a way of exploring this new life together, finding new ways of relating. This flexibility in relationships is always key.'

Resilience stands couples in good stead to deal with the biggest change, when children first leave home, but it's equally important in facing the other changes that inevitably follow. Couples can never afford to get set in their ways, whatever their age and whatever stage they're at. All good relationships develop and grow, and that's as important during the years together after the children have gone as it is at any other time.

It's a mistake to dismiss couples who have been together for years as smug. Most long-term couples have learnt painful lessons along the way about the dangers of taking their eye off the ball. They understand that the relationship needs as much attention as their growing children, something that's easily forgotten when they are in the thick of parenting. The psychotherapist Ian Argent says, 'I see many couples taking their relationship for granted, and seeing it as this unchanging and enduring thing that's just there, that exists in and of itself; they think they don't have to worry about their contribution to it. Well, that doesn't work. Couples need to see their relationship as something that is not static, that changes over time, and that we have a responsibility to monitor those changes and stay in touch with each other as the relationship changes.

'Many couples were a good fit when they first got together but something that started out as quite good has morphed into something else that doesn't feel so good, and yet they haven't adjusted to that. There isn't the facility to say, "OK, our relationship is different now, what are we going to do about it? How are we going to relate to each other from here on?" Both partners can become frustrated and resentful of their roles.'

On the plus side, years of dealing with the ups and downs of family life make parents expert in responding to change. The added advantage is that they have more time and emotional energy to shift their focus back to their partner and to their relationship. The first step is to acknowledge that change has a big impact and to think about ways of working through it. Psychoanalytic psychotherapist Elizabeth Hamlin believes that it's helpful to see the relationship as a separate entity: 'Ideally an individual can both be in the relationship and also think about the relationship, and has the capacity to move flexibly between these two positions. Being able to reflect on things is important. Both partners need to have a coherent narrative of life together, that doesn't make one partner wonder what life the other person has been living.'

Be curious about your partner – avoid misunderstandings

If you've been together for years it's natural to make assumptions about how the other person thinks and feels. You believe you know them so well, but you may have lost touch with how their values and interests have moved on, and vice versa. It's easy to think you're the only one who has changed. The best way to test assumptions is by being curious: listening and reflecting on what the other person has to say. You both may be pleasantly surprised to discover that opinions and tastes aren't set in stone.

Paul and his wife Toni had a classic misunderstanding. They spent a lot of energy and money doing their house up after their three daughters left home but later discovered they were both desperate to move. Paul remembers, 'I thought Toni would be happier if I made the house nicer, but I really didn't like living there after the girls left home; in fact, I used to do anything to get out of the house. It was only when we'd finished all the work that I found out that Toni didn't like the place either. She'd been going along with me because she thought I liked it! We've been much happier since we moved to this little house.'

Without the distractions of raising kids and the busy admin of family life, the couple relationship is exposed and that can feel uncomfortable. You're both aware that the relationship would benefit from the kind of honest talk that enhanced intimacy when you first got together, but now feels too risky. It's so much easier to push the serious emotional stuff aside and carry on as before, with safe discussions about what the kids are up to and what's happening at work, instead of what really matters between you. Serious issues get parked up until tongues are loosened by a few glasses of wine. That's a perfect recipe for a row: things get said in hurtful ways and it's hard to hear the other person's point of view. The other alternative is stagnation, which could end with one partner looking elsewhere for what's missing, by having an affair, for example.

It's not surprising that many couples lose touch with saying how they really feel. The psychotherapist Ian Argent says, 'Some couples I meet don't have a good channel of communication when it comes to resolving difficulties. They bang pots and pans around because they don't have a way of saying *I'm unhappy* or *I want to be close to you but it's difficult*, or *I'm angry* or *I'm sorry*. And if they don't have that facility, resentments just build until eventually they get cashed in. So a big part of my work with couples is trying to establish emotional literacy and foster more effective lines of communication. It's also important because, whether parents are aware of it or not, they're still offering a model for relationships. Even when the kids are grown up and living somewhere else they're still watching what their parents are doing.'

Make plans as a couple

Sitting down together and hashing out joint plans is a simple but effective way to embrace change, yet couples tend to get out of the habit after focusing on the children's futures for so long. It's never too late to start thinking about how you would like to spend the coming years together. Simply instigating conversations about what you would like to have achieved in five years' time, and where you'd like to be living, reinforces the sense of yourselves as a unit, moving together purposefully into the future rather than drifting aimlessly. This feels so much more optimistic than the vague ideas most of us have about getting older as a couple.

Shared goals and ambitions help parents steer their own course, distinct from their children. Everyone knows where they stand if parents are proactive, instead of constantly reacting to what the kids are up to and their requests for help. It allows parents to say yes – and at times no – without feeling ambivalent. Kids often say they feel better about asking if they know that parents feel able to say no.

At this stage in life it's time to seize the hour; there's no point self-censoring hopes and dreams. Be bold: tell your partner what you've always wanted to do and invite them to be equally honest. You may well have very different ideas: one partner longs to try out life on a houseboat or co-housing while the other dreams of road trips or wants to keep working until they're 100. Taking time to explore a range of different ideas together wakes you up as a couple. It won't end in tears if both sides can keep an open mind and recognise that compromise can lead to unexpectedly brilliant outcomes.

How couples are affected when children move back home

If adult children live at home it's harder to reignite life as a couple. Couples who've had a period of being back to just the two of them notice this most. Even if kids' lives are pretty independent, simply being under the same roof sends many parents straight back into Mum and Dad mode. The emotional space that opened up when the kids first left deflates. Children's presence can hold the couple relationship back in different ways; it makes people steer away from honest conversations because they don't want to end up arguing with their kids in earshot, even when they're grown up; it inhibits sex lives.

It often happens that one partner reverts to the parent role, leaving the other trying to keep the relationship going forward. Nicole says, 'After the kids left home I felt like our relationship had lost its way and I finally managed to persuade my partner to try couples counselling. It helped. We started to enjoy being just us again – we did more stuff together, we were much more in tune with each other, our sex life improved. That was a bit of an issue when the children kept moving in and out of home in their twenties and early thirties. I loved having them back as adults, but for us it felt like a bit of a backward step.'

BEING A COUPLE AGAIN, NOT JUST PARENTS

- Make a weekly date to talk properly. Be curious about what the other person is thinking and feeling.
- Don't allow minor resentments to build: think of a kind way to say what's on your mind.
- Look for a balance between joint and separate activities.
- Interests you shared when the kids were growing up are a source of continuity.
- A new joint project helps reignite the relationship and move it forward.
- Try something that you would both find a bit risky – it doesn't have to be dangerous! It could even be something quite simple that neither of you has done before.
- Make plans for the next year and for the next five years – things to do separately as well as together.
- Holidays are a wonderful opportunity to shake things up because they take you away from the domestic context. Go somewhere that's different, but not too challenging.
- If a child moves back home, try not to revert to Mum and Dad mode. Stick to the new habits you've established since they left, like weekly date nights and weekend breaks.

WHEN A PARENT MEETS A NEW PARTNER

It has become a staple theme of TV drama: a divorced or widowed vulnerable parent – it's nearly always a mother – stirs up conflict and consternation among her adult children by falling for a stranger whose motives appear decidedly dodgy. It may be fantasy, but it has its roots in reality. When parents start dating, or find a new long-term partner, they may be over the moon, but their children are anything but. It's understandable if adult kids feel disconcerted. It rocks a boat that once seemed so stable, perhaps for the second time if it follows a recent divorce or the death of a parent. It's a clear signal that good old Mum or Dad is taking off in a new direction that feels like it's got little to do with them. It's a staunch assertion of independence, a statement that parents have a right to be happy too.

'In the same way that the children's decisions really impact on me, so do mine on them, like having a new man in my life,' Anne-Marie says. 'Effectively my life is a bit like a married life again, but it's going in a whole new direction.'

But the reaction of adult children depends a great deal on the individual situation. They naturally feel protective towards a parent after divorce or bereavement and they don't want to see them hurt again. Stories of mid-life romances that end in tears are common, but it's not just concern that makes adult children uneasy. It's disconcerting for children of any age to feel a parent is being replaced; the difference with adult children is that they often have strong views about the new partner's suitability.

Anne-Marie, who met a new man a year after her husband died, remembers the family's reaction: 'At first the kids were clearly thinking, where has this man come from? Is he ripping you off? They were worried that I was jumping into the comfort of the first person I met because I was vulnerable and lonely. I had to make sure for myself. The kids took a bit longer. They were polite but they were clearly thinking, I'm not going to bond with you, you're not my dad. At first my son and his wife didn't want their kids to meet Scott, which meant I didn't get to see my grandchildren when I was with him. It was a dilemma and I couldn't tell Scott because it would have broken his heart. But over time they've got to know him and they can see that he loves me and looks after me.'

If the new partner arrives on the scene after an acrimonious divorce – or perhaps played a part in precipitating the parents' parting – adult kids may take time to warm to them. But equally they may take a dislike to the new partner for no apparent reason. In fact, there is good reason not to be enthusiastic: the new uncertainty about the future. They may feel anxious about being replaced in their parent's affections, about what will happen to the family home and their inheritance. It helps to be as straightforward as Anne-Marie has been: 'I didn't want the children to think I was leaving everything to Scott and his children so I sat them down and told them that I'd done my will and that everything is going equally to them. But I also said that at some point, I will have to put a bit in for Scott.'

Professor Lisa Doodson, who is an expert on stepfamilies, explains, 'When couples get together later in life there are suddenly complicating finances and emotions and all sorts of things. You meet a partner, you fall in love, but everyone else has got to catch up. The fact that you're happy doesn't mean your children are going to be happy too. If children see that the new step-parent is changing their parent, and they don't like the changes, it can make for a lot of resentment.

'The new couple have to be very sensitive to relationships with adult children and recognise that everyone has a different perspective. The new partner needs to step back and take a back seat. They should be careful not to jump in, but respect what's already happening in the family and let things happen slowly. The biological parent needs to make sure everybody has time to get to know their new partner and to understand the situation. It can take years, not months.'

The big advantage for adult children is the relief from responsibility. They no longer have to worry about a parent being lonely, or that they'll have to look after them if they get frail in old age. Mel was pleased when his father found a new partner after a divorce that upset the whole family and delighted to see him enjoying retirement with a woman who shares his interests. He no longer worries about his dad in the way he worries about his mother, who lives alone. Nevertheless, it's still complicated: 'My dad's partner is lovely but that has also brought difficulties with it. She's got two grown-up married daughters, and she is very family-oriented, and I think she had a sort of fantasy that my family would sort of be absorbed into hers, which is not going to happen. We've spent several birthdays and dinners with them but my dad now feels obliged to spend Christmas with her married daughters rather than with us. So I don't know if I'm ever going to get a Christmas with my dad again and that is hard.'

4

Meeting and Communicating

Good communication is the beating heart of any relationship, but when adult children and parents don't live together, it can no longer be taken for granted. Its importance is heightened and crystallised. The continuing evolution of the bond depends on how well you communicate about what you're thinking and feeling, and not just about the day-to-day stuff. How often you see each other plays a part, but it's the closeness of the connection that really counts, not only when you meet face to face, but also when you're apart. Good communication is the motor that keeps the relationship moving forward.

Deborah Merrill, Professor of Sociology at Clark University in Massachusetts, points out that patterns of communication are established in childhood and provide a template for adult relationships. Yet things have developed: talking to adults is not the same as talking to younger children. You're equals now, perhaps even friends. If adult offspring ask for advice they may not take it and you certainly can't tell them what to do. The language and what you feel comfortable talking about has changed. Parents today talk to their kids more openly about subjects that would have been off limits with their own parents.

When you live under the same roof conversations can be ad hoc, casual, fluid. Of course they can also be grumpy and grunty! A random chat in the kitchen about your day might go no further, or it could flow into something deeper and more personal. If you want to bring up a difficult subject, there are more opportunities to find the right moment. Above all, communication is not just verbal; a hug or a pat on the arm speaks volumes, while we all know people who can ice up the atmosphere with a mood.

When you live apart, all that changes. One sad father put his finger on the difference the day his daughter moved out: 'I'll never be with her in the same way again.' Limits are imposed by time and context and who else is in the room. It might feel a bit stiff, especially if you meet in public, and that's excruciating because it's your child and you know them so well. At least you thought you did. The danger is that without enough regular contact, it can be harder to maintain an emotional connection because you don't know enough about each other's daily lives. Talking about everyday details offers a way in to deeper things, like how people really feel about their job or the lack of romance in their life.

However, the fact that communication requires more effort and consideration is no bad thing. When contact is no longer woven into daily life, it has to be thought about and planned. Seeing each other becomes special rather than everyday. Decades of research consistently confirm that it's women who are the lynchpin of family contact. Mothers are the 'kin-keepers', who ring their kids and arrange to meet, organise gatherings and remember birthdays. That might explain why several studies found that adult children feel closer to their mothers and that mothers have more influence. The Norwegian sociologist Grunhild Hagestad wrote that women see themselves as 'specialists in family dynamics'.

But things are changing as men open up about their feelings. Steve, who was brought up in the north-east of England in the 1960s, has noticed a big change in the way parents and adult kids relate to each other. He says, 'My dad and I never had the kind of conversations where we were open with each other. I think he was proud of me, but that was never said. I think it's a lot to do with the way society was then, people were more clipped. But then people in the 1940s and 1950s had a hell of a lot more to deal with.'

As fathers become more involved in their children's daily care, they develop a new appreciation of adult family life. Paul, who describes himself as a typical East End bloke, wrote a book about what saved him from empty nest depression when his three daughters left home. Since then, things have changed. He explains, 'I don't feel ashamed to show emotions now. Since my daughters, and my mum, read the book, they look at me differently, they even talk to me differently. The way we communicate is more grown-up, because I'm not trying to put on my Batman cape any more, it's this is me, so let's be honest.'

THE DIFFERENCE BETWEEN SONS AND DAUGHTERS

Things are also changing with sons and daughters. Many parents still say there's a difference in the way they communicate and I'm aware of it in my own family. One mother told me that although she felt close to her sons, she had no idea what was going on for them emotionally. This echoes what other parents say, that sons don't volunteer much personal information and there's a classic male lack of communication. The standard riff is that daughters get in touch more often and they're more open about their emotions and what's going on in their lives. Mothers and daughters 'get' each other: one mother said she felt the contents of their minds overlapped. Meanwhile, the recurring theme is that sons don't return messages, don't get in touch enough, and when they do, it's usually for a specific reason rather than a nice long chat.

This correlates with the idea that it's women – daughters as well as mothers – who take responsibility for family relationships. Things change again when sons have a partner. It's common to communicate with sons through their wives, often through sheer frustration. It goes with the old saying 'A son is a son till he gets him a wife, a daughter is a daughter all of her life', which still has a ring of truth for many parents. A lot of parents connect with sons through a common interest, like movies or sport, or doing stuff together, like Theresa, who describes how playing golf improved communication with her two boys. Of course, this works just as well with daughters. It also helps if parent and child work in similar fields.

I've got two sons and a daughter, and while there's undoubtedly a difference, I think that in general it's becoming blurred as young men become more articulate emotionally. It's often when sons become fathers themselves that they want to talk to their parents more and conversation flows more easily. Corinne says, 'The journey with my sons has been really interesting. You think boys are these big blokes who just get on with things, but for me it's been about learning to understand that they have as many neuroses and frailties and concerns as women. And they still need supporting but in different ways. I think my sons' generation of young men is much more in touch with their feelings, because they've had positive female relationships throughout their lives. That's very different from boys of my generation; I don't think they did talk.

'I learnt from my parents, who were beatniks in the 1950s, not to be judgemental; they were always very open with me. I've always talked to the boys about my anxiety, which was debilitating for about 10 years when they were younger. And I feel very lucky that they always talk to us very openly, even when it's about things I'd prefer not to know about!'

Corinne's son Liam, 25, adds, 'I think we are more in touch with our feelings than our parents; perhaps that's why we are a snowflake generation! I would always ring my mum when difficult stuff was going on, like when I left university and when I split up with my girlfriend. And I know Mum talked things through with my brother when he had problems with his girlfriend. We definitely have that openness about dealing with things in my family.'

MEETING FACE TO FACE

How often you meet up depends a lot on whether you live on the other side of the city or the other side of the world. But geographical barriers to communication are breaking down, thanks partly to advances in technology and transport. Professor Karen Fingerman, who runs the Adult Family Project at the University of Texas, points to dramatic, and rather encouraging, increases in contact between parents and adult children over the past few decades. Studies published in 2012 found that an astonishing 55 per cent of young adults reported some form of contact with their parents either every day, or nearly every day. This is a marked increase since the 1980s, when studies indicated that about 50 per cent of parents had contact of any kind with their adult children once a week or more.

How often people meet up is also about how much they want to see each other. Parents can't force their adult children to include them in their lives. Once they leave home, it's up to them how much time they spend with their parents. Parents can make arrangements and pile on the pressure, but who wants to be visited out of a sense of duty? Perhaps as parents we have to accept that there will always be an element of obligation and it's probably true that parents want to see their children a bit more than the other way round. But most adult children value the connection highly, as long as it isn't stuck in the past.

I was surprised by how often the young adults I interviewed brought up the notion of respect. East Ender Paul's youngest daughter Leah, who is 29, was one of them: 'I see Mum and Dad more as friends now. When you are together, you're just there to have a nice time.

But they're still my parents at the end of the day – they brought you into the world and they brought you up – and you've got to respect them. Just because you're an adult doesn't mean you can speak to them like garbage. You might have a point that you want to put across but you'd never be rude.'

Where to meet

Where you meet is more important than you might think. Communication can only evolve if both generations keep adapting; you run out of things to say if you're stuck with the way things used to be. In the family home people often switch straight back into parent–child roles, which can either be comforting or stifling. One father says, 'I still bring out the child in my daughter – even now that she's 29 – and she still brings out the father in me, especially when she comes to visit us. I've noticed I get on much better with her if we meet for dinner or go to a movie.'

When parents visit their adult child's home there may be all kinds of new tensions if they can't resist making comments about the expensive new cooker or the way their child makes coffee, or if they tidy up or, God forbid, clean the loo. Tania, who is in her forties, says, 'My parents are very good at saying "Do you have to paint it grey…?" or "Wouldn't it look nice a different colour?" In my twenties I would have walked away, saying "For God's sake!", but now that I've formed a deeper relationship with them, I'm no longer irritated by it. I understand that they can't help it! They just have very strong opinions on homes and houses in a way that I don't.'

Meeting for lunch or coffee works well for some people, but you have to pack a lot into a short time, so it's quite intense and harder just to chill out together if the waiter is hovering with the bill. There might be awkward silences. Sometimes the best solution is to find a shared activity where you don't have to talk much, whether it's a bike ride or attending an art exhibition. One friend bought a ping-pong table because it was such a good way to chat with friends as well as her sons. I recently heard a woman in her seventies talking on BBC News about how she and her middle-aged daughter had played tennis a couple of times a week all their lives: 'Getting into a rhythm, hitting your rallies, chasing the ball, you are still communicating, but in a different way,' she said.

The family therapist Dr Reenee Singh encourages families who are having problems communicating to go for regular walks together as a 'therapeutic ritual'. Talk flows more easily when you're not eyeballing each other across a table and there's stuff to look at and comment on, which naturally takes the conversation in a different direction. Theresa, who has two sons and two daughters, found that playing golf together has made it much easier to talk to her sons. She says, 'I remember meeting Ben for lunch in a pub when he was in his early twenties and it was so stilted and awkward. It seemed ridiculous, so I rang him up about a week later and asked if he fancied nine holes of golf. He leapt at it and it was just a completely different situation because we were playing a game. We chatted for two hours and it was fun. I'm so thankful that I can play, because there aren't many other things I could do with the boys – they're not into art galleries or whatever. In fact, they laugh because there was a time when they could tell that I wanted to talk to them because I would only play with them one at a time – it was a fantastic way to catch up.'

Seeing your child one-to-one

Parents really value being able to see their children on their own but it's an increasingly rare treat if families get into a habit of meeting en masse and when there's a partner or grandchildren. For Lily, one of the unexpected pleasures of retirement has been more time with her son and daughter on their own.

'The other day my son was dropping something off on his day off and he said, "Why don't we have lunch?"' she says. 'It was such a treat. Because when the grandchildren are there, you're engaged with them and there are some topics you can't touch. Just having that one-to-one time with him was lovely – being able to meet up every few weeks has been really nice.'

That's not always easy to arrange if a partner always comes too, or if big family gatherings are the norm. It might seem a bit heavy to suggest you'd like to see an adult child alone. Clever parents find ways of making it happen, like Brenda, who offers to taxi her son to the pub on a Friday night. Sitting side by side in the car is a great way to have a proper debrief. Finding time alone is harder if your child doesn't get why it matters to you. If solo time is an established fact of family life it helps: one mother I know started taking each of her three away for a mother-and-daughter weekend once a year when they were in primary school. The habit has stopped now that they're in their thirties and now it's the girls who make a point of having quality time alone with their mum.

COMMUNICATING WHEN YOU'RE APART

When parents say they speak to their adult child on the phone every day it's usually seen as a sign of a strong relationship. Yet what really matters is not so much how often you communicate but the quality of the connection: what you talk about and how close it makes you feel. There are no rules: different families have different styles of engagement. Some have long conversations once a month, others communicate mainly by text. Family therapist Judith Lask says, 'The people who don't have so much contact might feel closer than those who speak to each other all the time. The amount of contact doesn't predict how close families are.'

Some know more about each other's lives than others. Even within the same family, a parent will communicate more with one child than another and there will be phases when they speak more often: if the adult child needs support through a stressful time, or if they're planning an event together, for example. Family therapist Dr Myrna Gower insists, 'How connected people want to be is particular to the individual relationship. It's impossible to say you should see or speak to them once a week or whatever. It has to be a negotiation.'

Adult kids have grown up with increasingly sophisticated ways of communicating, while we parents grew up with landlines and public phone boxes. Making a call was a big deal and private moments had to be carefully engineered. So it's not surprising if parents are taken aback, even irritated, by how casual communication is now. It's annoying when your son sounds distracted by screens when you want a proper catch-up. And adult children are notoriously bad at picking up and returning calls, which grates if they expect an instant response when they ring you. Renate got so frustrated that she decided to give her son a nudge: 'I get really upset that Nathan rarely responds to my texts – how busy can he be? It takes two seconds to send a thumbs-up emoji. In the end I emailed him saying it was fine if he didn't have time for a proper response, but that I did expect some kind of brief acknowledgement at least. That seems to have worked.'

It's never been easier to stay in touch, either one-to-one or in groups, whether it's a quick text to say good luck or a long in-depth phone conversation or a messaging group where everyone posts photos of the dog or the meal they've just eaten. This week an old friend celebrated her 65th birthday with a virtual disco with her three kids and friends dancing in their own kitchens. Families have discovered that a focus, like a quiz, makes things flow more naturally. Video calls feel like they bring you closer and the view they offer into a loved one's world boosts the connection, whether you're living 50 or 5,000 miles apart. Nisha's daughter lived in Ecuador for three years: 'Stella used to give me a virtual tour of her flat and stuff like that. Which was great, you felt really connected. But then you pressed the button and the chat stopped, and suddenly she was 5,000 miles away again. That felt quite dramatic.'

That's one downside of video calls – or indeed any call when you're far apart – the minute you hang up, you're left missing them even more and knowing that they probably don't miss you quite so much. The other downside is being caught in your pyjamas with no make-up! And it can be hard to judge someone's mood when you're not in the same room; it's terrible not being able to give them a hug.

Jacqui was living 100 miles away from her daughter when she was having IVF treatment; they were both on a rollercoaster of anxiety, hope and disappointment. She remembers, 'We couldn't just pop round and have a chat. It's all right talking on the phone but actually physically talking to someone face to face, you can tell by their reaction and facial expressions how they're feeling. I know Tru is the kind of person who would hide her feelings from me because she knows I get easily upset. If she rang with bad news, I would always try to be positive, even though I didn't feel that positive. I'd talk to her in the moment in a calm way but when she was off the phone, that's when your heart starts to beat faster.'

Social media is a boon, as long as it's used wisely – and that generally means sparingly. It's tempting to follow adult children on social media, particularly when they first leave home and parents want to know their kids are safe and stay involved in their lives. But it can feel overprotective and even a bit controlling – one daughter joked that it felt like she was being stalked, while another had to ask her mother to stop her effusive posts because they were a bit embarrassing. It smacks of a reluctance to let kids lead their own lives and while that's understandable, it doesn't help them, or you. Sensible parents choose not to be friends with their child on Facebook because they feel it's their world. Instead, they turn their gaze on to their own lives and friendships, and allow adult children to get on with theirs.

HOW TO HAVE GOOD CONVERSATIONS

Good communication between parents and adult kids doesn't come from nowhere. It's a continuation of patterns established in childhood that ideally develop as the child grows into adulthood. But we all know families where parents talk to their adult children as if they were still children. And other families where, for whatever reason, people don't connect when it comes to the stuff that really matters.

'Some families aren't that good at communicating,' says Judith Lask. 'There isn't an intimacy between them which is built by knowing how each other is feeling about something, or what's going on in their lives, what's important to them and so on. Some families aren't very intimate in that sense; people are quite distant and almost a bit formal. When they become adults the children may stay like their family, and see it as perfectly OK, and they don't look to their parents for that sort of intimacy. But other adult children might feel upset that they haven't been able to talk about feelings or share things.'

This doesn't mean that we should gush on about our emotions or continually ask 'How did that make you feel?' It's more about making it perfectly normal to say when you feel a bit miserable rather than pretending everything's fine all the time. Parents and kids should be able to say they had a bad day without it being either glossed over or turned into a big deal. Acknowledgement is usually enough.

When Lindsey was a young adult, her mother used to get angry if she was feeling a bit down. She says, 'When I was growing up, the communication wasn't there to say you were fed up. My parents were emotionally distant, it was all stiff upper lip. The channels of communication were never established in childhood, so they weren't there when we became adults. As an adult, I communicated with my mother in the same way as I had as a child: not very much. So with my own daughters, I was very aware that if you don't communicate when children are little it's very hard when they are adults. I've always been open with them about how I felt about things, and I always wanted to know how they felt and be tuned in to what they were doing and thinking. I think my children are aware if I'm cross or not happy, just as I'm tuned in to how they're feeling, without intruding too much.'

How to have good phone conversations

We're all familiar with that initial awkwardness on the phone to someone you don't see every day, as the person who has been interrupted shifts focus away from what they were doing. Getting a conversation going can be hard because you're not so tuned in to the ordinary dilemmas and problems that come and go in people's lives. And even though parent and child are equals now, it's usually up to the parent to make the effort.

Corinne, who has two sons in their twenties, accepts this: 'I think as a parent it's down to you to find things to talk about that they'd be interested in and you have to work harder to draw them out than when they were at home, so I try to think about what's going on in the world that would interest them. It helps that Liam is a furniture-maker, which overlaps with my work as a designer; if he was a doctor, the things that interested him would be right over my head!'

It helps to get in the zone before you make a call by focusing your thoughts on the other person, even visualising them. Be curious about their lives and how they're feeling. Think about things you've noticed that might interest them. There's a fine line between being curious and being too intrusive. Too often, adult children find their parents' questions annoying and clam up – I know I used to with my mum's gentle enquiries. I can't put my finger on why, because it's not that kids don't want their parents to be interested in their lives. But no one wants to feel like they're being interviewed or interrogated.

IF AN ADULT CHILD RARELY GETS IN TOUCH

If an adult child doesn't contact you as much as you would like it hurts because it makes you feel insignificant, that you are not in their thoughts. In fact, there could be all kinds of reasons. Practical obstacles, such as a long and expensive journey, are likely to make visits difficult. There are other things you can't do much about too: saying they're busy is not just an excuse, they genuinely are preoccupied with work and family. It should be reassuring to remember that there are times when life gets so consuming that when people do get time to themselves they just want to relax. I've learnt from experience that there are periods, which sometimes last a couple of years, when adult children aren't around much, but they undulate into phases when they are more present. However, some issues are within your control:

- Do you expect too much contact?
  There are no rules. Some kids text three times a day, others call every couple of months. If friends' kids ring every day it might give you a pang of envy, but what really matters is how well you connect when you do speak. Every parent and child has to work out what suits them. Parents generally like to see their children more than their children want to see them: that's a fact of life, but it's still sad. Judith Lask adds, 'Of course expectations are highly influenced by peer pressure among parents. There is also an issue of what your expectations are and they will differ between different people; how much you need to be in touch in order to feel OK will depend on your experience and attachment. If the attachment feels secure, you don't get so worried if you don't hear from your child because you have a sense that they care about you and that they'll contact you when they want to. And vice versa.'

- Are you making them feel guilty?
  No one likes being made to feel guilty, least of all adult children. If parents pressurise their kids to visit or to attend family gatherings, or make remarks that unintentionally make them feel bad for not being in touch more often, it will probably make them stay away even more.

- Does your child feel that they aren't living up to your expectations?
  Quizzing people about job hunting or success at work, however well-intentioned, can make people feel inadequate, or even worse, that they've let their parents down. The same goes for questions about their love life or hints about wanting a grandchild. These subjects don't have to be avoided outright, but they need to be approached with care and sensitivity.

- Do you treat them like an adult?
  Adult children enjoy home comforts and being a bit spoilt when they visit, but if they're treated like children, they'll behave like children. It's just not on to have a go at them or correct their table manners. It's no longer appropriate to impose limitations on young adults that were part of life with teenagers. Why would a child want to come home if they feel their parents get at them the whole time? Language is important. An acid test is to ask yourself whether you would talk to a friend in the way that you ask your child to lay the table. Children aren't the same as friends, but they do deserve the same respect.

GIVING ADVICE

The basic rule is, don't offer adult children advice unless they ask for it. Once again, it's about trusting them to find their own way and making sure they believe you have faith in them. At the same time they need to know you're available. If they do want advice, whether it's about buying a car or a difficult situation at work, parents need to accept that they may not take it. Often all they're really looking for is a sounding board. They don't want parents to fix things, or to be told what to do, but simply a chance to talk things through with someone they love and trust.

It's the same approach that good life coaches use. We all know how useful it is when making a difficult decision to weigh up the pros and cons with an objective outsider and then work things out yourself. Lucy, a psychotherapist whose two children are in their late twenties and live at home, says, 'Cat and Duncan ask for our advice occasionally, although they don't always listen to it! Sometimes it's quite straightforward, like when Cat was looking at postgraduate economics courses and asked us what we thought. What's harder is if Duncan says he's going to email his boss to complain about a colleague. Internally, my husband and I are both going, *Oh My God...* and I look at Angus and he says, "Well, Duncan, I think it's probably best if you just speak to someone about it rather than sending an email, because that could get really up somebody's nose."

'And because the advice is given in a thoughtful way rather than an accusatory way, Duncan is able to take it. Sometimes he comes back and says that was really helpful, it made a difference. It's really about can they receive the advice and that's about how you offer it. It's like a bird with a crumb, or a baby with the breast – you can't force it down by saying *you really should do this*. If they can process it for themselves, they can make the idea their own and digest it.'

As children develop through adulthood, they are just as likely to give their parents sensible advice and support as vice versa. It's one of the many signs that the balance between you is shifting all the time. One day you notice how wisely and calmly they handle situations that might have made them panic in the past. As Brenda says, 'I no longer always assume I've got to be the one who sorts things out.'

5

Living with Adult Children

One of the biggest demographic changes in family life over recent decades has been the dramatic rise in the number of adult children living with their parents. A large-scale study by the Centre for Research in Social Policy at Loughborough University, published in 2020, found that nearly two-thirds of childless single adults aged 20–34 in the UK have either never left home or have moved back in with their parents, an increase of a third over the past decade. It's no longer only graduates who return to the nest after university while they find their feet and get jobs; these days many young adults spend most of their twenties living at home. Disconcertingly, parents never quite know whether their children have left home for good. They can expect their kids to return in their twenties, thirties and even forties, perhaps several times, and for all kinds of reasons: they're between jobs, or saving for a flat, or they've split up with a partner. The actor Rupert Everett announced he was moving in with his mother at the age of 59. American pop artist Andy Warhol lived with his mother from his mid-twenties to his early forties.

The COVID-19 pandemic accelerated the trend, forcing adult children of all ages to move in with parents when they lost their jobs, even their homes. Although the phenomenon is primarily driven by economics, it's likely to have a lasting impact on the quality of individual relationships. Hopefully it's largely positive, because it gives parents an opportunity to really get to know and understand their children as adults. Yet the feeling persists that there's something not quite right if a child moves back, or doesn't leave home in the first place. In most Western countries launching independent young adults into the world remains *the* benchmark of success for both parents and twenty-somethings. Even in Italy, where it's not uncommon for people to live at home in their thirties, a government minister called for laws in 2010 to encourage young people to leave home, as a way of tackling the 'culture of mummy's boys and big babies'; there's even a term for them: '*bambiccioni*'. So when kids move back in with their parents, there is often a nagging sense of failure on both sides.

Over the past few years research has focused on the downsides, particularly for parents. A study of 17 European countries by the London School of Economics concluded that when adult children returned to an empty nest it caused a noticeable decline in parents' quality of life. But when you talk to parents and adult kids the picture is more nuanced. Most parents feel ambivalent. It's true that they worry about holding their kids back and regret giving up aspects of their recently rediscovered freedom, but at the same time they're keen to help their kids in whatever way they can and they can see that it's tough out there.

Most parents enjoy having their kids around and see the benefits of living together on more equal terms. Lucy is typical: one minute she really hopes her son, who's 29, will move out soon, the next she's worrying that he might feel pushed out. Both her kids have moved in and out of home throughout their twenties. She says, 'You have to observe your own motives and whether you're fearing the empty nest. I'm not! Having said that, it is very nice having them around, but I'd be equally delighted if they had their own places. I think it would be better for my son if he was doing his own thing somewhere else. I think he thinks that too, although I haven't actually raised it.

I'm worried he'll think that we don't really want him here. There's an element of truth in that, but not because we don't like him.'

Adult children have mixed feelings too, although generally they are more positive than their parents, according to an earlier study by the LSE. The vast majority of adult kids see living at home as a temporary stopgap, yet many kids appreciate the emotional support as much as the financial benefits – they just don't want to be treated like children. Interestingly, one study found that daughters were much more likely than sons to say that living at home made them feel like a child.

As a result of this huge change in adult family life, people are finally questioning the automatic link made between independence and leaving home. There is a dawning acknowledgement that there are mutual benefits as well as difficulties and a new interest in the way other cultures view the transition to adulthood. There is a recognition of the value of seeing it as a more gradual process with the emphasis on continuing interdependence. Dr Reenee Singh, Director of the London Intercultural Couples Centre, says, 'It is a very Anglo-Saxon, Eurocentric idea that children should leave home at the age of 18 and that adult families should form their own little units. Ideas of autonomy and independence are valued much more in Western society, or have been until recently. A part of it is economic. There isn't enough money for young people to move out, so they don't have a choice. That's partly why in the Western world the whole notion of adult families is changing. The idea of freedom and autonomy is quite different if you're also bound up financially.'

There is also a growing number of families where two or three generations make a positive decision to set up home together and mutually support each other. It has long been an established norm in many cultures, where parents expect to help with grandchildren, while adult children expect to support their parents in old age. It's now the fastest-growing household type in the UK. According to the Office for National Statistics (ONS), multi-family households have grown by three-quarters to 297,000 over the last 20 years, although to be fair, they still make up a small proportion of all household types – just over 1 per cent in 2019.

Why parents feel uneasy about kids living at home

One reason why parents can't help but have doubts is that our generation's experience of leaving home in the sixties, seventies and eighties was so different to our children's. The urge to break away from parents is what many of us understand in our bones, but it's not that helpful now. Back then the generation gap was wider and parents were generally less tolerant: everyone was desperate to escape the small-minded suburbs and head for places with cool, like-minded people, parties, sex, drugs and liberation. Generous student grants and a surge in university places made it easy to leave and never come back.

The landscape for young adults has changed utterly. Young people have been profoundly affected by the global financial crisis of 2008 and its subsequent repercussions. Student fees have risen and rents have escalated, while the COVID-19 pandemic made the job market even more competitive and unstable. Most kids live at home primarily because they can't afford their own place, but emotional support and a sense of security come into it too. Liam, 25, recently moved back home while looking for his second job. He says, 'This is my first time moving back for six years and I'm really enjoying it. Living at home is not just about being able to get the train to London for job interviews, although that's a blessing too. Now that I'm looking for my second job, I'm finding that employers are asking for more than I can offer, like two or three years' experience, so this is a difficult time. I've suffered from anxiety since I was a student and having my parents' emotional support has been really important. So has the familiar feeling of home: we've lived in this house since I was young, so it's coming back into the nest I have known my whole life.'

There's clearly a danger that living at home can infantilise adult children by protecting them from realities like council tax and electricity bills. If the living's too easy, there's little motivation to leave or get a proper job. Parents naturally feel torn between supporting their offspring and successfully launching them as independent adults. But people are now waking up to the idea that the two things aren't mutually exclusive and that by supporting their children, parents may in fact be giving them a better chance of launching successfully. Many psychologists now believe that a supportive family setting can help nurture independence and make the transition to adulthood more gradual and easier to navigate.

Living with a child in their early twenties who is fresh out of the student bubble is very different to living with one who has lived away from home for a while, perhaps even for several years. Lucy sums it up: 'It's different living with Catriona because she worked and lived independently for a few years before she came back. I know she's viable. And she feels that too, very much so.' It's different again when a child moves back in with their partner. (More on page 90.)

What works for one family is a question of individual circumstances, temperaments and behaviour, so it's best to trust your instincts as a parent and avoid being influenced by what anyone else thinks. Parents and kids know in their hearts when living at home feels right and when it really is a backward step. Everyone will feel more comfortable if they know there's an end in view, even if it's a few years down the line, so it's good to discuss and agree on a rough time limit, which can be reviewed every few months. If adult kids have their sights set on finding their own place, and are taking steps to make that happen, they'll feel less frustrated and no one will feel that life has stalled. If there's not much sign of that, and the young adult seems almost too content with home comforts, parents may need to give them a nudge.

Living with adult children in their early twenties

About half of new graduates boomerang back home after university, according to various sources, including the London School of Economics. These days, they may stay a couple of years rather than a few months. In many families, this works well, giving adult children a secure springboard. Anyone who is going through a challenging transition benefits from familiarity in some aspects of their life. Home should be a place where adult kids know they can relax and be themselves. Parents need to feel that too, but sometimes there is a clash. Lucy says, 'There are times when I get in from work and there are at least six of Cat's friends in the kitchen and you think, *Oh God, I'd really like to go in there* but you know you're intruding. That's a bit of a drag. And sometimes I go to the fridge looking forward to a glass of orange juice and the kids have drunk it all. So I text Cat and her brother saying will one of you please replace the orange juice and while you're at it, think about what you're eating because all the cheese has gone – I don't let them get away with it.'

When an adult child first moves back, the inevitable settling in period requires adjustment and compromise on both sides. Things are bound to get tense at times as everyone adjusts to their new roles and works out different ways of rubbing along together. Parents often complain that children expect to be treated as adults, yet they don't do their bit around the house or take responsibility in other areas of their lives. Meanwhile, young people resent the loss of freedom and feeling more dependent on their parents than they were at university. And if kids try to impose their own new values and eating habits on the family, it rarely goes down well.

From the start, life with adult children needs to be on a very different footing from life with teenagers. That might sound obvious, but it's far from automatic. Breaking old family habits requires effort on both sides. Liam, who had lived with friends for six years before moving back, says, 'Just by being at home you're being looked after.

Although Mum doesn't go over the top, you can't help but slip back into those old childhood patterns and all of a sudden you find yourself getting annoyed with your parents and feeling like a sulky teenager. I know that's why some of my friends don't like being at home. It makes them feel like they're a kid again, because they can't help slipping back into those patterns.

'That's why I've made a conscious effort to act differently and be a part of the house. I came back a different person. Mum and Dad see I've changed and I feel like they treat me like an adult, but they still have that nurturing towards me and I like that. Being at home is not the same as when I left – having done all my own washing and cleaning, I can't slip back into letting Mum and Dad do everything.'

It helps if you can both change expectations. The theory is that if parents treat their emerging adult children like adults, they'll behave like adults. Equally, if your child behaves like an adult, it's up to parents to respond to the change. But of course it's more complicated than that. Most parents find it hard not to revert to hands-on parent mode at times, even with children in their thirties and forties.

Nisha's 30-year-old daughter has moved in and out of home a few times on her own, as well as with her partner and more recently their baby daughter. She says, 'The other day I asked my daughter if she wanted a cup of tea and she said, "Mum, I can look after myself!" I thought, but I'm your mum, that doesn't stop. At what point in your life am I going to stop caring about you? You do those things naturally, it's part of your relationship.'

It takes nerve to stand back and let them make their own mistakes when you're living cheek by jowl. It's too tempting to chip in with advice. You can't help but purse your lips when they keep reaching for the bottle of wine; it's hard to get to sleep until you hear the front door shut in the wee small hours.

What's confusing is that while sometimes kids get really irritated by the nurturing, at other times they love it – indeed they positively demand it. A young adult who has just started a full-on first job won't complain about help with cooking and laundry, and that's fair enough in the first few months. But for the relationship to feel more equal, parents have to let kids look after themselves, even if it feels petty to make a point by not shoving their washing into the machine for them. The flipside is that parents need to pursue their own independence too. The aim is to allow adult children to be as self-sufficient as possible under the same roof. They need to take on the tedious everyday tasks they would have to do if they lived elsewhere. That's not just about housework but helping sorting out council tax admin and dealing with a power cut and finding a plumber. The other side of the coin is the freedom to come and go, while respecting the household.

LIVING WITH TWENTY-SOMETHINGS

- Don't just drift into things. The arrangement will get off to a better start if it's grounded in a clear-sighted discussion about the pros, cons, expectations and practicalities.
- Don't make assumptions about how your partner feels about an adult child moving back. It helps if you're more or less on the same page.
- Agree on a flexible end date and review it periodically.
- Parents' biggest complaint, according to LSE research, is that children want to be treated as adults but don't behave like adults when it comes to the domestic stuff. Parents are partly to blame if they don't allow their kids to look after themselves in the way they would have to if they had their own place.
- If parents change their expectations, adult children usually respond.

- Give adult kids an idea of the bills they'd have to pay if they left home, from regular utility bills to fixing a blocked drain. You could do this by going through the household bills together or asking them to organise the washing machine repair.
- Go away for a fortnight and leave them to it.
- Parents' independence is a pivotal part of the equation. If you're preoccupied and fulfilled by other stuff in your life, your child will have to step up on the domestic front.

Moving back home in the late twenties/thirties

The big change in recent years is that adult children now keep boomeranging in and out of home in their twenties, thirties and even forties. This coming and going is an emotional rollercoaster for parents that their kids are blissfully unaware of. Parents who have got used to a new life without children and perhaps reconnected with their partner – or found a new partner – have to change gear, although hopefully not into reverse. And just when they get used to having adult kids around, they have to say goodbye again.

The primary impetus to move home is still usually financial or practical necessity rather than a desire to live together. It might be divorce or redundancy or homelessness, or even something more mundane, like being in between flats or having a new kitchen installed. Nisha's older daughter moved back with her three-year-old when a problem was picked up in her second pregnancy. Nisha says, 'My kids see me as a safety valve. I never feel they're taking advantage and I'm glad that they feel comfortable enough with me. It's not *Oh God, we've got to move back with Mum*. We all get on fine.'

Clearly, different situations require different levels of emotional and practical support. Life in the household is bound to get stressful if the return is due to a relationship breakdown or redundancy or illness and parents have to judge how to be helpful without interfering. Tania moved back home for a short time when her marriage ended in her thirties after living independently for 17 years. She remembers, 'I was in a physical and mental state of shock and my parents had to deal with that. It was a very difficult and humiliating time. You are thrust back to being a child and that's deeply uncomfortable. It was nonetheless very comforting and I felt very lucky that they were there.'

When I met Paul, who suffered badly from empty nest sadness, his eldest daughter Kealy had just moved back home after leaving her husband. Her two young children were there for half the week, spending the other days with their dad. Paul says, 'Overnight, our relationship with Kealy changed. Suddenly she was my little girl again and I know it sounds selfish but I became a father again: she came to me because she needed her dad. But at the same time it's a more grown-up relationship between us. Kealy has been through a divorce; she has experienced something that I haven't, and which I don't understand, so I'm asking her questions. Sometimes it's like she's never left, but it is different. Last night, she came down and said, "Is it OK if I have a bath? And can I take a little drink up with me?" It's not like the teenage days when you were putting a mark on the vodka bottle! She's 34, she can do what she wants.'

When older adult children move back there should be less conflict, if only because they've got more experience of sharing with other people and don't need prompting to tidy up the kitchen. Parents have become used to seeing older offspring as independent; there's less need for the kind of friction that's common when young adults are trying to assert their individuality. But older children are just as likely to feel uncomfortable about a return to dependence and this inevitably gives rise to tension. They're used to their own way of doing things and accustomed to having their own space.

Lucy says, 'We don't have a lot of arguments, but my son and I did have a run-in about six months ago – I can't remember what it was about but I got totally exasperated and he got really angry and in the heat of the moment I went for mass destruction and said, "This is our house and if you don't like it, you don't have to live here!" I think it hurt him. I really regretted it and I retracted it later.'

Living with adult kids and their partners

Life with an adult child is different again if a partner comes too. With an incomer there is inevitably more at stake than there is with your own child: you both want to be liked and approved of. It's not easy for an outsider to get to grips with a family's unfamiliar quirks. It helps if you can put yourself in their shoes and recall a time when you were in a similar position, perhaps on holiday with your own in-laws or staying with another family. If you can be yourself, and see them as part of the family, they'll relax too. Rather than offering endless cups of tea, which is friendly but actually makes people feel like a guest, it's much better to encourage them to treat the kettle and the house as their own. This goes with expecting the other person to do their bit around the house. You know things are going well when you no longer feel the need to thank them when they automatically take out the bins.

Living with a couple brings challenges – and I don't just mean their sex life, although that is undoubtedly a thing. There's more a sense of them and us, and while it feels natural to a young couple to spend most of their time in their room, it can come across as unfriendly or make parents feel awkward. Parents worry the partner doesn't like them or that they should be more welcoming, but Nisha has worked it out: 'I've noticed that all my children still treat their bedroom like their space. So even though there are communal spaces, and even though they're grown-up, they need that space to be theirs – I think that's essential when you live with people. My mother wasn't like that. If you were in the house you all had to be together, and if you left the room it was, where have you gone? I always thought that was very claustrophobic and I'm much more accepting of people just needing to go off.'

Clearly there's a lot of luck involved. A great deal depends on how well you get on with the new person and how compatible you are when it comes to things like domestic standards and TV habits. One father I know, whose stepson and his wife have lived with him for a couple of years, admits his own standards are lower than theirs. Nisha thinks it's been easier for her because she's been a single parent since her three children were young: 'For my own children as well as for their partners it's been much easier to move into a place that has just me, not a team of Mum and Dad. As a single person I can be adaptable and I've learnt to make allowances in a way that would be almost impossible for a couple. I've had a lot of experience of adult males living in my house and luckily, I've always got on with them. Your own children grow up and change and you just get used to it and go with it. But it's a bit different introducing new people into the house who don't know the house rules and maybe don't wipe the shower and things like that. At first, I used to say something and it would feel awkward and I'd wish I hadn't, so over the years I've learnt that actually it's best to leave it. My house is a lot untidier than it used to be because I've just had to relax and think, it doesn't matter. What does matter is us all feeling happy.'

However, it's no good pretending you don't mind about things if they really get to you, because too quickly minor stuff builds up and creates a permanent undercurrent of resentment. No one wants to have to tell their son's girlfriend not to overload the washing machine or to pick up her dirty coffee cups. Writing notes is a bit cowardly and winds people up. One alternative is to communicate the house rules through your child, but it's probably better to be direct – and choose your battles carefully – if you feel the need to say something. Take a calm moment to think about what really bugs you and then set aside time for a discussion without being too heavy about it. Be clear, straightforward, don't be apologetic – and take their suggestions on board too. One of the bonuses of adult kids in the house is that they shake things up, introduce new ideas and generally prevent their parents getting into a rut.

And there's another bonus of sharing everyday life with your child's partner: it's one of the best ways to get to know each other properly. Casual conversations in the kitchen or in front of the telly, no matter how trivial the chat, build the kind of relationship you don't get from meeting up, however frequently. You get to know ordinary things about their lives and gain insights into their likes and dislikes. If the couple go on to set up their own home and build a life together, it will give your future relationship a solid grounding and a mutual understanding that's harder to achieve in other ways.

MONEY: WHEN ADULT CHILDREN LIVE AT HOME

Financial issues get more complicated when adult kids' lifestyles are in your face and you can see what they spend their – or in some cases *your* – cash on. It's also obvious how much effort they're putting into looking for a job. Money is bound up with emotional issues that tug at parents' hearts, like safety and health, and so knowing when to chip in and when not to can be a dilemma. Most parents aren't quite as hardline as Keith, who says, 'If my daughter says she can't afford to get her bike fixed or whatever, I wouldn't hesitate to tell her to get her priorities right. If she thinks having a beer is more important, that's her lookout. I would never bail her out for anything basic like that because it would feel like I was treating her like a child.'

If adult kids move home because they're out of work and in dire financial straits, most parents do whatever they can to support them and don't expect them to pay rent. It's a different matter if they seem a bit too content to be unemployed, or if they're sniffy about jobs they think are boring or beneath them. Parents of young adults want to feel that they are doing their best to get a foot on the career ladder, while at the same time acknowledging that the job market is tough.

If their children are employed, most parents go along with the idea that they should pay rent, however little they earn, although we've come a long way from the days when kids' wages were automatically syphoned into the family budget. In practice, though, I've come across only a few parents who ask for a contribution and that's backed up by LSE research in 2016 that found that even the minority of adult children who do pay make only a nominal contribution. In many families, cultural norms mean that a contribution is not expected; parents feel it goes against the grain. What's also fascinating is that in so many families the subject is rarely discussed; instead, assumptions are made on both sides.

But it's undeniable that asking for rent or a weekly contribution to household costs keeps things real. It doesn't do your child any favours to get used to a lifestyle way more lavish than they could afford if they didn't live at home. Lucy, one of the few parents I've met who does ask for a contribution, explains, 'Ever since Duncan started work six years ago, when he was 23, we've charged him rent, even though he wasn't earning much then. I think it's probably best for him: it's saying, don't take us for granted, and that's important. Now that he's earning quite well, he pays us £450 a month, which we put in an ISA for when he moves out. But it seems a bit unfair to us because his younger sister doesn't earn enough to pay anything; she works part-time while she does an economics MA.'

IS IT OK TO SAY NO OR ASK CHILDREN TO LEAVE?

Most kids take it for granted that if there's enough room in the house they'll be welcomed back with open arms. Many adult children have no idea that their parents have reservations about relinquishing their empty nest freedom, according to LSE research. But many parents, even if they hate to admit it, are keen to get on with their own lives. After years of child-rearing, it's natural to want to do your own thing and explore a direction beyond the family. Some parents feel that having kids at home holds them back both emotionally and in practical ways. They feel frustrated that their plans to downsize, or take in a lodger, or go on dates, are put on hold.

A few parents, like Jenny, are brave enough to say no. She says, 'In our son's final year at university we sat down with him and said that we didn't think it was a good idea for him to come back and live at home when he graduated. He had come home one vacation and when we went away, he and his mates had wrecked the house. At the time he said it was a bit harsh, but now he says it's the best thing we could have done. It helped that he's very independent. We said we would support him financially until he found his feet and within about six months he was self-sufficient. I didn't feel I was being brave, I just felt it was the right thing to do.'

If you don't want your child to move back, it's only fair to give plenty of warning so that they've got time to make plans. Helen has already brought up the subject with her younger daughter, who is currently in her second of four years at St Andrews University. She says, 'I've been observing from friends that moving back home is not necessarily a very healthy move, on the whole – I don't see many people very happy about it. I have been drawing my daughter's attention to the fact that it could be a real possibility. As a result, she is being much more active in building her CV and visiting the careers department, so that she can avoid it happening at all costs.'

Asking a child to leave

Asking a child to leave when they're already living at home brings similar dilemmas. Most parents hope their child will move out without needing to be asked. I've heard of parents who waited so long that they gave up and moved out themselves! Of course, for most people that's not an option. Lucy, whose son and daughter have lived at home for most of their twenties, says, 'There are times when my husband and I say to each other, *Duncan's got to go, no question*. But it's a sensitive subject. He told us recently that he's been offered a room in a friend's flat, but he doesn't want to start paying for it until the end of the summer, while the flat starts in May. We both went, "No, Go! Go now, we'll help you with the rent." Maybe he'll feel a bit pushed out, but too bad. He's 29, for God's sake! I really hope it happens.'

Suggesting that it's time to move on is a lot easier if you've already agreed a deadline, albeit a flexible one. That way, both sides know where they stand and expect the situation to be reviewed every few months, so that there are no sudden surprises and both sides get plenty of warning that change is on the horizon. It's tough for parents if a child suddenly announces they're moving out next week, even if they are relieved. Equally, parents should be upfront about their possible future plans to move, or rent the house to go travelling, or take in a lodger. It's also fair enough to simply say that you think the time's approaching when you both moved in a new direction.

HOW KIDS AT HOME AFFECTS PARENTS' RELATIONSHIP WITH EACH OTHER

Mothers and fathers often have conflicting views about whether it's a good idea for a child to move back home and how long they should stay. Generally, it's fathers who seem more reluctant, but that's not always the case. One father I interviewed was happy for his daughter to stay at home because he worried she had been unsettled by his divorce; his new wife was less keen, but did her best to be understanding. Step-parents are usually inclined to take a more objective, less indulgent view and want to get on with their own lives, particularly if it's a new relationship. So, before kids move back home, parents need to talk through how it might affect them, as well as how it will be for their child.

Lucy and her husband have learnt the importance of being on the same page: 'We've realised it's better to talk to each other before we talk to either of the kids about something we're not happy about. Occasionally I say to Angus, would you support me if I insisted that we did x?, and he'll usually say, good idea. Or he'll say, I don't think they should be doing x. It's really important to present a united front.'

Sharing a home with adult children is bound to have an impact on your relationship as a couple. One of the huge benefits of an empty nest is that parents have more time and emotional space to give their relationship the attention it badly needs after the child-rearing years. But with kids back under the same roof, couples who had got back into the habit of putting each other first find themselves in full parent mode again. It's all too easy to slip back into the way things were, unless you're clear in your own minds that from now on, things will be different. If parents can allow their adult children to lead independent lives, albeit under the same roof, that should give their own relationship the space it needs. They'll still have quality time with each other and continue to nurture their relationship as a couple.

Privacy is part of it. There is an estate agent's advert doing the rounds at the moment that hits the nail on the head: 'The best thing about finding your own flat is no longer having to share a wall with Jake's parents'. It's addressed to the younger generation but they're not the only ones who need their own space. Again, it's not just about sex, but there is usually an impact. A lot of couples feel inhibited when their adult kids are in the house and women in particular can find it hard to switch from mother to loving partner. As one woman said, 'A Saturday morning lie-in is not the same when there's a 37-year-old crashing about downstairs.'

6

Crises in Adult Children's Lives

A crisis in your child's life can feel like your crisis too, and that's the case whether they're 14, 24 or 44. When your child is ill or upset or in trouble, it sparks an instinctive, gut response. The anxiety that gnaws in the middle of the night is a sharp reminder that you never stop being a parent and that your relationship is still underpinned by a kind of primeval protectiveness. You might have thought your job was done when they left home, but that's never really the case. A friend's 92-year-old father recently remarked, 'One of the good things about getting older is that you don't worry about the children *quite so much.*'

Some crises hit like a bolt from the blue, with one of those dreaded phone calls that slices into an ordinary day with news of a house fire or a divorce or an accident. But crises are just as likely to be ongoing struggles that rumble on and periodically explode into a meltdown: stress at work, loneliness or lack of romance, disordered eating. Apparently ordinary circumstances, such as a difficult boss or problems moving house, can build into a crisis. For parents who sense something's wrong, the anxiety nags away: you can tell something's not right with your daughter's marriage or your son's drinking, but you keep hoping for the best...

It's often said that what really matters is the way people deal with difficult situations. Some fall apart in the face of minor disasters, others never get out of the habit of expecting someone else to sort things out for them, while some people simply roll up their sleeves and get on with it. To some extent it's a combination of temperament, experience and resilience. As adult children get older, resilience builds as they become better at dealing with difficult situations.

Emerging adults in particular often see minor calamities, like a broken laptop, or a battle with bureaucracy, as the end of the world. It comes as a surprise to parents when children who are fiercely determined to be independent suddenly demand their help. Helen, who has two daughters in their early twenties, says, 'The big drama last week was when Jessie got a fine for not having the correct railway ticket. She rang out of the blue, totally outraged, saying, "Mum, it's a disaster!" I could see it was tough, but I'd been having a quiet, uneventful day at the computer and suddenly my emotions were on high alert. I still get very drawn in emotionally.'

It's at this stage that parents can help emerging adults to build resilience and an emotional toolbox to deal with challenges. Their role is to put things into perspective. Adult children need to know their parents believe that they can handle things on their own, but at the same time that they're always there to give support when needed. Yet stepping back is hard because parents are acutely aware of their children's vulnerabilities and weak spots, and naturally want to protect them from situations that might dent their self-confidence. In fact, if parents always sort things out, it's even more likely to dent self-confidence, and unless it's a serious emergency, it's best to resist the urge to don the Batman cape. Janet Reibstein, Professor Emerita of Psychology at Exeter University, says, 'Being supportive is being able to step back and understand what your child's needs are.'

Helen's training as a coach has proved a big advantage when dealing with her daughter's pleas for help. She says, 'I just stay on the phone while she vents and give her space to think round ways of getting the problem sorted. If she can sort out the problem herself, I think it can be quite powerful in improving her understanding about herself and in boosting her self-confidence, so we don't rush to help unless it's a real emergency. I suppose we are the baseline, the safety net.'

The problem for parents is that they don't stop worrying until things get sorted out, yet young adults often forget to let them know. It's not deliberate: once they've sorted out the problem they just move on to the next thing, and forget that their parents might still be concerned. But that doesn't make it any easier!

CRISES YOU DON'T HEAR ABOUT

Some crises – like divorce – are in everyone's face. The whole family gets caught up in the emotional fallout. Other crises you don't hear about until after the event. Adult children are selective about the areas of their lives they open up about. Parents can't be blamed if they feel hurt, particularly if siblings or in-laws have been in the know for a while. The consolation is that their children have other people they can rely on – and that's the way it should be.

Paul is proud of the way his three daughters support each other and tell each other everything. Nevertheless, he sounds a bit wistful when he says, 'Kealy's sisters knew she was having problems in her marriage before me and Toni, just as they knew she was having a baby before we did. That's great, but sometimes you can't help feeling, why couldn't we be part of that initial conversation? There's a bit of jealousy perhaps. We could see the marriage was in trouble for about 18 months but I said to Toni, just leave her, don't talk about it, when she needs us she'll come to us. We just have to be ready.'

If parents have an inkling that something's wrong, but their child doesn't say anything, it's difficult to know whether to broach the subject or wait to be told. There are all kinds of reasons why adult children prefer to keep things from their parents. They may not want to worry them and have their anxiety to cope with on top of their own. Or they may be too proud to admit that things aren't going well. They may fear parents' reaction: that they'll disapprove or blame them or say 'I told you so'. They may even feel guilty or foolish, that they're a failure or disappointment.

Tru explains why she was reluctant to tell her mother that she needed fertility treatment: 'I thought she would see it as failure, especially after I'd experienced other frustrations in life. That was a lot to do with feeling nervous about telling her. I didn't want to feel I was a disappointment. But then I couldn't *not* tell her. If I hadn't, what would the fallout have been? It would have been, "Why didn't you say?"

'My mum can be quite emotional and can sometimes get very stressed and worried, which is natural, but it wasn't necessarily helpful for me. I had to cope with her stress and anxiety as well as my own. I could have shielded her from having to go through it with me, but I'm so glad I didn't, because I would have had to deal with the whole thing by myself.'

What's tough is that parents have to manage their own emotions while helping their child manage theirs. Their concern is not only with getting through the crisis itself, but also about how their child is coping with it. Are they drinking too much or eating enough? Are they sleeping? Are they lonely or isolated? Professor Janet Reibstein advocates a direct approach: 'I think you should be honest about your concerns and say something like "We're your parents, we're thinking about you, we're wondering whether you're looking after yourself. And we're here to help you to do that. If it's too much, just tell us to shut up. Or reassure us, and then we won't ask you any more."'

SEEING THE CRISIS FROM YOUR CHILD'S POINT OF VIEW

Parents also need to think about what it must be like for the adult child to be thrown back into a dependent role after years of independence.

That's particularly hard if children have to move back home, perhaps because they're seriously ill or they've split up with a partner and they've got nowhere to live. But what's wonderful about parents is that their love and support is unconditional and that's just as well, because people in crisis can be challenging company, as Tania is the first to admit. Her parents have seen her through two major crises: divorce and redundancy. They cut short a holiday in Spain the minute they heard about her divorce and flew straight home to support her: 'As an adult child you're thrust into a situation where you need your parents again – in my case for the first time in 17 years. It's very difficult because you are back to being their child. My mum's a big talker rather than a listener so what I could always rely on when I turned up was that she'd be talking about my divorce. Which sometimes I didn't want! But perhaps that underlying feeling of returning to being a child and wanting my life back as an independent adult was no bad thing. It probably spurred me on to get my shit together, to find a new place to live and get a job, to carry on and start again.'

In a crisis people often go into what my GP calls 'coping mode' – when they don't want to talk or even think about their problems because all their energies are focused on getting through. Parents need to be sensitive to this and make space for their child to talk when they're ready, rather than ask too many direct questions. That's still the case when the immediate crisis has passed: the parent is still worried but the adult child wants to shake off their concern.

Anne-Marie's daughter, Siobhan, who is now 31, has suffered anxiety since her father died of cancer when she was in her late twenties. Siobhan accepted her mother's help in the early days, but six years on, things have changed. Anne-Marie says, 'Initially, Siobhan came to me a lot because she was unhappy and extremely anxious about everything. Every time she had chest pains or numbness in her arm she thought she was dying. I did my best to help her because I know myself how crippling anxiety can be and since then she's had CBT [cognitive behavioural therapy] and that has helped. Now she's a bit loath to come to me and she gets a bit impatient if I mention it too much. She's quite firm when she says, *Mum, I don't want to talk about that.'*

In the long term a crisis usually brings families closer and changes the relationship in unexpectedly positive ways. That's partly because to be genuinely helpful, parents have to stay curious and open-minded about what's going on for their adult child. Curiosity is not about prying or asking questions, but about thinking empathetically. Parents need to be flexible, prepared to reassess their own assumptions and adaptable to change. The resilience they've built up through their own past experiences should stand them in good stead.

Tania says, 'I would never have guessed that the parents who raised me with quite black and white rules would be so accepting of me doing things differently. They were able to go through all these things they had never experienced before, and had no understanding of, and would therefore want to reject, really. I feel they are much more open-minded now than they were when I was growing up. And my mum is more able to change, even though she's nearly 80. My relationship with her has moved on in a way my sister's relationship with her hasn't, because my sister has never needed her.'

HOW PARENTS CAN HELP IN A CRISIS

- Try to keep your own emotions in check. That's a big ask, but the last thing your child needs is your anxiety as well as their own.
- Try not to be judgemental and never say 'I told you so', even if that's exactly what you're thinking.

- Focus on practical help that would make life easier or simply boost morale. A thoughtful gesture, however small, carries a weight of emotional support: lifts, food parcels, babysitting, a bunch of flowers.
- Practical help also creates opportunities for an adult child to open up about how they're coping and what they really need.
- If you're worried about how your child is coping, it's better to be direct, rather than dropping hints or locking up the wine. All you need to say is 'I'm your parent, I can't help worrying...'
- Remember to say 'I think you handled that really well'. People need affirmation, particularly in a crisis when so much seems to be going wrong and self-esteem is low.
- Parents also need to take care of their own well-being and find sources of support outside the family. It's important to keep life going as much as possible, most of all through activities that give you a break from your child's problems.

DIVORCE

'When my husband left three years into my marriage everybody was in huge amounts of shock,' says Tania. 'My parents were in pain as well.' A child's divorce is a crisis for parents too. Emotions run high: you're sad that an era of family life is over as your hopes for your child's future are dashed. You're anxious about how your child will cope, angry with their ex, yet sorry that your relationship with your in-law will never be the same again. If you didn't get on, you'll probably have mixed feelings. If your child ended the relationship, it's even more complicated. And if there are grandchildren, there is huge anxiety about the impact on them. The big fear, particularly for parents of sons, is that you won't be able to see them so often, or you might even lose contact altogether.

Yet however upset parents are themselves, they need to keep their own emotions out of the mix as much as possible, according to the psychologist Professor Janet Reibstein: 'Divorce is always an emotionally disturbing time for everybody, even though it has become more normalised than it used to be. While there is no rule about exactly what parents should do, the golden rule is that they need to be available and try to ascertain what is the best role they can play in offering to help. Of course emotions get in the way – your fears for your child and your fears for yourself if there are grandchildren. But it's not your divorce, and the most important thing is not to become so emotional that you are unable to think clearly.'

Parents often feel helpless. They may feel they should not get involved. But in fact there is a lot they can do: above all, they are a source of reassuring stability when the adult child's whole world is in turmoil. When emotions are boiling over, parents can take a long view of the need for relations with the former partner to remain civil. The received wisdom is that parents shouldn't take sides, but that's asking a lot, particularly if their child is the one who's been left. Parents are naturally biased, and may well have had strong views for or against a child's partner, even before problems emerged. But they need to keep their views to themselves: no one wants to hear that their relationship was doomed from the start, or that their parents never liked their partner. What they *do* need to feel is that their married life wasn't a total waste and that they did their best to make it work. Parents have learnt from their own experience that no one knows what goes on inside a relationship. With couples there are always two sides to a story and it is never helpful to blame one person. Professor Reibstein says, 'Divorce is painful for all sides, even for the person who is initiating it. Yet research shows that very little attention is paid to that. The worst thing is to be judgemental.'

Life experience gives parents an advantage when dealing with most crises, but divorce is less common in our generation than it is in our children's. Baby boomers still remember when divorce was legally tortuous and scandalous – even as late as 1978, when Princess Margaret's divorce hit the headlines. Deborah Merrill, Professor of Sociology at Clark University, points out that statistically parents are less likely to be divorced than their children.

Paul's family is not untypical: until his eldest daughter's marriage ended in 2020, divorce was unheard of in his family. When we met at his house in Essex, he had just spent his day off putting up shelves and making his daughter's room homely, because she had recently moved back with her two young children: 'I come from an old-fashioned family where it doesn't matter how bad the marriage is, you just crack on with it. You've made your bed, you've got to lie on it, kind of thing. Kealy has broken the mould in our family. She has been through something that we haven't, an experience that I find hard to understand, so I'm learning from her. I look at Kealy in a totally different light now. I think she's been very brave and very strong. She was unhappy in her marriage for a long time and she got out of it. I'm really proud of her for doing that. We have a more equal, adult relationship now.'

Parents may feel at sea with no reference points and no one to talk to in their own family or their peer group. Tania, who divorced 10 years ago, says, 'We grew up with the understanding that marriage was the absolute seal of security. So when my husband left, the family's whole value system was shaken. No one understood what to do. My parents were exposed to stuff they had never had to deal with before. At one stage my mother-in-law wrote my mum a letter that really upset her and made her feel quite attacked. And there were some difficult scenes when my parents had to host my ex-husband's family at their home in order for them to see my daughter. That was really hard for everybody and I leant on my parents heavily at that time. My mum was on the phone a lot to her friends. Both of her best friend's daughters were divorced, so that was helpful for her – it was almost like joining a club! That's how she coped with the whole thing.'

How to support a child through divorce

While it's comforting for adult children to hear parents say, 'We're always here for you', specific offers of practical help are more useful. When people are in survival mode in the first few weeks and months, they don't really know what they need. So while in normal circumstances it's better to wait to be asked, in a crisis parents are justified in being more proactive. Professor Reibstein says, 'When people are in the midst of difficulties they're often not thinking straight, so asking what they need often draws a blank. So parents need to ask themselves what they can offer and what's appropriate. Having thought through the various options they can make practical suggestions that their child can accept or reject. They could offer to pay the first few months of a new place to rent or ask if it would help if they were around when the children come for the weekend. They could also say, is it intrusive if we call once a week, just to check in? If it is, just tell us.'

Practical help also keeps the door open for emotional support. There's more chance of coinciding at a time when a child happens to feel like talking if you have regular contact about practical issues. Steve understands this. He paid the first few months' rent on the flat his daughter and grandson moved into when she left her husband. He says, 'I wanted to give Samantha a fresh start. And because she is a bit vulnerable, I make sure I make contact by dropping something off at least once a week, just to keep that thread there.'

While a child's divorce often strengthens the bond between parent and adult child, it can also increase the tension. Some adult children move in with their parents while they get their life back on track. Home remains a safe place to let your guard down, lick your wounds and be yourself; there's less need to keep up appearances in the way you have to at work or with acquaintances. Yet it goes without saying that anyone who is in the middle of a relationship breakdown isn't easy to be with. Their moods may swing from misery to wild optimism; sleepless nights make them tetchy; they're hypersensitive to the slightest perceived criticism. They need to rant endlessly about their ex's behaviour or the latest outrage from the solicitor. That's understandable, but it demands oceans of patience and understanding from parents who are managing their own painful emotions at the same time.

Many children feel uncomfortable about needing their parents' support, whether they have to move back home or not. Research by Professor Merrill into the impact of children's marriage on families is revealing. She says, 'Some adult children felt they had failed, that they had been incapable of maintaining the marriage and were a disappointment to their parents. The parent may not have intended to make them feel that; they may have internalised it.' One divorced daughter in Professor Merrill's study said that although her mother meant well, her insistence on paying for everything made her feel inadequate, and that increased the tension between them. Another daughter said she felt guilty about being divorced and added that she didn't really like to open up to her mother because she feared it would prompt questions. That's so telling. Adult children are caught in a cleft stick between needing their parents but at the same time wanting a degree of privacy about the painful details.

At the beginning of this chapter Tania described how it felt to be dependent on her parents in her late thirties. They had moved from a different part of the country to be on hand to help look after her baby daughter. She says, 'I was so lucky that they were there but at times support felt like it came at a bit of a cost, because my mum was front and centre of my business at a very difficult and humiliating time in my life. Expectations came back. She would say things like, "You won't be doing that, will you?" or "You will be doing this, won't you?" You feel a bit obliged to do what is being advised because the support is being given. It was fine with my dad, because he tends to remain in the background. And it was very comforting. It wasn't only that they relieved some of the practical burden of a one-year-old. Just being in their company was comfortable.'

How involved should parents get in a child's divorce?

For their part, parents often feel unsure about their role and how involved they should be – or whether they should butt out altogether rather than be involved at all. Treading on eggshells is wearing. Divorce brings up all kinds of personal stuff that kids would rather their parents didn't know about and that parents don't want to hear about either! It's always best to take the child's lead if they don't want to talk about their relationship or what went wrong. It may feel too raw; they may prefer to discuss the painful details with friends or siblings; they may want to protect you. They may feel you disapprove or blame them if they initiated the breakup.

Steve's daughter told him she was going to leave her husband two years ago, when her son was seven. His immediate response was to persuade her to give the relationship another chance, while her response was that he was being unsupportive. But Steve had good reason to offer an alternative view: he knew from his own experience how tough divorce is on the whole family and what a struggle being a single parent can be: 'Initially I did wonder whether Samantha was trying hard enough. Up until then her marriage seemed to be going rather well and I don't really know what happened but she suddenly wanted out. I found it quite sad that it all came to grief; there was a lot about her ex-husband that I liked. I used to meet Samantha regularly for coffee and I'd say, look at it this way, Brendan's got a difficult job, maybe he just needs you to throw some familial support behind him while he's building his career – maybe that's where he's coming from. I didn't mean she should be at home cooking his dinner, I just meant marriage is a partnership, he's seen you through your degree, now you see him through this. I was looking for reasons to hold the marriage together. Those were the natural thoughts of a parent, but I was accused of not supporting her. My attitude changed when she said he was emotionally blackmailing her.'

Grandchildren and divorce

Research by Judy Dunn at the Institute of Psychiatry in London shows that grandparents are key to young children's adjustment to divorce. But of course that is only possible if parents are able to maintain reasonable relations with their child's former partner. The psychologist Professor Reibstein says, 'Grandparents are an extremely important resource of stability for children. It is very important for them to know that they have that constant relationship and that relationship is not going to stop or fundamentally change. So that means parents have to maintain a relationship with the ex. It's tragic for everybody when that doesn't happen.'

Yet it is all too common for grandparents to have no contact with their grandchildren, as the heartbreaking forums on grandparenting websites testify. Avoiding a breakdown in communication is a big challenge if one partner feels betrayed and angry and the other fights back. Parents have to overcome their natural instinct to defend their child against the accusations that inevitably fly about. Divorce is rarely totally amicable and when children are involved, everyone needs to behave like a grown-up. The grandparents' role is to help their adult child to appreciate the long-term benefits of a workable relationship with the ex and to support them in keeping their eye on the prize – the grandchildren's well-being – when they're furious and never want to see their ex again.

It obviously helps if parents have previously established a good relationship with their son- or daughter-in-law, and they like each other (see Chapter 10). That should make it easier to have a difficult conversation, explaining that they hope that supporting their own child won't rule out a lasting relationship with them and that they want to work something out for the sake of the grandchildren. But it's equally important to make it clear from the start that their first loyalty is to their own son or daughter. According to Professor Reibstein, grandparents don't always get this right. She says, 'I know many parents who have got it wrong by saying to the ex "We love you too and we will stick by you". They haven't made it clear to either side that their loyalty to their child has to come first. It can be misinterpreted to mean the parents will take the ex's side against their own child. This comes up particularly when an ex wants their in-laws to get in the middle and take their side when there are disputes. That would obviously upset the child.'

HOW TO SUPPORT A CHILD WHOSE RELATIONSHIP IS ENDING

- 'We're always here for you' needs saying, but specific offers of practical help are important too.
- Before rushing in with offers of help, think carefully about what would make your child's life easier and what you can realistically do. Then present them with options and don't be offended if they turn them down.
- If they need to move back home, think about how to avoid making them feel like a child again.
- Don't expect an adult child to take your advice, even if they ask for it.

- If your child instigated the breakup, they need to know that your love and support is unconditional. However, if you think they've behaved badly, you don't have to condone it.
- It's never a good idea to be rude about the ex even if your child slags them off. They no doubt feel bad enough about their choices already.
- It's even more important to avoid making disapproving remarks about the ex in front of grandchildren.
- If there are grandchildren, it is essential, if at all possible, to stay on civil terms with the ex. Your child's former partner will always be their parent.

INFERTILITY

One of the questions parents don't like to ask is about grandchildren. The time comes when you long to know whether your child is planning to start a family, or whether they're having problems conceiving, and you begin to wonder if they'd tell you if they were. The trend towards later first pregnancies makes parents a bit twitchy – nearly half of women born in 1989 were childless when they reached 30 in 2019, compared with 38 per cent for their mothers' generation, according to the ONS. There's a nagging concern that they might leave it too late, that they're in denial about the unpalatable truth about the decline in female fertility from the early thirties which becomes more significant from the mid-thirties. One in seven heterosexual couples have difficulty conceiving, yet the subject is often the elephant in the room. With a gay child, parents often feel they don't know where to begin.

Once again, a parent's concern is double-edged. It's not only for their child's well-being, but also for their own. As parents, we make so many assumptions about what the future might look like, and even if they're a bit vague, they often involve the possibility of grandchildren. When that's cast into doubt, the future has to be reassessed. Some people are outspoken about their longing for grandchildren, which must be painful for their children if they're trying unsuccessfully to conceive. However, a conversation on Radio 4's *Listening Project* gave me pause for thought. A man who was unable to have children said that part of him wished his parents had asked 'Where are the grandchildren?' because he felt that more open conversations would normalise infertility and make childless couples feel less like outsiders. But most parents don't dare to broach the subject and they may not even admit their longing to themselves.

Jacqui says, 'It's odd when your friends are grandparents and your daughter's getting on a little bit and you think you're not going to have any grandchildren and you think it doesn't bother you... But when Tru told me they were trying for a baby it was like Wow! I was over the moon.'

And it's true that couples who are having difficulty conceiving are often reluctant to talk about it. Inevitably, daughters are more likely to talk to their mothers than sons. 'I'll never forget how I felt when my daughter-in-law told me they'd been trying for a baby for over a year,' says Bryony. 'It hit me in the pit of my stomach. I only heard about my son's feelings second-hand – I wish I could have talked to him about it. I couldn't stop thinking about what a hard road lay ahead if they needed treatment and how it would be for them – and for me, selfishly – if they couldn't have children. It was a shock to realise how low it made me feel.'

At the other extreme I know mothers who have been closely involved with their daughters' attempts to conceive. They've researched diets and paid for alternative therapies. They shared the heartbreak when things didn't work out. An increasing number of parents, like Jacqui, help to fund their children's fertility treatment. Her daughter Tru told only two people when she embarked on IVF: her closest friend and her mother: 'I told my mum because she would have known something wasn't right, and it would have been too stressful to have kept something so important from her, to keep up a pretence. I didn't even tell the people I worked with, because I couldn't deal with others knowing. People can be very glib about IVF; they underestimate the impact it has. It was hell; I'm surprised I didn't end up with mental health issues. To be my complete self I have to be with someone I'm really comfortable with, and Mum was there for me emotionally throughout. Mum was always there on the other end of the phone, and she called me every night to make sure I was all right. And she used to drive down to Oxford regularly. She's not the most confident driver, so for her that was huge. It was my parents' idea to help pay for the treatment; I didn't ask. I'll always be so grateful to them for that.'

Our generation tends to have a more pessimistic view of fertility treatment than our children. While our kids probably know at least one friend who's been through it, we generally don't have access to the same kind of first-hand info. That's partly because fertility treatment has changed dramatically since the first 'test-tube' baby was born in 1978. It's more widely available now, although not always on the NHS, with 2.6 per cent of all children in the UK (2.1 per cent in Europe) born via assisted reproduction. Meanwhile, birth rates from IVF have tripled over the past 30 years, with the average birth rate per embryo transferred 24 per cent in 2019 (32 per cent for women under 35), compared with just 7 per cent in 1991.

But fertility treatment is still a huge ordeal and parents understandably feel daunted and anxious about how to help an adult child through something they have no experience of themselves. The future is horribly uncertain. One thing they can do is to read up about the subject, using reliable sources of information, such as the Human Fertilisation and Embryology Authority (HFEA) website, rather than random internet searches. Talking to friends can be helpful, but only up to a point, because each problem is individual. Anecdotes about successes, failures and alternative treatments can make you either over-anxious or unrealistically optimistic. With a firm grasp of the facts, and a basic understanding of the procedures involved, you're better placed to offer calm support, even when you don't feel calm yourself. Fertility treatment is an emotional rollercoaster, with nerve-racking waits and potential complications. It feels odd and special to know the time that your grandchild is being conceived – or not – in a Petri dish. It's hard to concentrate on anything else in the days that follow, when you're hoping and praying for good news.

Although Jacqui was still working, and Tru then lived two hours' drive away, she supported her daughter through three gruelling cycles of IVF. She went to every hospital appointment and even held Tru's hand while the eggs were inserted. At one point, Tru was admitted to hospital with ovarian hyperstimulation syndrome, a rare complication of IVF, which in severe cases can be dangerous. Jacqui remembers, 'We drove home after visiting her in hospital but I was so worried that I couldn't sleep. I had read that OHSS can be fatal. I just couldn't cope with being at a distance, so we drove back first thing the next morning.

'I was very anxious a lot of the time. The first cycle failed and you think, Oh well, we'll try again. But then the next attempt failed and Tru got deeper and deeper into feeling that it was never going to happen. I would talk to her and try and put her at her ease. I would try to be positive, even though I didn't feel that positive myself.'

The third cycle was successful, but the stress didn't stop with the positive pregnancy test. One afternoon, Jacqui's phone rang when she was in Waitrose. She remembers, 'Tru was in a terrible state. She said, "Mum, I'm bleeding, I'm not sure what to do." I suggested she went straight to the hospital. I was so worried. My heart was beating, but I was trying to talk to her in a calm way. I just couldn't stop thinking about it, but I couldn't actually do anything because I was 200 miles away.'

After a difficult pregnancy and labour, Tru gave birth to healthy twins.

WORK-RELATED STRESS AND REDUNDANCY

Stress at work has long been a widespread problem. A survey for the mental health charity Mind in 2013 found that work was the most stressful factor in people's lives and one in five people developed anxiety as a result of work-related stress. The economic turbulence of recent decades has piled on the pressure. Now it's not only tougher to find a job but to hold on to one too. It's much harder for emerging adults to find even stopgap work, let alone get a foot on the career ladder. At this stage parents are getting more used to the possibility that they may have to step in with both emotional and practical support. Things can be just as tough for older adult children. Burnout, meltdowns and stress-related sick leave are all too common. Parents are understandably concerned for their overstretched adult children's well-being and look out for signs that the pressure is getting too much.

Brenda's son was in his mid-thirties when the combined pressures of a stressful job and his wife's ill health nearly precipitated a breakdown. His sons were four and two when his wife had major surgery, followed by months of recovery. Brenda remembers, 'Chris went through hell. He was profoundly stressed. At the same time as dealing with anxiety about his wife, and taking care of the boys, he was also under intense pressure at work. At one point he almost became nocturnal; he wasn't sleeping and was close to collapse. We discussed the situation quite a bit, with him taking the lead, and he decided to resign from his job and take the family on holiday. I was so relieved; I thought a few weeks' complete break was all he needed to get back on track and that his resilience would be boosted by the holiday. But I was wrong. When he came back, I've never seen him so close to collapse. He was totally stressed out, both emotionally and physically. I've never been as worried about him as I was then.'

Yet despite her concern, Brenda managed to be pragmatic. She decided that the only way for her son to avert a complete mental and physical breakdown was to take a break from full-time work. She offered to help support the family financially on her pension to give him a breathing space to find his feet and she has stuck to her resolution not to pester him about job interviews: 'For me the most important thing is that he gets better,' she says. 'Nothing else matters.'

Lindsey's daughter Esther, 31, works in public relations in Washington, DC, where she moved with her husband a couple of years ago. Everything seemed to be going well until one autumn weekend, when Lindsey was staying with friends, she got a call from her daughter. She remembers, 'It's very unusual for Esther to ring out of the blue. I asked how she was and she said "Everything's fine" and burst into tears. It was very upsetting. She said she'd been having trouble at work. She had been suffering from anxiety and panic attacks for some time, and had just been signed off for two weeks' sick leave.' Lindsey offered to pay for her to catch the next flight home and by the next morning, they were drinking tea at the kitchen table.

Lindsey continues, 'My husband was still in bed and we got straight down to talking about Esther's anxiety. She told me she'd been getting in a panic about not being good enough at work, worried that she hadn't been promoted, and anxious about how she was going to cope. She didn't ask for my advice directly but I think she expected it. I think she got permission from me not to strive for promotion; that we wouldn't think less of her and that she shouldn't worry about it. She stayed with us for nearly two weeks, and that's really what she needed: to be with her family, being looked after at home. The medication soon kicked in and she got some CBT, and when she came home for Christmas a few weeks later, she seemed fine.'

Parents often invest heavily, both financially and emotionally, in their children's careers. They've supported them through GCSEs and A-levels, helped them find work experience, panicked over their dissertations and helped fund university degrees and further training. They're rightly proud that their children have got good jobs. In some families, children are expected to follow in their parents' footsteps. At the other extreme, parents look to their children to achieve their own unfulfilled ambitions vicariously. If, after all their hopes and dreams, work is making their child miserable and stressed, it's a huge disappointment. Parents who fought hard to achieve a good standard of living themselves can't understand why a child would give up a well-paid job for the sake of well-being and a better work-life balance.

Elliott, who had wanted to be a lawyer since primary school, was doing well until an epiphany at work changed everything. One particularly difficult day, his boss burst into tears and he realised that he wasn't the only one who felt stressed and out of control; the pressure-cooker corporate environment just didn't suit him. He handed in his resignation and within weeks had successfully applied for a job in an IT firm. But he was so nervous about his parents' reaction that he didn't tell them until the deed had been done and there was no going back. To his relief, his mum, Anne-Marie, just laughed – in a good way! She remembers, 'We had just got back from a holiday in America when Elliott said, "Mum, I've got something to tell you." I thought something terrible had happened. He said, "I don't want you to be upset, but I've changed my job." He was really worried, but I just laughed and said, "Darling, the number one thing as a parent is that you want your child to be happy. I don't care if you're a road sweeper."'

You may have heard the saying that the Chinese character for 'crisis' means both 'danger' and 'opportunity'. Tania would agree. Made redundant in her thirties, she now runs workshops to help companies and individuals manage redundancy and other major transitions. When it happened to her, she remembers her parents being more upset than she was. That's perhaps because the precarious working landscape she takes for granted is so unfamiliar to her parents' generation; now in their late seventies, they grew up expecting jobs to be for life. Yet their response was textbook supportive. 'My parents' reaction was nervousness,' she remembers, 'especially when I made it clear that I wasn't going to look for similar jobs. Unlike me they have always been extremely conservative financially and they asked me a lot of questions about how things were going to work out. But they had faith in me: they said we know how important your work is to you and we know that you will be resourceful and sort this out. And since I started my own business they have played a kind of cheerleading role.'

Brenda has been through a few challenging and traumatic events with her son over the last 10 years, culminating in the near breakdown she described earlier. She even gave up her own plans to support him, as so many parents do when adult children need help. She had always dreamt of spending her semi-retirement in a house with room for friends to stay, in a city she loved. All that changed when Chris and his wife came back to England unexpectedly after a contract in Singapore collapsed. He was shell-shocked, with no job, no money and nowhere to live.

Brenda remembers, 'The decision to come home was a real crisis for Chris, because he had seen Singapore as a great opportunity. I needed to be as supportive as I could without saying "I told you so", as much as I wanted to! That was hard at times and I admit there were some lapses, but I was quite good at providing practical help.'

She acted as guarantor for the flat they rented, and when they mooted the idea of buying an old farmhouse with outbuildings where they could all set up home together, she didn't hesitate, even though it meant swapping her dreams for a converted cowshed in the middle of nowhere. Brenda believes that the crises they've been through have brought unforeseen benefits. Above all, she feels closer not only to her son, but to his wife and her mother – and of course her two grandsons.

Tania feels the same. Her relationship with both her parents has been strengthened by tough times. She says, 'My parents weren't big on praise when we were growing up, but that's changed since we've become adults. Now they say things like "I think you handled that brilliantly". That has been really positive. As an adult child, you need to hear those things, especially when everything can feel like doom and gloom. I have a very good relationship with both my parents and that's a direct result of me needing them and them being there.'

7

Parents' Crises

Every crisis or major change in a parent's life affects their adult child and often more than they might think. It sometimes seems that from middle age onwards life is full of crises, from bereavement and redundancy to cancer. Some involve adult kids directly, such as the illness or death of a partner, or divorce, which has a much greater impact on adult children than people expect. Other crises not so much: parents' own elderly parents needing care, the death of an old friend, retirement. In these situations, adult children can be concerned and supportive, but they are not so directly involved.

Some crises are strictly the parents'. Perhaps the most painful is when adult children announce that they're moving to the other end of the country or even the other side of the world. Emotions are poles apart: an exciting opportunity for the adult child is a dagger in the parent's heart.

Brenda, a single parent, will never forget the day her only son announced he was moving to Singapore: 'My mother said I went completely white. I knew I couldn't interfere but I was desperately hoping someone else would advise him not to go. A wise friend told me to relax and let him go. And she was right. It was a very low period, but I got through it, and after a year he came back.'

Parents often have little choice but to bite back the tears and find consolation in having raised an adult who feels secure enough to explore and take risks. Yet the uncomfortable truth is that being together matters less to children than it does to their parents. That's the way it should be, but it still hurts.

Any crisis brings possibilities as well as challenges. Parents and children learn about themselves and about each other. Adult children see their parents' flaws and vulnerabilities, as well as their strengths. That might not feel comfortable for anyone at the time, but it's all part of building a more rounded, equal relationship. Both sides have to reassess their roles and responsibilities.

Facing a challenge together often brings parent and child closer, not least because they start talking more frankly about the stuff that really matters. Tania's divorce, which she talked about in Chapter 6, forced her family to develop a new emotional resilience that continued to grow through subsequent crises: 'My divorce shone a light on the fact that bad things happen, and there's no shame in it, and that it's how you deal with things that matters. It enabled us to talk about stuff in a way that didn't happen when we were growing up. I feel like my relationship with my parents is a lot more equal now, because of difficult things my mother has been through herself since my divorce. She had a horrible falling-out with her sister, which has completely shaken her world. It helped that we now have a history of dealing with bad and difficult emotional situations as a family.'

The big problem is that when parents are struggling with their own issues, whether it's with relationship problems or dying parents or illness, they don't have the bandwidth to think about anything or anyone else apart from their own needs. Sometimes the only way to get through is by going into denial about the impact on adult children. But if their needs are ignored at the time, they may have to be faced further down the line.

WORK CRISES, RETIREMENT AND REDUNDANCY

When parents have problems at work, or if they are struggling with redundancy or retirement, they often try to hide how they feel from their kids. Perhaps they feel protective and don't want to worry them. Parents naturally feel it's their problem and that it's their job to handle difficult stuff on their own. But adult kids are alert to signals that something's wrong, whether or not they live at home, and they pick up clues from their siblings.

Rupa's youngest son had moved back after university when her husband was going through a major work crisis. She remembers, 'Aran lived with us through the stress of his dad running his own company – the trauma years, I call them, because we ended up in so much debt and it was mounting all the time. I don't think people fully understand the stress when one partner is behaving like a runaway train, spending money and bankrupting you. You love them, you see that they're having a crisis, but you don't want to support the crisis. You end up arguing to try and sort the crisis out and because it's not of your making, you resent them to some degree. It was a real strain and Ahmed was heading for a breakdown.

'It was difficult to hide these conversations from Aran – it wasn't like we could wait until he was in bed – he was 24! But with hindsight, I know we upset him a lot. It all came to a head five years ago, but he still talks about it now. The other day he said, "Mum, that was really upsetting when you used to argue." I felt he was criticising me and I explained that I didn't want to argue. He said, "I know it wasn't your fault, I realise you were just trying your best to sort things out, but it was very hard." At the same time it helps that he knows what I had to go through.'

If parents feel negative about leaving work because they've been made redundant or elbowed out, their confidence will have taken a knock. Money is part of it and that is also tied up with identity, because it gives a sense of control. It can be hard to relinquish the role of magnanimous parent who takes adult children out for meals and bails them out financially, but there are many other ways to be supportive and show love, most obviously through gifts of time. And while many adult kids are sensitive about the financial repercussions, some might need a gentle reminder that things have changed.

Retirement doesn't always precipitate a crisis, although in some cases it can lead to depression, and that is obviously a huge concern for the whole family. But whether or not it goes well, leaving work is one of the biggest changes people ever go through. It's a huge adjustment on many levels: it affects everything from how you spend your time to how you feel about yourself. Like redundancy, retirement can take its toll on self-esteem, particularly if people struggle to find new purpose and meaning. The loss of work identity and status is bound to affect how parents feel about themselves in relation to other people, and that includes their children.

Coming to terms with the fact that you're no longer a player in the working world can take time. Letting go of your image as protective breadwinner and head of the family isn't easy. Many people pretend they're doing fine because they don't want to appear weak or vulnerable, particularly to their children. But it's much more helpful to all concerned to be direct yet positive in acknowledging that it's not easy. Throughout life, parents are modelling behaviour to adult children and if you allow them to see how you cope with challenges, it will help build their own resilience – and that's just as true if it's a struggle.

WHEN PARENTS DIVORCE OR SEPARATE

Over the past 30 years, divorce among the over-fifties has risen. Yet while a great deal of thought and research rightly goes into the effects of divorce on younger children, the impact on adult children is largely ignored. There is still an assumption that if children have left the nest by the time their parents divorce, they won't be so deeply affected. Indeed, that's why so many unhappy couples put off parting until the children leave home. Yet even relationships that seem OK struggle when it's just the two of them. The impact of the empty nest on a marriage starved of attention because the children's needs took precedence is often the final nail in the coffin.

Psychologists, psychotherapists and adult children are unanimous: the idea that adult children are barely affected by their parents' divorce is unhelpful nonsense. In his autobiography, the tennis player Rafael Nadal talks about his heartbreak at his parents' temporary separation in 2009, and the effect it had on his performance in the French Open. He was defeated for the first time ever in that tournament, and says he pulled out of Wimbledon that year because of problems not only with his knees, but also his state of mind.

Ian, a psychotherapist whose parents divorced when he was 38, says, 'My emotional response was unexpected. I became very low and a lot less productive at work. I was moody and distracted, went to bed early and slept a lot more. At first, I didn't connect it to my parents' divorce, I just thought I was miserable. I recognise now that I was suffering a kind of grief reaction. At times I was out there in the world and functioning quite well, and at other times I couldn't do anything. It bled into my everyday life in ways I hadn't anticipated.'

Just because adult children have their own independent lives doesn't make their parents' breakup any less painful. Adult children of divorce feel angry, sad, abandoned, destabilised; they question the past and worry about the future. They face the huge adjustment to a new landscape of family life, in which relationships with a secure, stable parental unit have to be recalibrated. Siblings may be drawn together by the crisis, but they can also be divided by it. If one parent has a new partner, adult children worry about being displaced in their affections and how they fit into the new status quo. But they also worry about how the other parent will cope on their own. Dr Reenee Singh, Director of the London Intercultural Couples Centre, says, 'What's quite difficult for adult children is not only the breakup of the family, but the fantasy and image of the family as they understand it. In some ways I think it's almost easier if they're younger. Because younger children are more flexible, they don't know of this institutionalised family that adult children are craving or clinging to.'

Adult children feel even more isolated and confused if they, as well as their parents, buy into the popular myth that they won't be greatly affected and that they should just get on with their lives. This is such a contrast with younger children: the impact on their daily lives, routines and emotions is so blatant that parents have no choice but to focus on mitigating it. With adult children there's no ferrying between households, no moving schools or sharing a parent with stepsiblings. Signs of distress may be less obvious too, because adult kids have learnt to hide their feelings and may want to protect their parents. They may not connect their own low feelings with the divorce. They may not admit how they feel, even to themselves. Janet Reibstein, Professor Emerita of Psychology at Exeter University, explains, 'Mostly people think adult kids understand, they can adjust, because they've moved on and have their own lives. It's true that because an adult child has more freedom, they can make choices about where they live and when they see the other parent, so it's less traumatic in one sense. Nevertheless, divorce shakes the adult child's whole model of what they think they have depended on. Adult children have an internal model of how you have a secure and stable relationship. They have never had to question that, because they've always had that model in their heads. Suddenly they go back over the past and there are all sorts of things they might question. They're at sea.'

When parents part: a child's grief changes but doesn't go away

The grief triggered when parents split up can last years, yet it's rare to hear the adult child's perspective. I met the psychotherapist Ian Argent after coming across a moving article he had written for the website welldoing.org about his parents' divorce when he was 38 and they were in their sixties. For a long time, he thought his reaction was abnormal until, after endless searching for support, he stumbled on a book by the American journalist Brooke Lea Foster that made him realise his experience was all too common. He says, 'The grief changes but it doesn't go away. In my teens I thought my parents would never get divorced. Although my mum and I spent endless cigarette breaks on the patio when she would confide in me about her difficulties with Dad, I thought they would carry on, unhappy, a bit like that couple in *One Foot in the Grave*. But as the cracks became more visible, I felt this persistent sense of foreboding, a dark cloud always there in the background.

'The divorce made me look back on my childhood and my parents' relationship and realise that it was not what I thought it was. The story that you hold inside yourself about your family, the experience of growing up and being part of this family, all that gets changed. There are still times when I remember my childhood and think, that was really nice, but immediately reality kicks in and says that's gone. There is always that echo that gets added on. That's hard.'

At the same time assumptions about the future of family life are shattered for divorced parent and child: weddings, graduation ceremonies, celebrations and holidays will never be the same again. If a parent has a new partner, they are in a bind, because they know their new spouse would be deeply hurt if they are not invited, yet they know that it will upset their ex if they are. It's equally tough on the child who is struggling to do the right thing and keep everyone happy. Some parents put on a brave face for the sake of the kids, but one woman I interviewed stayed away from her grandson's naming ceremony because she couldn't face the other woman. It was such a sad story; she spent the family's special day trying her best not to think about it. When it came to her younger son's wedding, the other woman was not invited, so again, no one was happy.

Professor Janet Reibstein advises parents not to make assumptions or demands, and to be ready to compromise. Your child will hopefully discuss the guest list with both parents, and take your views into account. If you are also able to have a reasonable discussion about guests with your ex, that could really help your child deal with a potentially tricky situation. Above all, remember that it's their day, not yours.

When children become parents themselves this can trigger renewed grief and a deep sense of loss. Ian, whose daughters were born since his parents' divorce, says, 'The old image of family life necessarily had with it a sense of what family life was going to be like in the years to come. I had to surrender my ideas and fantasies about the future. That was really hard and it's got harder since I became a dad. It really hit me one Christmas, when I had my heart set on taking my daughter back to the family home. I wanted to recreate some of that joy that I had felt as a child for her: it's a lovely house to have Christmas in. When I heard that neither of my parents would be there I collapsed in tears when I was talking to my wife about it; my overwhelming feeling was, *it's gone, it's all gone...*'

Some divorces come like a bolt from the blue, while others seem long overdue after years of misery. Sometimes it's a huge relief. What's surprising is that adult children who can see that their parents are unhappy, like Ian, assume that they will continue to rub along indefinitely. Perhaps that's because divorce, like sex, is unthinkable in relation to your own parents – it's what other families do. Even adult children who breathe a sigh of relief when their parents finally call it a day can be poleaxed.

Like many couples, Amalia's mother waited until her youngest child went to university to end her 30-year marriage. Although Amalia has never doubted that it was the right decision, she can't help crying when she talks about it, 10 years later: 'I felt so many different emotions. I still get emotional about it, even though it was a bit of a relief at the time because I was always expected to be the mediator and being stuck between the two of them was very stressful. Before the divorce, Mum was always complaining about Dad to me. And it's true that Dad had so many opportunities to change but he didn't. The divorce has brought me closer to my mum. She's back to her old self now, the one I never knew. Now when we meet we can get straight on to the nice stuff, there aren't so many issues.'

How parents' divorce changes their relationship with adult children

Even unhappily married parents can represent a solid unit of support and stability that adult children take for granted. Divorce shatters the unit by transforming them into single parents. Both parents are knocked off their pedestals: it's deeply disconcerting to see their flaws or weaknesses so exposed. Ian remembers, 'My dad is not an emotional man but he was visibly tearful when he showed me the divorce papers, which were pretty shocking and damning of him. He said, "I feel like I've failed." That was a shock to the little boy in me who saw my dad as big and strong.'

It's equally shocking if divorce gives parents licence to behave like teenagers – although fair play to them! A parent who embraces the single life wholeheartedly, dating, partying and all the rest, may be oblivious to their children's concerns about their behaviour. And while the kids' worries might be justified, the reversal of the protective role is disconcerting for both sides. One mother said that her children found her single status after 23 years' marriage much harder to adjust to than she did, even though they were grown up and had their own lives.

The sudden role reversal is particularly unsettling and worrying if parents are depressed, vulnerable and needy. The parent who wanted to stay in the marriage naturally needs more support than the one who ended it, particularly if they have a new partner. Adult kids may have no idea how best to help their parents. They may feel a new sense of duty to go home more often and that's tough when they have been spreading their wings and have their own commitments and responsibilities. Where there used to be one home to visit, now there are two. They face an unfamiliar new worry about how their parents will cope alone, not just in the immediate aftermath, but in the future: what will divorce mean to them as older people?

Amalia's parents both needed support after the divorce, although she admits that she and her siblings saw her mother more often than her father. Both parents had financial difficulties; her father was lonely and isolated while her mum's confidence had been knocked and she needed her daughters to help her take charge of her life. 'Mum has been trying internet dating and I'd be really pleased for her if she met someone new,' Amalia says, 'but at the same time I don't want her to make a mistake.'

If there is a new man or woman on the scene, adult kids are torn. They feel guilty about spending time with a parent's new partner and anxious about dividing their time fairly. They fear that if they spend time with one parent, the other parent will be hurt or angry, and dread their intrusive questions about their ex's new life. Yet parents are bound to be inquisitive, even if it's torture.

Malorie, whose husband left her for another woman after 30 years of marriage, says, 'My son visited his dad not long after the divorce, when I was at that stage when you want to know everything about what's going on with the other person, although it only makes you feel worse. My son refused to tell me anything about him or his mistress and that really annoyed me. But now I can see that my son was right, that the relationship was between them, not me.'

Professor Janet Reibstein says, 'You must always avoid putting the child in a loyalty battle, no matter how old they are. Children don't want to be caught in the middle, they don't want to be judge and jury. And they don't want one parent to feel alienated because the other needs more support. So again the onus is on the divorcing couple to think about what it means for their children and how their children need to be freed up and assured that nothing has to change in terms of their love for them, and that they don't have to make choices.'

Guilt doesn't go away, not just for parents but children too. Emerging adults often feel guilty that their parents stayed together for their sake. All adult children are prone to feeling bad for not supporting their parents enough. The director William Nicholson's film *Hope Gap* (2019) is a nuanced examination of the painful everyday details of the breakup of a long marriage and it's inspired by his parents' separation when he was 29 and an only child. He told *The Guardian*: 'If you're the child of separated parents, you can't escape the guilt. I sometimes have flashes of memory and think how lonely [my mother] was and how hurt and that I didn't do enough to support her.'

Eight years on, Ian feels the same kind of regret. He says, 'My father said to me, "Look, this is not your battle". When I look back, I wonder if he was just being kind. In some ways I regret not getting more involved and supporting him.'

How can divorcing parents help adult children?

When it comes to parents' divorce, I make no apology for focusing on the experiences of adult children, because their voices aren't heard enough. And hopefully what they say will give parents some insights into what adult children need. In the thick of relationship turmoil it's understandable if parents are too preoccupied to think about how their kids might be coping, although as Professor Janet Reibstein says, 'Even if you're heartbroken, you are still the parent.' And many parents look back with regret for not supporting their children more, because at the time they had no idea that they could be so deeply affected. So the first thing is simply to acknowledge that the divorce will have some impact, even if on the surface the adult child seems to be coping well. Parents need to make it clear that they're available to listen whenever children want to talk. They also need to be wary of depending on their children too heavily in the long term, whether for company or other kinds of support. While children are a lifesaver in the immediate aftermath, this can only be a temporary stopgap.

Adult children should be kept in the loop about practical matters like selling the family home, finances and inheritance, to combat the feeling of helplessness and that things are being done to them. Even if they left years ago, the family home still represents much more than bricks and mortar: it's a symbol of stability and a concrete reminder of the family's history that has been undermined by the divorce.

Ian has a vivid memory of the period just before his parents separated: 'My brother called me at work to say that Mum was getting family photos and objects out of the dresser to take with her. I was furious. I emailed her to say that she was dismantling the history of my family. I wanted her to understand that it was not just about her, but that what she was doing had an effect on the rest of us.'

Don't expect adult children to take sides

Adult children can be judgemental: if they think one parent has triggered the divorce by an affair, it can create a rift that takes years to heal. As adults, they may feel they have a right to interfere in a way that younger children don't. Meanwhile, parents don't always know how to tell their children that they don't understand the full picture.

It can be tempting to fan the flames, but parents need to bear in mind that it is just as important for adult children as it is for younger kids that they remain on civil terms with each other. They should certainly avoid arguing in front of them. Parents should never expect or encourage children to take sides, nor ask them to act as a go-between, or make them feel disloyal for seeing the other parent. And while it's so tempting to quiz them about what the other parent said or did, or what the new partner's like, it's just not fair. Besides, that kind of information will only make you feel worse. They should also be wary of confiding too much, however tempting it is, because it is likely to involve disloyalty to the other parent and again, that's unfair.

Professor Janet Reibstein says, 'You may be longing to say, "I'm not to blame for him messing up". But you need to avoid giving the message that the marriage ended because the other person had an affair, because it's usually a complex of things. What you can say is, "We might have been able to work things out but we reached a point where there was no choice." It is the joint responsibility of the parents to release the child to accept the ending.'

Besides, adult children really don't want to hear the gory details of their parents' marriage. It's much wiser and more dignified to save those kinds of discussions for a good friend.

The added danger of encouraging adult children to take sides is that it could drive a wedge into sibling relationships at a time when they most need each other. Research shows that siblings are a key support for each other when parents divorce and the intensity of going through the experience leads to closer and stronger sibling relationships. Parents need to take care that they don't get in the way.

Adult children often feel that if things can go wrong for their parents after so many years, there is little hope for their own relationships. They worry about repeating their parents' mistakes. But people can learn just as much from negative experiences as positive ones. And as time goes by, adult children gain more understanding of their parents' past behaviour. Even children who have put a distance between themselves and either one or both parents may start to come round: experience brings greater awareness that relationships are nuanced and that things are never black and white.

The director William Nicholson said that his parents' example made him understand the importance of candour in his own 32-year marriage. Ian Argent has built on what he learnt from his parents' divorce in his work as a couples therapist: 'One of the problems between my parents was that resentments would just build and build, until finally, 40 years of stuff got cashed in. Things might have been different if they had had a way of saying *I'm angry*, or *I want to be close to you but it's difficult, I'm sorry*. If my mum had found a way of talking to my dad about what she used to tell me in our cigarette breaks, there might have been a way through.'

HOW DIVORCING PARENTS CAN SUPPORT THEIR ADULT CHILDREN

- Acknowledge that your adult child will be affected just as much as a younger child, whatever their age and stage in life.
- Make sure they know you're always there to listen and want to know how they feel.
- Some parents are looking forward to a fresh start after divorce; they may be head over heels in love. Recognise that your children are unlikely to share your enthusiasm.
- Be clear about plans and practical arrangements: include adult children in discussions if possible.
- If the family home has to be sold it's important to acknowledge its significance to adult children as well as the practical implications.

- When family occasions – weddings, christenings, graduation ceremonies – are being arranged, be reasonable and open to compromise. Discuss guest lists with your children and with your ex, if possible, and don't make assumptions or demands. It's their day, not yours.
- Try to stay on good terms with your ex, especially when the kids are around. Never argue in front of them.
- Adult children have busy lives and commitments. Visiting two parents takes up more time than when you were together. Do your best to fit into their plans.
- Don't expect your children to take sides or act as a go-between.
- If your ex needs more support than you, be gracious not jealous. Tell your child that you understand if they need to spend more time with them.
- If you have a new partner, respect your child's loyalties to the other parent. And be patient: it may take them time to adjust to seeing you with someone new.

WHEN A PARENT IS ILL

When a parent is diagnosed with cancer or some other life-changing condition, the whole family is thrown into a nightmare of panic, uncertainty and anxiety about the future. Hope alternates with despair on the emotional rollercoaster of tests, treatment, good news and bad news. Parents are frightened and anxious, yet fear becoming a burden. This is a particular concern for single parents who have no partner to hold their hand when they go for tests, or help them recover after surgery.

Since her husband died, Brigid's eldest son drives her to hospital appointments. She says, 'I've suddenly realised I'm no longer invincible mummy pack leader, I'm much more vulnerable now. The tide has turned; the children are the strong ones. It's really weird because as a mother you always look after them, always. And I think I always will feel that instinct, that I'm in control. But I realise with my health issues, they are much more anxious about me now and worried about me as an old person. That is the number one thing that has changed the balance between us.'

Breaking bad news about a diagnosis is one of the hardest things a parent ever has to do because it goes against the deeply ingrained instinct to protect your children, whatever their age. It's easy to understand why people put it off as they agonise about how and when to do it, but there are general guidelines that emerge from listening to parents and adult children who have been through the experience. The overwhelming message is: be honest, don't delay, and don't keep things back for fear of worrying the children. It's much more worrying if they find out the truth later – they might understandably question whether their parents are still covering up the full picture.

The time is never right to break bad news. Sometimes there is no choice: the call comes in the middle of the night. 'Adrian had a massive seizure, just as he and I were going to bed,' Anne-Marie remembers. 'The hospital told me to call all the children to his bedside at 4 a.m. We were all in shock. The next day, they found a tumour on his brain.'

If the child is preoccupied with something stressful, like starting a new job or taking exams, the temptation to put off delivering the news may well be justifiable. At the other extreme, parents dread spoiling a happy time, whether it's Christmas or a family gathering or a new baby. If kids live too far away to break the news in person there's another barrier; we all know the unbearable sadness of not being able to give each other a reassuring hug. The general consensus is that while a short delay is acceptable, it's vital not to keep putting it off. If children are kept in the loop from the beginning, they are able to come to terms with the situation gradually.

Parents' illness: role reversal

Parents hate being dependent on their children and find it hard to quash their protective instinct. We all dread our adult children having those 'What shall we do about Mum?' conflabs behind our backs. At the same time, there is pride as well as gratitude when a child steps up to the plate.

The actor Sheila Hancock has written about her admiration for her daughter's 'core of strength' when their roles were reversed when she had breast cancer. For Brenda, a single parent who has always been fiercely independent and self-sufficient, illness was a revelation: 'I realised I don't always have to assume I've got to be the one who sorts things out. I'm well known to be indestructible but I ended up with critical psoriatic arthritis, a debilitating autoimmune condition that flows to different parts of the body. It happened so suddenly that my son had to cut my rings off. He was an incredible support. I was on crutches and couldn't drive for a long time, and had to have both hips replaced.'

The role reversal can be uncomfortable for children too. They're hard-wired to see their parents as strong and effective, and it's disconcerting to adjust to the new vulnerability caused by an accident or illness. Anne-Marie says, 'The children suffered as much as I did, seeing their father go through the stages of brain cancer. There was one phase when he used to get really angry, with them as well as me, because his brain was affected, and the children were quite nervous of his temper. With hindsight, we realised it was a phase, and it passed.'

Adult children are used to receiving support, not having to give it. Their lives are disrupted in different ways. That often varies within individual families, with one sibling spending more time at home or even moving back to help with day-to-day care, or lifts to hospital, or general moral support.

Parents like Anne-Marie, who are caring for a sick partner, have several balls to juggle. They have to manage their own anxiety while at the same time supporting their children, who are in turn trying to keep their own lives on track. They may be haunted by the prospect of a future alone and fear becoming increasingly reliant on their kids. It can feel very lonely for each person in the family, even when they are supporting each other.

Many adult children say they feel isolated when caring for an ill parent, that they have no one to talk to outside the family, and that few people understand what they're going through. Age and peer group play a part. People in their twenties are less likely to have many friends whose parents have been seriously ill than those in their forties or fifties. They're conscious that they're not much fun to be with. They may feel helpless, angry, irritable, sad and anxious about test results and decisions about treatment. They don't want to burden their parents or friends by talking about how they feel. Yet often this turns out to be the best thing to do. I came across some really helpful and heartfelt advice about communicating cancer to adult children on an American website, www.patientpower.com. It's written by Paula K. Waller, who suffers from multiple myeloma, a type of bone marrow cancer that is currently incurable, although manageable. She has three adult children. Like most parents she dreaded telling them about her diagnosis, but ultimately she says that communicating about how they feel has brought new meaning to their relationship.

Anne-Marie agrees: 'We all used to sit and talk about how we were feeling, and that helped,' she remembers. 'We all sympathised with each other. It was quite an eye-opener for me, because you get selfish. You think about yourself and forget that it hits the kids just as much. My daughter's fiancé was a great help to us all. He's quite a hippy chap, into Buddhist thinking and meditation, and he used to come to the hospital with us and talk for a long time. He put together a little book of meditations called "Anne-Marie's little help book", which I still treasure.'

Adult children are torn between wanting to support their parents, both now and in the future, and giving their own relationships the attention they need. A parent's illness can put a huge strain on life at work and at home because, however understanding an employer is, employees are usually expected to keep going. Anne-Marie's youngest son was in his final year at university when his father was ill and although he was granted dispensation for one of his projects, no allowance was made for his final exams. However, it's also true that although keeping the rest of life on track can be an added source of stress, the grounding of everyday routines can help people to keep going.

Illness draws families together and brings a new dimension to the relationship between parent and adult child. 'I know it sounds strange, but there were lots of really happy family times after Adrian's diagnosis,' Anne-Marie says. 'The kids paid us more attention and came home more. The steroids made Adrian super happy, like a rock star, blogging about what he had for breakfast and things like that. He never felt sorry for himself or thought he was going to die, right until the end. I did. So, for me there was always the thought, this will be the last Christmas, the last birthday…

'When the tumour came back, it came back with a vengeance, and Adrian finally said, "I'm going to die, aren't I?" In those last weeks he was very sad. He wanted to die at home, so we had a hospital bed in the front room. Elliott used to bring his new baby son to show Adrian and he really loved the time with his new grandson.

'I kept trying to persuade Adrian to write letters to the children, but the saddest thing is that he didn't do that when he still had the ability. He started writing little notes to all of us, but by that stage his brain had gone so far that he could only manage one little scrawled sentence to each of us.'

WHEN ONE PARENT IS ILL: SUPPORTING ADULT CHILDREN

- Don't put off breaking bad news. Be honest about the prognosis and as positive as you can.
- Make it clear that you will keep children up to date about test results and decisions about treatment; some families set up a WhatsApp group. If kids don't feel they're in the loop, they may worry that things are worse than they're being told.
- A child should never be a parent's only source of support. Talk to friends: people want to help but often don't know how. Make specific requests, such as lifts to the hospital or homemade apple pie. Remember that children need support too.
- Counselling, therapy and practices like meditation and yoga build emotional resilience and contribute to a rounded network of support, which makes parents less dependent on kids and more able to support them.
- Don't allow the illness to dominate every conversation. Focus on the things you've always enjoyed doing together and stay curious about what's going on in your children's lives.

BEREAVEMENT: WHEN ONE PARENT DIES

The death of a partner is devastating. The death of a parent is equally devastating, but it's different. The parent faces life without a soulmate, perhaps after decades of marriage, and as a single parent. They have to adjust to a future that's very different to the one they had looked forward to, with plans and dreams of more time together in retirement shattered. In the second half of life it can feel that everything will be downhill from now on.

For an adult child it's fundamentally different, not least because they are nearer the start of life's journey, with so much ahead. They have career ladders to climb, work ambitions to fulfil, partners and perhaps children of their own to give life meaning. But it's a mistake to think that dealing with loss is any easier. Whether a child is 26 or 66, whether the relationship was close or distant, the death of a parent has a huge impact, both in the immediate aftermath and in the years to come. Anne-Marie's four children were in their twenties and thirties when her husband died at the age of 57 after 33 years of marriage. She says, 'Adrian's death has totally rocked their world. The children only have one dad. They are never going to have another dad who cares for them and is genetically part of them, who puts their interests first, who would die for them. I almost think his death devastated the kids more than me.'

When one parent dies: role reversal

While parent and child both need support, it is usually the adult child who steps up to look after the parent, not just in the early days but in the months and years ahead. At the funeral, it is often an adult child and not the surviving parent who gives the tearful eulogy. This is the opposite of what happens with younger children. Then it's the parent who puts their own grief on hold while they devote all their energy into supporting the child.

Sue Gill, a bereavement volunteer for Cruse, the UK's leading charity for bereaved people, says, 'I think the expectation from society is that a child's grief is not as great as the parent's, because they have lost their life partner. You hear people at funerals say to adult children, "You'll have to look after your mum/dad now." It's almost expected that the adult child will support their parent. The parent often lets it happen because in the depths of grief they need that support. It's a strange role reversal. The child almost has to put their own grief on hold and finally deals with it two or three years down the line, when they've got the time and space.'

This role reversal signals a significant shift in the relationship that may be permanent. Both parent and child have to adjust to unfamiliar roles. 'I don't want to be a burden' is every parent's mantra, yet bereaved parents don't have much choice.

Anne-Marie has been struck by the way the balance has shifted in the six years since her husband died: 'The tables have turned; the children are looking after *me* now. If Adrian was still here, I think they would take us for granted more. Instead they're all a bit more precious with me; they recognise I have problems, they see I'm very vulnerable, they've seen me mourning and crying and they're aware of my financial difficulties. It grew them up a lot. Elliott, the eldest, is now the daddy figure. He helped me wind up his father's company and took a lot off my shoulders.'

Children may feel deeply anxious that the bereaved parent will fall apart because they can't boil an egg or hate driving or they've never spent much time alone. Many parents have to work out how to go forward with their new life; adult children can help them to gradually reinvent their life and get back to some sort of normality. However, Cruse volunteer Sue Gill has found that with the best of intentions, adult kids can be a bit bossy, a bit too eager to organise. They may encourage the surviving parent to throw away clothes or even move house before they're ready. Parents may be at their lowest ebb, but they need to resist pressure to make changes too soon and help their children to understand why.

Supporting bereaved adult children

In the immediate aftermath of the death – for at least a year, according to Cruse – it's totally understandable if parents have little room to think about anything beyond their own grief, including the children's needs. As Anne-Marie says, 'You get selfish. You think about yourself and losing your partner and me, me, me, the widow. And you forget that it hits the kids too.'

But as time moves on, the parent needs to be alert to signs that the child needs more support and space to cope with their own grief. A quarter of the people who sought help from Cruse in 2000 were adult children of all ages.

Yvonne, whose mother died 15 years ago, says, 'I realised I had never really grieved for my mum, because looking after my dad and work took all my time and focus. Finally, I've got time to grieve and it's a very conscious process, through meditation and counselling.'

Out of the blue, some small thing – a death in a movie or a sad song – might trigger an overwhelming emotional reaction. Yet an adult child may be reluctant to admit they're struggling, particularly if they think their parent has got enough on their plate. They may not even identify what they're feeling as grief, because grieving is such an individual process and manifests itself in so many different ways. It is likely that a child's grief will look very different to their parent's.

Bereavement: how to open up the conversation

There comes a time when parents are able to reflect on whether they could rely on their children less and give them more space to grieve. Their own experience of grief, still raw, should offer unique insights into what could help adult children most. Cruse bereavement volunteer Sue Gill suggests simple ways to open up the conversation: looking through old photographs and treasures together prompts all kinds of different memories and what she calls 'all those daft tales that every family shares'. She adds, 'The problem is, people don't talk and that applies to young and old. So it's important to make use of opportunities to talk, like sorting through the dead person's clothes or putting together a new photograph album. And above all, listen. Proper listening, when you're not just mentally composing your shopping list, is really tiring. Allow the other person to talk, don't butt in with your own ideas or memories, wait until they've finished. A child's memories will be very different from a parent's. And with adult children, you can talk more easily; you can have different conversations than you would with younger children. If it was an unpleasant death, talking keeps bringing it down to size.'

It can be helpful for parents who have already lost a parent themselves to reflect on how it affected them. It won't be the same, but it can provide clues. It's also useful to think about what the adult child will miss about the other parent. Even the most successful and together adult can feel like an abandoned child when a parent dies. They face the absence of a role model who has always been in their lives, who helped shape their personality, who offered guidance and a moral compass – even if it was something to kick against. If they didn't get on well, it can be unexpectedly painful and the grieving process more complicated; there could be more than a twinge of guilt. And inevitably there's a shift of identity and status as adult children are catapulted into the next level of adulthood and assume a new role and new responsibilities within the family. You often hear people in their forties and fifties say they didn't feel grown up until their mother or father died. There's a new awareness of mortality and of life's fragility.

The adult child's age when a parent dies

The age of the adult child, the stage they've reached in life and their life experience all have an impact on individual experiences of grief, as does the age of their parents. My dad died when he was 69 and I was 29 and had no children, whereas my mum died when she was 89 and I was 53, with a supportive partner and three children on the cusp of adulthood. There was a huge difference. I brushed my dad's death under the carpet and swiftly moved on with my life, ignoring the fact that underneath it all, I felt totally at sea. When my mother died, I had my own family to support me; they loved her dearly and missed her too. By that stage I had learnt that if you deny the big stuff, it never really goes away until you deal with it.

Sue Gill of Cruse believes the age of the adult child makes a significant difference and that needs to be acknowledged: 'People in their twenties may be very vulnerable, because they might not have been living independently for long, they might still be at home, they're starting a new career, they might not have a long-term partner. By their thirties and forties, adult children are usually more settled, they might have a partner and children of their own. They're still heartbroken and suffer all the usual feelings, but they've also got a busy life to carry on. In your twenties you look ahead and think, Dad's not going to be there when I get married... or Mum's not going to be around when I have my first baby...whereas in your forties, hopefully your parent has been there for those first bits, so you look at things differently. But however old you are, the death of a parent is always traumatic and incredibly sad. You never get over these close deaths, you just learn to live with them.'

Anne-Marie thinks that each of her four children has been affected in different ways and that's to do with their age and circumstances as well as their personalities. Her eldest was in his early thirties with a new baby, while her youngest was taking finals and still based at home. At first, her daughter appeared to be coping well: she was in her late twenties, newly married and loving her job. But after about a year everything changed: 'She started coming home a lot and saying she was worried about her health, thinking she was dying all the time. At first, I thought her symptoms were physical, but I soon realised that having told her to go to the doctor, she wasn't getting consoled; it didn't matter what expert she saw, she was still anxious. I didn't want to be rude, but I felt I had to say, I think this is in your head, not your body. Since then she has had a lot of counselling and therapy, and she's got much better. But it's been a tough time for her and it has affected her a lot.'

Facing the future as a single parent

The bereaved partner now faces the future as a single parent. Clearly, that doesn't carry the same practical burdens as it does for widows and widowers with young children, but it is still a massive upheaval, both emotionally and practically. The surviving parent may feel lost and ill-equipped without the support of a partner. That goes for lovely events as well as crises: weddings, birthdays, Christmas, graduation ceremonies.

Anne-Marie has a poignant memory of sitting by herself in a vast hall waiting for her youngest son's graduation to begin: 'I had a little cry because I was so sad that Adrian wasn't there to see his son graduate.' There will be times when the surviving parent struggles to offer the unique support the other parent would have provided: when an adult child has a baby, or needs advice on buying a flat, for example.

The widowed parent doesn't just miss their partner at times like these, they miss *being parents together*. For their children too it can be a surprising adjustment to relate to their parent as an individual after years of seeing them as part of a solid mum&dad unit. Each parent is a separate and unique role model, and their personalities often complement each other. For example, it often happens that one parent's anxiety about the kids is balanced by the other's calm encouragement; the loss of that equilibrium leaves both parent and child at sea.

'Adrian was a good balance to me, we were very different,' Anne-Marie says. 'There were a lot of areas the children turned to him for, like music, which he loved. Now, when they get a new job or they're expecting a baby, they want to rush home and tell their dad. I've got to try and be everything to them.'

How a parent's death affects siblings

You expect grief to bring families together, but tension and even conflict between siblings is surprisingly common. In fact, when you think about it, it's not so surprising, given the depth of emotion. If there has been tension or rivalry in the past, a death is likely to bring it to the fore. But even the most amicable sibling relationships can become strained and that's hard to deal with because it's so unexpected. Each person in the family is caught up in their own grief and may find it hard to understand the needs of the others, or recognise that everyone grieves in different ways. Cruse bereavement volunteer Sue Gill says, 'The way people deal with grief is individual and it can differ within one family. Some people naturally deal with it more easily, while others are still struggling with it five or even 10 years down the line.'

One child may feel they've got to be the strong one, supporting another sibling at the expense of their own need to cry and talk. One child may have done more for the parent when they were ill and that can create resentment. Sometimes the whole family keeps a lid on grief for fear of upsetting each other and repressing such deep emotion adds to the tension. And I think we're all guilty of thinking we knew our parent best: we know which tune they'd like at their funeral, or who they wanted to inherit their wedding ring. According to Sue Gill, sibling conflict is common: 'We get clients coming to us a year after the death saying that they're still fighting. Meanwhile, the poor parent is trying to keep the family together as well as grieving. They know it's all going on, but they just haven't got the headspace to try and resolve things.'

There is one consolation, at least, although it's sad too. Adult children are a constant reminder of the dead parent in their mannerisms, appearance and behaviour. The resemblance often becomes more marked as they get older. Anne-Marie's children have reached the age Adrian was when they first married and they remind her of him more and more. She says, 'The weirdest thing is that Adrian's legacy carries on in the children. They have become my reflections of Adrian; he's gone, but he is in them. There are moments when it feels very intense.' This echoes what the film director William Nicholson told *The Guardian*: 'The presence of the child – the living embodiment of a marriage – is both a joy and a torment to the parents.' He was talking about divorce in his film *Hope Gap*, but there are resonances when a parent dies too.

SUPPORTING A BEREAVED ADULT CHILD WHEN YOU'RE GRIEVING TOO

- Be aware that your child may bottle up their own grief so that they can look after you. The time will come when they need space to grieve themselves.
- A good way to talk is by sorting through family photos or looking through family treasures together.
- No parent wants to rely totally on their children and they need to mourn too. Your friends will also be ready to offer solace and support.
- Resist pressure from your child to make changes too soon.
- Think carefully before relocating near your children. If you do, explore opportunities in the area to build your own social networks and pursue both new and existing interests.
- Remember, grief is individual. Your child's grieving may be very different to yours.
- Get together as a family – either in person, or virtually – on the dead person's birthday or the anniversary of their death, to honour and remember them.

8

Conflict, Tension and Disagreement

Not long ago, I found myself wagging my finger like an old crone at my daughter during a row. 'Just look at yourself, Mum!' she said. I was horrified – I might have got away with finger-wagging when the kids were young, but it's clearly out of order with a 28-year-old.

Disagreeing with adults is very different to disagreeing with younger children. Parents can no longer tell their children off, even if they want to; rather than punishing them by grounding them or withdrawing privileges or pocket money, they have to find other ways to show disapproval. Meanwhile, their adult children have ways of expressing their own disapproval of their parents' foibles and inconsistencies – and it hurts! Adult children can touch a nerve in a way no one else can.

Disagreements are part of family life. Families express conflict in different ways: some like getting things off their chest in a big row, while others tend to sulk or withdraw altogether. Some families argue and get nowhere, others argue and get somewhere. In many families, people get tense, irritable and distant from time to time, but they don't actually argue much. This chapter is about this kind of everyday disagreement, but also about the fractiousness and conflict that gets so intense that it puts kids off meeting up with their parents and in extreme cases leads to estrangement.

Ultimately, more is at stake. If adult children decide not to see you because you disagree, there's not much you can do about it. Professor Lisa Doodson, an expert on stepfamilies, says, 'Parents have no control. Adult children can decide to cut you off, or to be rude or disrespectful to their parent or step-parent. That may cause problems for the relationship between parents as well as for the relationship with the adult child.'

When you no longer live under the same roof, grievances can more easily persist, unresolved, and take on too much significance. When you don't see the other person regularly, it's hard to tell whether they've forgotten all about a dispute or are still upset and seething. It takes a conscious overture to make amends: you can't just make peace over a casual cup of tea or when you give someone a lift. But on the whole, adult children are more reasonable than their younger selves, although emerging adults are still battling to assert a separate identity with parents who may be resistant.

The family therapist Judith Lask explains, 'With a younger child you have different arguments than you would have with an adult. There is a big power differential that gets in the way because there are lots of things that both parents and teenagers can use to get their own way in an argument. When children are adults you might have to learn to argue in a different way. It's much more like an argument you might have with a friend or a work colleague or a partner, when you're on more equal ground.'

All the hype about snowflakes warring against their baby-boomer parents suggests there's a new conflict between the generations, but research into relationships in several European countries found that only a fraction of adult families – just 5 per cent – speak of frequent conflict. And of course the generation gap, with all its implications of conflict, is as old as the hills, even if it didn't emerge as a sociological theory until the 1960s, when the younger generation, who are now baby-boomer parents, rejected everything their parents held dear: politics, culture, dress, music, morality.

In this context I find the work of the social psychologist Professor Vern Bengston, who died in 2019, reassuring. His research into intergenerational relations pointed to the eternal tension between parents who favour continuity and hope their children will uphold their values, and their adult children who are naturally driven by a desire for change and to be distinctive. He concluded that 'continuity often resides within innovation'. I like to think this means that while adult children might appear to be rejecting their parents' ideas and values, what is actually more likely is that they are expressing, reflecting or developing them in their own new and distinctive ways.

KEEPING CONFLICT TO A MINIMUM (WHILE STILL TALKING ABOUT THE DIFFICULT STUFF)

It's neither possible nor desirable to avoid arguments completely, but it is possible to keep conflict to a minimum yet still talk about the stuff that needs saying. These things can help:

- Agree to disagree
- Identify what you argue about and reflect on why
- Choose your battles
- Find non-confrontational ways to raise difficult issues

Agree to disagree

We bring our kids up to have their own views and be independent, but this can be infuriating! Differences that you might relish in a friendship can jar with an adult child. Agreeing to disagree amicably is a sign that your relationship is developing and becoming more equal. It's about respecting adult children's choices and accepting – even enjoying – difference. Each side can learn from disagreements, both about each other and about handling conflict generally. But the fact remains that no one enjoys arguing with their adult kids and many parents do their best to avoid it. Helen, whose daughter is in her early twenties, says, 'My daughter and I don't have many arguments but that's partly because I'm working so hard to avoid them.'

We've all been there: steering away from subjects that touch a raw nerve, especially at stressful times. You don't get much more stressful than IVF, not least because fertility drugs can affect mood. Jacqui's daughter Tru went through three rounds of fertility treatment in her thirties and she remembers: 'Tru is a sensitive person. Sometimes I can say the wrong thing and she'll respond in a direct fashion, but it just goes over my head because I've got used to it. When she was going through IVF, I realised that all the stress that she was under would naturally make her much more sensitive, and there were times when I was conscious of having to be very careful.'

Learning to argue, and respecting difference, is part of being an adult family. Judith Lask explains, 'If you are direct, you are probably going to develop a more intimate, meaningful relationship with your adult child. If you're constantly treading on eggshells, there's a big gap between you because certain issues aren't being taken up. And then one of these issues comes up when you're having an argument about something else, and you're not feeling on very good terms with each other, there isn't time to talk about it properly and it all ends badly. If you're tiptoeing around topics, it also means that things don't stand a chance of getting resolved as they would if you were able to argue.'

Identify what you argue about and why

An important first step is to identify the issues you argue about most and think about why. It's essential to reflect on your own role in the conflict and how much you are contributing to the tension. Don't automatically assume you're right and your adult child is wrong. Relationships with adult children are ambivalent and complicated.

Arguments are usually about much more than what's on the surface. When you're hanging around waiting for your child who is late (again), you're not merely irritated as you would be with a friend, you feel taken for granted as a parent but also anxious about whether they're always this disorganised. You might even blame yourself for not bringing them up to be more considerate. Parents' irritation about trivialities is often rooted in underlying anxiety. They may be concerned about how well an adult child is coping at work or in their personal lives, and about whether they're lonely or stressed out or partying too hard. Past anxieties refuse to go away: if a child has been depressed or bulimic or had problems making friends in the past, it's hard not to be alert to the smallest signs that the problems might be coming back.

Lucy, whose son and daughter are in their late twenties and both live at home, believes her experience as a psychotherapist has given her a better understanding of sources of conflict and how to keep it to a minimum. She says, 'There are so many emotional undercurrents. Any understanding or awareness that gives you some insight into how another person might be thinking or feeling can be really helpful, so is anything that helps you step back a bit and not act out. You have to monitor yourself and think, am I asking a question that's going to really piss him or her off? Is this going to result in a massive explosion and if so, I won't say it! You also have to resist the natural tendency to get rid of a feeling by passing it on to the other person and walking away feeling a lot better.'

Choose your battles

It's generally agreed that it's best not to sweat the small stuff but to save discussion – and possible confrontation – for the issues that really matter to you. Most parents learn this lesson when their children are young. It's an entirely individual thing, because what seems like a big deal to one person looks like nit-picking to another – and that probably includes your child! Some people are by nature easy-going, while others are sticklers for standards. One stepmother I know found it really upsetting that her stepson and daughter used to turn up without warning, walk straight into the kitchen and raid the fridge. Resentment built because she couldn't say anything: her husband shared his kids' view that they should treat the house as their own.

I'm not suggesting that minor irritations don't merit discussion, because otherwise they can build into deep resentment. And they often have an underlying emotional significance, which may need to be addressed. It's a question of working out what really matters to you. Nisha used to get fed up when her daughters' boyfriends left the bathroom in a bit of a mess, but in the end, she decided it just wasn't worth creating bad feeling and lowered her standards for the sake of family harmony. Judith Lask adds, 'If you find yourself wanting to criticise or snipe at everything, you probably ought to do a bit of self-reflection and think about what it is that would be worthy of a good discussion. You always have to ask yourself, is this worth having an argument about? It's the same with other situations throughout life.'

Find non-confrontational ways to raise difficult issues

Nobody goes looking for an argument, but if tension keeps getting in the way, it has to be better to talk about things and hopefully clear the air. Otherwise grievances build and there's a real danger that they could eventually explode in an apocalyptic fallout that will be hard to recover from (see also Repairing the damage, page 162).

It helps to think carefully beforehand about what you want to bring to the table, how best to broach the subject and where to meet and when. Often it's best to choose somewhere neutral like a café or a walk in the park. Judith Lask advises being clear in your mind about the one issue you've decided to focus on: 'Never ever throw everything but the kitchen sink into the argument: stick with what you want to talk about. Never say, "You never do x" or "You always do y" – it's these little things that can very quickly throw a discussion into a nasty-ending argument. That goes for adult children too: they need to resist the temptation to say things like, "You never want me to do what I want, you never understand my feelings". You need to give precise examples of what you felt upset about, not vague blanket statements. Always remember that saying what you think and listening to the other person are of equal importance.'

The language you use and the way you talk to your child generally – and vice versa – really matters. It's a clear sign of how you see each other. No finger-wagging permitted! It's bound to create tension if you talk to an adult child in the way you would speak to a younger one. That might sound obvious, but when you're irritated or cross, it's easy to slip back into old habits. If you've ever taken an adult child out in the car for driving practice, you'll probably know what I mean! It's just as bad when adult children are rude or talk down to their parents in that slightly patronising way we're all familiar with.

The family therapist Dr Myrna Gower says, 'The most frequent behaviours you see when families are fighting can be interactions where parents address their adult children as if they were still younger children as in former times; they might even tell them their table manners are appalling. Being critical and harsh with children seldom is strength-building and such interactions with adult children can be further humiliating and harmful to self-esteem. This would be indicative of a limited evolution of the relationship into phases of adulthood, blocking potential joy and respect that could be shared for a lifetime.'

It also goes without saying that it is essential to listen properly: really pay attention to what the other person is saying. Rather than leap straight into outraged defensiveness if your child says, 'You *never* listen!' – a common complaint – take a clear-sighted look at your behaviour and ask yourself whether they could have a point. The award-winning dramatist Mike Bartlett's play *Snowflake* features an estranged daughter who has broken off contact with her father for many reasons, but it is his failure to listen to her – and to recognise that he's not *really* listening – that lies at the heart. It touches a nerve because the audience can see she's right.

STEPFAMILIES

The general assumption about step-parents is that they are more likely to create conflict with adult stepchildren than biological parents: Olivia Coleman's magnificently manipulative stepmother in *Fleabag* is a fine example. But that's not always the case. It can be that the absence of that intense umbilical connection takes the heat out; the underlying emotional complications are different. Adult children often find it easier to discuss difficult issues, and hear advice, from a more objective adult who is nonetheless entirely on their side. I know of one woman in her early thirties who readily took up a career suggestion from her stepmother that she had dismissed when it came from her mother.

When there is conflict, it's up to the parent or step-parent to think about whether they're contributing to it. If the step-parent is new to the family, it's particularly important to see the adult child's perspective. For example, any adult child who is used to their father's undivided attention is bound to be upset if they rarely get to see him alone. Professor Lisa Doodson, an expert on stepfamilies, says, 'It's up to the step-parent to think about how they could improve the relationship. Conflict is often about misconceptions and it may be simply a question of spending more time to get to know each other. It's about being sensitive about the status quo that already exists with adult children and not just jumping in. You may have to take more of a back seat and allow them to have their relationship with your partner, rather than insisting on always coming along.'

If a step-parent is relatively new to the family, they may get irritated – even outraged – by behaviour that the biological parent takes for granted: adult children assuming they can move back home without asking, or expecting financial bailouts. Meanwhile, it's bound to give rise to tension if adult children are expected to welcome a new person into the family, with all the potential repercussions about home, finances and inheritance. Rivalry between siblings and stepsiblings can also create conflict with parents. There are obvious practical conundrums: if both parents have children from a previous relationship, they may all want to move back home but there's not enough room; they may all need help with a deposit or grandchildcare at the same time. If possible, parents need to come to an agreement well in advance and work out ways to divide their energies and money fairly.

Professor Doodson adds, 'The issues are all eminently fixable as long as couples work together. But it's like anything: unless the other person can see that there's an issue, it's not going to get solved. In stepfamilies it's particularly important that the parents keep talking to each other rather than allowing minor resentments with adult children to build up. Things can become very difficult if people sit on minor issues which then build up, and after a while there's a tidal wave.'

COMMON SOURCES OF CONFLICT

- Anxiety about adult children's lives
- Adult children's disapproval of their parents
- Unfair treatment
- Money
- Issues from childhood and the past

Anxiety about adult children's lives

When parents express concern about their children's lives – their work, their stress levels, their partner, returning to work after a baby, childcare – it's not always that welcome. Blunt parents have no qualms about saying exactly what they think and that's fine if kids are strong enough to stick up for themselves. But other parents, who acknowledge that some things are none of their business, face an internal conflict about whether or not to say anything and that just makes them feel more tense and anxious. They don't want to intrude or provoke a row but even if disapproval is not expressed openly, it's obvious from parents' behaviour: an involuntary pursing of the lips, a thinly veiled hint or a lukewarm response to something their child is excited about. After all, adult children have been reading their parents' body language since they were babies. They are likely to be even more irritated if their parents' concern touches a nerve because they are already feeling unsure themselves.

The dilemma for parents is that while they never stop worrying about their kids, they need to recognise that even if they think they've got a solution, it's nearly always better to let children find their own way. Some parents remain so closely invested in a child's decisions that they fail to allow them to find their own path and accept that the choices they make may be very different from their own – and indeed from the ambitions they've nursed on their behalf. If a son or daughter opts to be a stay-at-home parent when you worked full-time, for example, it can feel like criticism. So it's important to question how much your concern is to do with an adult child's understandable reluctance – or even refusal – to fulfil *your* dreams rather than their own.

Dr Ruth Caleb, an authority on young people's mental health and well-being, says, 'Every parent says they want their child to be happy, but we only believe they can be happy in the way we would be. Actually, we have to listen to them and let them decide for themselves.'

Sources of conflict: adult children's disapproval of their parents

I'm not sure why an adult child's disapproval should be so painful, but it is. A trivial remark about the way you dance or say sorry all the time can still smart months later. Because they know you, warts and all, they never fail to hit an emotional bullseye. When Lindsey's daughter accused her of drinking too much (she really doesn't), she was devastated: 'All the family had been together for the weekend and a few hours after everyone had left, my daughter rang and said, "Have you got a minute?" I thought it was really strange. She had this speech prepared about an incident eight years earlier when I'd given an elderly relative a lift home. It was literally two minutes up the road and although I'd had a couple of glasses of wine, no one else offered. From this, and a couple of other incidents, my daughter was implying that I drank too much and that I was irresponsible.

'I was in shock for several days. I felt it was a wider criticism of my behaviour as a mother. The worst thing was that she gave the impression that her siblings were in on it too: I felt completely isolated. I thought I had been deluded about my relationship with my whole family and I couldn't see how we were going to survive or what the future was going to be. It was really horrible.'

Divorce is one of the most common causes of adult children's disapproval; it can lead to years of conflict and tension. If an adult child blames one parent for the split, they may even refuse to have any contact and that's tragic for everyone. Judith Lask explains, 'When parents separate there are all sorts of things that can create a rift that then doesn't get crossed. At one extreme there might be alienation from one parent, or there can be distancing or lack of trust. If there are no bridges made, it gets wider and wider.' I've come across many fathers – and mothers too, but it seems less common – whose adult children won't see them because they've had an affair or taken up with a new partner. Caught up in their own turbulent emotions, parents often fail to acknowledge that their adult children will feel as torn, upset and angry as younger kids.

After Ian's parents divorced eight years ago he had no contact with his mother for a couple of years, while his brother didn't see their

CONFLICT, TENSION AND DISAGREEMENT

father. 'Mum attempted to contact me a few times in the year or two after the divorce, but I just wasn't ready,' he says. 'I was very angry with her and with my brother. I felt they had effectively joined forces against my dad. That was one of the most painful things for me. Towards the end, I told Mum how I felt. In my view she should have been the parent and told her sons to stay out of it, because it was her problem.'

Sources of conflict: unfair treatment

Sibling rivalry is a fact of life in every family with more than one child. If adult children think their parents have treated them unfairly, either in childhood or more recently, it can create friction not only with their siblings, but with their parents too. They might feel that another child has always been the favourite, or that they've been given an unequal share of money or opportunities. A child who doesn't have kids could resent the energy and money their parents invest in their grandchildren. It's often an issue in stepfamilies. Parents, meanwhile, may be blissfully unaware that a child feels hard done by and mystified by what's causing tension between them. Whether or not perceptions of past unfairness are justified, they need to be acknowledged and discussed: that at least gives parents a chance to explain and for a dialogue to open up. And when it comes to the future, parents need to be open with their children about the decisions they plan to make. (More on adult siblings in Chapter 9.)

Sources of conflict: money

Money is a classic source of tension and disagreement, because it's so knotted up with guilt, control, attachment, dependency and letting go. It's not only parents who disapprove of the way their children spend their money. Adult children can be just as judgemental of baby-boomer parents with final salary pensions and paid-off mortgages who drive gas-guzzling cars and love long-haul destinations.

Loans or gifts to kids usually come with strings attached, even if that's not really supposed to be part of the deal. Research at Birmingham University into intergenerational financial giving found that help often comes with a negotiation about how the money is used. Kids are grateful, of course, but they may also feel irritated if parents exercise too much control. Meanwhile, if parents expect undiluted gratitude, they may well be disappointed. And if they have to bail a child out of financial difficulties, a parent's attitude is dictated by circumstances. If an adult child runs up a crazy credit card bill for no good reason, their parent might be furious but also anxious. Yet in other situations, whether they acknowledge it or not, they may rather like – perhaps even need – the continuing bond that writing a virtual cheque represents. It's different if a child is struggling with debt after redundancy or divorce: then parents just do whatever they can to help – although they need to resist the temptation to say 'I told you so'.

Perceived unfairness about gifts to siblings is a common cause of bitterness among parents. One mother I spoke to was in despair because her husband had secretly doled out ad hoc sums of money to some of their children and paid the school fees for some grandchildren and not others. Unsurprisingly their middle-aged children were still squabbling among themselves and with their parents – and not just about money. Dr Reenee Singh says, 'Unfortunately money is the idiom through which a lot of feelings are expressed. Money comes up as a theme with so many of the adult families I work with. It's never just about the money, it's about acceptance and belonging, whereas the theme of unfairness or injustice often expresses itself over conflicts about money.'

Parents are clearly right to agonise about being as fair as possible. And if circumstances arise when one child needs more financial help, like Tru, whose parents contributed to her fertility treatment, it's important to lay your cards on the table with their siblings. Couples also need to discuss what they think is fair, both now and in the future. Professor Lisa Doodson says: 'You want to avoid those horrible conversations where the child says "He got x, what about me?" Fairness is even more important in stepfamilies than in a biological family. I disagree with the idea that if you give one child something, you have to give the others exactly the same. I don't think it's the adult child's right to say *you owe me this* or *she got that*. But parents do have to let their children know that they will balance things out at some point in the future, when it's appropriate. If you can have a conversation about what you think would be fair, it takes children's anxieties away; they know they can trust you. It's when children don't trust their parents to be fair that the situation becomes difficult.' (More on money in Chapter 2, see page 41.)

Issues from childhood and the past

Sometimes resentment has been brewing for years, but it's only in adulthood that a child feels able to talk about why they felt let down, betrayed or hurt. It may surface in a row about something totally unrelated, which adds to the anguish and misunderstanding. It's also common for issues to emerge during individual therapy or counselling. Often the parent is unaware, or doesn't realise the full impact, of what was said or done in the past. The family therapist Judith Lask says, 'The parent might think it's something very trivial, that it's in the past, that the adult child should get over it. But it isn't in the past for the child, it's still in the present, and that's why they want to sort it out.'

It could be that the child was bullied or had problems with stepsiblings and felt the parent's response was inadequate and they failed to protect them. Perhaps the child feels aggrieved that they were sent to a school they hated or moved house too often. Renate says, 'I'm sure there were times when Nate looked at us and wished he had another family! He said it was very traumatic for him moving around so much – although in fact we didn't move that often.'

A young or teenage child might have felt let down or confused when parents divorced. There may be darker issues: if the child was abused, for example, and feels the parent failed to protect them. If a parent had a physical or mental illness it might have been hard for the child to make sense of what was going on. Conversations that would have helped a child cope at the time may now need to happen in adulthood.

In Dr Reenee Singh's experience as a consultant family therapist, it is more often the adult child than the parent who initiates the therapy, because they are looking for a safe place to talk about issues from their upbringing that are still holding them back. She explains, 'The past colours the present continually. If there are secrets floating around, or issues that haven't been spoken about in a helpful way, that impacts on the relationship: the adult child and parent often drift apart. Often the parents don't have a clue what their child went through, simply because the child hasn't been able to talk about it.

'Some of the work I do with families is thinking about the present interactions and what parent and child can do to interrupt the unhelpful patterns they might have got into, such as never inviting their parents for a meal, or never spending time together. Actually, the adult child might be sitting on a whole lot of anger, upset and resentment; they might feel really let down or betrayed by a parent. It's only when they have a way to express those feelings that parent and child can move on.' She adds, 'I always emphasise that parents were doing their best, often in a difficult situation. But at the same time, parents just really need to slow down and listen.'

REPAIRING THE DAMAGE

Arguments can clear the air, but only if they are followed by some form of reconciliation and a willingness to take on board each other's point of view. At the other extreme, a bad row can cause huge rifts and, in the saddest cases, estrangement. And while we all know it's best to avoid getting into a row after a tough day or a few drinks, we've all done it. We've all said things we didn't mean, as well as things we meant to say, but came out all wrong. It's then a question of repairing the damage. Saying sorry might be enough. If not, it's usually up to the parent to make the first move, whatever the adult child's age, and even if they feel they're the more injured party. Parents always need to look at their own role in any disagreement.

They also need to be clear-sighted about their motives when they make overtures to make amends. Family therapist Judith Lask says, 'You always need to be sure that what you want is the communication with your child – or your parent – and that you're not actually wanting to punish them, or prove how bad they are, or get them to admit what a terrible child/parent they are. It has to be approached with a gentleness and openness, an exploration to see what's possible rather than an assumption.'

Even when parent and child seem to be drifting wider apart, and the rift seems entrenched, Judith Lask believes it is possible to repair enough of the damage to allow the relationship to move forward. If at all possible, it obviously helps if some kind of communication can be maintained, because otherwise it will be more difficult to build new bridges. If relations are either hostile or have completely broken down, it's much harder to take the first step. In a vacuum of communication, grievances get out of all proportion: you find yourself rehearsing arguments in your head and attributing feelings and attitudes to the other person that simply aren't there. Often when you eventually meet face to face, you realise they're not as stroppy or unreasonable as the two-dimensional picture that's built up in your mind.

Sometimes time and circumstances are on your side. For example, when children become parents themselves and see their parents as loving grandparents, it often breaks the ice and triggers a willingness to reconnect. Having a child of his own made Ian view his mother's past behaviour in a more forgiving light and he agreed to meet her after a long period of estrangement. His work as a psychotherapist also contributed to a more tolerant view of her. He says, 'I realised that in spite of my ambivalence I couldn't refuse to let my mother have a relationship with her granddaughter. It was a bit awkward to begin with but then it was really pleasant, and of course she was cock-a-hoop to meet my daughter. Since then we've met every few months and text each other from time to time. She would probably like more, but at this point it's enough for me.'

Judith Lask believes that in order to build a workable relationship after a period of distance or estrangement, both sides need a level of recognition about the perceived hurt and the experience of the other person. Parents have to be willing to accept that they could be in the wrong and examine their role in the disagreement. She says, 'It usually needs one person to be a bit of a saint. It's almost like a truth and reconciliation exercise where the parent admits they didn't do something very well, but they want the child to know how they felt at that time, so they understand why they made the decision. Conversely, the parents may blame their children for doing something they disapproved of, or for not managing something well. There can be forgiveness, as long as people understand why something happened and they're not being blamed for it.'

STRATEGIES TO HELP REPAIR THE DAMAGE

I'm not suggesting that the only way to resolve conflict is through family therapy, although it can be incredibly helpful, particularly when people feel stuck. But there is a lot to learn from the way experienced therapists enable adult families to talk about really difficult issues and move forward. The first three suggestions and exercises below come from family therapist Dr Reenee Singh. Even if you don't follow them to the letter, they provide useful clues to more constructive ways of communicating.

Listening

Listening is just as important as saying what you think. It's the only way you can start to understand the other person's position. But it's not as simple as it sounds and we're all too easily distracted by phones, screens and what's for supper. It's important to be fully focused on what's being said, rather than mulling over what you're going to say next, or jumping in with an experience of your own. It's extremely painful to feel blamed and criticised, but parents have to sit with it. Dr Reenee Singh explains, 'When your adult child tells you about something difficult from their childhood, just listen and validate their experiences. Hear what they're saying without defending yourself and explaining why you did what you did. There is something powerful about just listening: simply making that space for the child to say, this was really hard for me when you did whatever it was…'

Paraphrasing

Parent and child take it in turns to talk while the other person listens. The listener is then asked to paraphrase what the other person has just said. They have to speak from an 'I' position so there is no blame attached to what the other person did, it's purely about their experiences.

Therapeutic rituals

Make a date to meet up once a week or once a month and go for a walk or do something together. 'There is something about being alongside someone rather than facing each other that is really helpful,' says Dr Singh.

See things from your child's perspective

Arguments make people self-righteous and defensive: they blame the other person and refuse to acknowledge that they must have contributed to the conflict. But, particularly when the disagreement is with an adult child, parents have to be prepared to accept some of the blame and do their best to understand the child's point of view. Professor Lisa Doodson, an authority on stepfamilies, advises, 'Disagreements often come from misunderstandings. It's about taking a step back, whether you're the step-parent or the stepchild, and trying to see things from the other person's perspective. We often don't do that if we're feeling aggrieved or resentful, we're just focused on how we feel.'

It's best not to fall into the habit of relating a child's feelings and experiences to situations in your own past. What they need above all is acknowledgement and understanding. That requires a much bigger imaginative leap, according to Jenny Langley, who works with parents of young people with mental health issues.

'It really comes down to empathy,' she says. 'Stepping into the other person's shoes does not mean thinking about what we were like when we were young adults, but looking through their lens as if we were young adults *now*. This is a life skill for everyone: we should all be seeking to apply empathy all the time.'

A family meeting

The Guardian's agony aunt, Annalisa Barbieri, once told an interviewer: 'Almost every problem I get could be sorted by the family sitting round and talking. Communication is everything.' Some people would baulk at the idea of a family meeting – it sounds a bit drastic and awkward – but it's a sensible solution if an issue arises that affects the whole family. After the argument with her daughter that Lindsey described earlier in this chapter, they met for a slightly sticky lunch, but the argument remained the elephant in the room.

So to clear the air, Lindsey's husband suggested a family meeting with one essential ground rule: each person took it in turns to speak, without interruption. This avoids stronger characters dominating and takes the heat out of the situation.

'Everyone was very nervous,' Lindsey remembers. 'Esther repeated the story about the incident eight years ago. I was able to explain that I was aware that my generation drink more than hers, but that didn't mean I had a problem with alcohol. I also said I really had done my best as a parent and I was sorry if Esther thought differently. It was clear from the meeting that the other two children hadn't been ganging up on me and that was a huge relief. I think it helped Esther that she was able to talk about what had clearly been on her mind for a long time and that her concerns were totally unfounded.'

Write a letter

If parent and child don't speak, or are estranged, an old-fashioned letter may introduce the chink of light you long for. 'A letter can be a good way of starting something off if there really hasn't been any communication,' says family therapist Judith Lask. 'It's much easier to explain things in a letter: you can be lengthier, you can look at all sides. And it can be re-read, which a phone call or a conversation can't be. You can look again and think, when I read it last time I took that meaning, but maybe there's another meaning.'

Letters should be written from the heart, but with caution. The written word is open to misinterpretation. Letters and emails are one-sided: they don't have the flexible to-and-fro of a face-to-face meeting, where people can respond to each other and explain exactly what they mean. And while their inky indelibility can be a bonus, it's always there to be held against its author. Judith Lask warns, 'I've seen this happen with parents who want to get back together with an adult child: they start the letter with something like, "You don't know how much pain I've had because you haven't been in touch with me..." Immediately the child reading it will close down and think, *it's the old story again, I'm to blame, that's what I escaped from...* So it's tricky because falling into those old patterns is what we're most likely to do.'

9

Adult Siblings and New Family Dynamics

People rarely talk about siblings without the word 'rivalry' getting a mention. There's a fascination with celebrity spats and fallings-out, from Prince William and Prince Harry to Liam and Noel Gallagher. At the other extreme, parents dream that their children will be best friends. But the reality in most families – both with our own siblings and with our adult children – usually lies somewhere in between.

Sibling relationships are special, even if adult children don't get on particularly well or see each other all that often. I'm not close to my own siblings, largely because there's a big age gap and we live miles apart, yet there's still a solid bond at the core; siblings literally understand where you're coming from. There's a comforting feeling of touching base when we all get together – as well as pushing each other's buttons in a way no one else can! Put simply, they're family: a connection that continues long after individual members stop living with their parents and even after their death. And there's something reassuring about knowing the bond exists, and that when the chips are down, they are there for you. Friendships and even marriages may not last, but sibling relationships endure even when you don't see each other very often.

Parents like to think of the family unit they've created lasting long into the future. They naturally want their adult children to get on well and support each other. So while they accept a degree of sibling rivalry as par for the course when kids are growing up, the hope is that it will dissipate as they become more independent. And it's true that many siblings get on better when they're no longer in the family home.

That's happened effortlessly in Paul's family. The youngest of his three daughters, Leah, 29, says, 'Things have definitely changed since we left home. When we were younger, we squabbled more – we used to wind each other up about petty things. We literally don't argue at all now we're older; there's nothing to argue about. We're much closer, even though we're living separate lives. We're best friends, not just sisters.'

But some siblings aren't close and perhaps they never will be. Some naturally drift apart as adults. That might be to do with rivalry, which doesn't automatically disappear with maturity. Dormant tensions often resurface when everyone gets together; jostling for parental attention can continue throughout life. But it could simply be that geographical separation leads to less communication and closeness. And some siblings just don't have much in common: they are naturally different from each other in temperament, personality and interests. Leading researchers in the field agree that, although they share about 50 per cent of the same genetic make-up and grow up in the same family, many siblings are remarkably dissimilar, not only in physical traits like hair colour, but in personality traits and mental abilities too. Psychologists now believe that the way parents tailor their responses to each individual child's personality, needs and stage of development may also help to explain why siblings are so different.

So, parents are setting themselves up for disappointment if they're desperate for their children to be bosom buddies. If siblings are not particularly compatible, it's surely better to accept that even if they aren't close, the bond between them still has enduring value. The family therapist Judith Lask says, 'Some siblings have always got on, they love each other, they have the same interests, they're best friends. But I would say that's probably the exception. Some siblings are just different.' She adds, 'My two boys have always been different from the moment they were born. They have different ways – one is very ambitious while the other is focused on quality of life rather than achievement. They don't understand each other's values – they don't fight or argue, they just don't have much in common. I would love it if they did more things together but I have to accept that is not the case. I think you have to be careful of expecting too much closeness between your children.'

Like any relationship, the sibling connection ebbs and flows over the years. Most parents are relieved to know that the rivalry that often peaks in the teenage years generally decreases through adulthood. Most adult siblings remain in some sort of contact throughout their lives and generally they draw closer, while arguments and competitiveness decline. That's according to the psychologist Professor Victor Cicirelli who, after devoting his long career to the study of sibling relationships across the lifespan, takes a very positive view of their unique value in offering companionship and support. In one of his studies of adult siblings, 78 per cent said they got along well, while only 4 per cent said they got on poorly.

Judith Lask explains why adult sibling relationships fluctuate: 'It's quite normal for siblings, just as it is for parents and children, to grow apart a bit over life. Often when you're in your twenties you want to be away from your family, to be yourself. But as people get older, they really see the value of family and siblings often draw closer. Families have this characteristic where they move apart and move back together; they're not the same all the time. It's the flexibility that's important.'

INFLUENCES ON ADULT SIBLING RELATIONSHIPS

- Personality and interests
- Age difference
- Birth order
- Number of siblings – close relationships seem to be less likely in large families
- How siblings got on in childhood
- The relationship with parents, both when siblings were growing up and as adults
- Geographical distance and how often they meet up
- Shared experiences
- The death or illness of a parent
- Inheritance disputes
- A new partner
- Family, religious and cultural expectations
- Differences in income and lifestyle

In adult life, siblings are drawn together – or apart – by circumstances such as where they live and how often they can get together. There are other influences: shared experiences both in childhood and adulthood, and shared crises such as their parents' divorce or a death in the family. Marriage can drive a wedge or bring siblings closer together, while the birth of a baby acts like a magnet to bring a new cohesion to the whole family. Family expectations, as well as wider cultural norms about how often siblings should see each other and how they should get on, also have an impact. But according to psychologists at the University of Cincinnati, the factor that contributed most to closeness between adult siblings was the behaviour of the family in which they grew up, along with a lack of favouritism and an appreciation of each individual's particular qualities. So it seems that the way parents manage family dynamics when children are young plays a key role in adulthood. This in turn is just one part of a complex jigsaw of factors that also influence sibling relationships, from birth order to age difference and the number of children.

BIRTH ORDER AND LABELS

Birth order has an impact on the way parents treat their children from the word go. Most of us remember feeling nervous and uncertain with our first baby, and more confident with the second, and believe that this has influenced what they're like as adults. Studies also indicate different levels of discipline within the same family: usually the eldest is disciplined more, whereas by the time the youngest comes along, parents are more laissez-faire. Preferential – or at least differential – treatment seems almost inevitable, with the eldest enjoying the parental spotlight, at least until a sibling comes along, while the youngest tends to get more attention and the middle child just has to get on with it.

The idea that birth order has a profound impact on personality was first proposed at the turn of the twentieth century by theorists including the Austrian psychiatrist Alfred Adler. Although it has since been disputed, the idea still influences the way we think about family roles: the eldest is bossy/controlling, the youngest is spoilt/rebellious, the middle child is easy-going/diplomatic and so on. There is often a clear link between birth order and the family labels we get stuck with. Lindsey, the eldest daughter in a family of six, remembers her own label: 'Little Mother'. She says, 'Of course I loved that role, but it became a duty. It was expected of me and it's not nice to feel you have to look after people, especially since my brothers weren't expected to.'

The problem with labels is that they confine a child's evolving abilities or characteristics to a nutshell. Often, they're an extreme version of what the child is really like – or used to be like many years ago. And labels can be hard to shake off in adulthood, particularly when the whole family gets together. Family dynamics become fossilised if they fail to catch up with changing realities. Adult children are influenced not only by their parents, but by the whole family's preconceptions of their strengths and weaknesses, their expectations of the choices that would be right for them and of the way they should behave. It's not uncommon for people to feel that they took a certain path in life to live up to family expectations. A friend said recently, 'I often look back and think I would make very different decisions if I had my time again. I think I just lived up to how the family expected a good daughter and sister to behave. It wasn't just my parents, it was my whole family.'

THE WAY PARENTS MANAGE FAMILY DYNAMICS

What's special and puzzling about siblings is that they can wind each other up like no one else. It's hard to work out why seemingly innocuous behaviour, or an innocent remark, elicits an over-the-top emotional reaction. Sometimes the wind-up is intentional, but more often people have no idea why their behaviour hits such a nerve. The interaction is so automatic and visceral – presumably because it's been ingrained since we were very young.

Anthea, who is in her fifties, says, 'My sister and I are civil but occasionally she floors me with some nasty comment that makes it clear she really doesn't like me. I think our relationship was set when I was born and she was three. With my younger sister, I have this fierce protectiveness that suddenly wells up and I have no idea where it comes from.'

Parents are just as baffled as their adult children, but there are clues in their childhoods, as well as in the present. A study of over 700 adult siblings by the American sociologists J. Jill Suitor and Karl Pillemer found that mothers' preferential treatment of siblings while they are growing up can have a lasting impact on how well they get on as adults. They found that adults' memories of how their mothers treated them and their siblings as children were more likely to lead to tension with adult siblings than what they saw as mothers' favouritism in the present.

Lindsey's experience with her five siblings echoes these findings. She says, 'I didn't feel like a favourite, but looking back, I can see that I was and that my siblings resented me for it. My sister and brothers continued to try to win my mother's approval and the resentment built up and got worse and worse. The way my siblings behaved as adults was a continuation of when we were younger: it was set in stone. In some ways it's nice to be part of a big family, but when you fall out, people shaft you; it's like *Game of Thrones*! We were like a bunch of puppies, being naughty together and making in-jokes at each other's expense. My brothers were terrible bullies but my parents never intervened – they thought children had to fight their own battles. I really felt the injustice of it.'

Children's antennae are finely tuned to differences in the way their parents relate to them and their siblings, not just when they're young but throughout their adult lives. It's not just a question of unfairness or favouritism, but different levels of interest and affection. It starts in infancy. The developmental psychologist Judy Dunn's observational studies in Cambridge in the 1980s found that 'babies as young as fourteen months were vigilant monitors of their mothers' relationship with their older siblings. They were particularly attentive to any interaction where emotion was expressed.'

Even when adult siblings seem to get on well, a perception of differential treatment may be an undercurrent. It's not merely that adult children hold inside them a sense of being treated differently as children. As adults, they continue to be alert to difference, which they might interpret as favouritism. To some extent it seems that unfairness is in the eye of the beholder, so it seems that parents need to be vigilant about their own behaviour too. Even if we don't think we're guilty ourselves, most of us have come across adult children who look crestfallen when a parent's eyes light up and their attention shifts when a sister or brother walks into the room.

Hilary has noticed new tension between her son and daughter since he moved back home after university. She says, 'I'm aware that when Izzy comes home for the weekend, she's watching to see how I get on with her brother. He and I have grown a lot closer because we share so much daily life, whereas in the past it was Izzy and I who were closer. So I suppose she's bound to feel a bit left out.'

CLASSIC CAUSES OF SIBLING FRICTION

There are two classic causes of friction between siblings: money and attention. Perceived unfairness in either can cause lasting resentment. While you occasionally hear of shocking exceptions, most parents go to great pains to be fair with gifts and loans, and what they plan to leave to their children when they die. However, being fair is becoming more of a challenge now that adult children increasingly have to look to their parents for different kinds of support throughout adulthood. One child needs funding to retrain or take a further degree, another needs cash to get the car repaired, while another moves back home and enjoys all the perks of life under the parental roof. Some children need more bailouts than others; parents often help a child who earns less than their siblings or has lost their job. The Parable of the Prodigal Son says it all. When he returns, having blown all his father's money, he receives a hero's welcome, leaving his hard-working brother resentful at the unfairness of it all.

It's also becoming more of a juggling act for parents to divide their time and energy equally between adult siblings. Each child needs different levels of parental support and attention in adulthood, depending on their circumstances and personalities. I can't help thinking of Tru (see Chapter 6, pages 112–115), who perhaps inevitably received more financial and emotional support than her brother when she was going through IVF. Many adult children benefit from regular grandchildcare, while their sibling lives too far away for parents to help out on a regular basis. Another sibling who doesn't have children might feel left out, both financially and emotionally.

And increasingly, parents who have the means help adult children get a foot on the property ladder. It's estimated that around a quarter of property purchases in 2020 were made with financial help from parents and other relatives, an increase from a fifth in just one year. For parents it would seem that the most straightforward thing is to dole out equal amounts to their children, but it's not always that simple, as Lindsey has discovered with her three daughters: 'Over the years we've given the girls different amounts of money to do various courses and qualifications. When Amy buys a flat, we're aware that it will cost more and she won't get exactly the same amount as the others. But we always make it up in some way and we're careful to talk through the issues together and make sure they understand. The girls know they can voice any concerns so they don't build up. I'm very aware of fairness, because I know how much trouble that sort of thing can cause. It's important not to have secrets and to be completely transparent and equal.'

She's right, of course. The best way for parents to pre-empt resentment is to be transparent and explain their reasoning. Adult kids need to feel that they'll be listened to if they complain about unfairness. For their part, parents have to be crystal clear in their own minds about their decisions, but at the same time flexible enough to respond if their child makes a fair point.

Dr Reenee Singh, Director of the London Intercultural Couples Centre, works with many families where money has created problems, including many stepfamilies. She stresses how important it is to take on board the significance of money and why fairness matters so much to siblings, stepsiblings and half-siblings: 'Money comes up as such an important theme with so many of the adult families I work with. There is often conflict between a sister and brother because they won't inherit equal amounts of money, so they are also squabbling over gender roles and what that means. And it's particularly complicated in stepfamilies. As a therapist, it's almost as if one can't just work at the symbolic level. It's also really important to go into the practicalities and the specifics of the money, like wills and inheritance and what it means to the adult children.' (More on money in Chapters 2 and 8.)

HOW PARENTS CAN PROMOTE HARMONY

Given that childhood patterns have such a big influence on the way siblings get on as adults, you might think there's not much parents can do to promote harmony. But there is. Parents can keep a watchful eye over their own behaviour with different children. They also need to judge carefully when it would be helpful to give the sibling relationship a gentle nudge. Often the best advice is to stand back and, as the family therapist Judith Lask said earlier in this chapter, to be realistic rather than over-ambitious for the sibling relationship. That doesn't mean parents shouldn't organise family gatherings or keep siblings in the loop about each other's lives, but it does mean accepting that attempts to engineer closeness might be counterproductive. Adult children can usually work things out for themselves without parents to complicate things.

The mistakes parents should avoid if they want their children to connect as adults are the same as when they're young. It seems so obvious: treat them equally, don't compare them – and the big taboo, don't have favourites. The problem is that it can be even harder to divide your time and attention equally between adult children than it was when the younger sibling was born and sucked up the lion's share of attention, leaving the older sibling puzzled and put out. Rather than try to treat children the same, perhaps it would be better to acknowledge how difficult that is and that what really matters is being fair.

Treating children differently is not the same as preferential treatment, unfairness or favouritism. A parent has a unique relationship with each child; each child's experience of us as parents is different. If you feel closer to one child because they share your interests or live nearby, it doesn't mean they're your favourite. Professor Lisa Doodson's advice applies to biological siblings as well as stepsiblings: 'If you have more than one stepchild you may have a closer relationship with one than another. That makes parents feel guilty. But it's really down to personalities and what you've got in common. It might just be that you're the same sex, or you're both into films or whatever. I really encourage people to accept that and to enjoy the relationship. It doesn't mean you're unfair to the other children, and it's not that you're mean or treating them unfairly.'

What parents do need to guard against, however, is the kind of unconscious bias that leads to unfair treatment and in turn, rivalry. This is often grounded in ideas about kids that may have held true back in the day and labels that have got stuck and failed to take on board the way they've changed. You might be more indulgent towards the baby of the family, even though he's 38, or towards a daughter who was more needy when she was growing up. It might equally be that you automatically expect children who have always seemed fiercely capable to just get on with things, when in fact they're crying out for more indulgence and support.

Mel confesses, 'My husband often says that I treat my son, who is the youngest, differently to his two sisters. I used to get irritated and deny it, but now I can see that he's right. I *am* more indulgent towards my son, because he's my baby and he had a troubled adolescence, and I suppose I feel a bit guilty. I help him with stuff I expect his sisters to sort out themselves. I suppose it's because I worry about him more. I know it's unfair, but it's hard not to do it.'

Family patterns aren't necessarily bad simply because they stem from childhood, but it's important to be aware of them. The key is to question and reassess family labels and roles, like 'the sensitive/ rebellious/neat/clumsy one', which are often linked to birth order. Family members tend to absorb and perpetuate outdated myths about each other. Labels are rarely helpful, but especially when they no longer have any basis in reality. Again, getting beyond them comes down to flexibility and an openness to seeing things with a fresh eye.

The family therapist Judith Lask says, 'We all fall into roles in families. And we tend to go to default situations in relationships, partly because the feeling of going back to an earlier stage can be comforting for everyone. The problem is that it may come with a lot of resentment, so it is much better to renegotiate. This sometimes means quite a bit of work for parents in getting over their assumptions. Parents have to do quite a bit of self-examination, to ask themselves, *What is the evidence for this? Have I given this child a chance to be different?* They need to have an intention to reassess themselves and their relationships, and not just be proving they're right. Otherwise nothing will shift.'

Promoting harmony: don't compare one sibling to another

It's clearly important to avoid making comparisons, not just obvious ones like 'Why can't you be more like your brother?' or 'Your sister was fine about it', but subtle comparisons too. This is not just about what you say but how you think. If a child feels that they are often judged in relation to a sibling rather than in their own right, it's bound to create resentment, whatever their age. However, it's not always a mistake to talk about one child to another: it's a question of how the conversation is framed. After all, in a lot of families it's the siblings who keep their parents in the loop about what's going on in each other's lives. If one child doesn't communicate much with their parents, it's acceptable to ask a sibling how they're getting on, as long as you don't pry or expect them to betray confidences. In many ways this flow of information feels very natural and it contributes to the reassuring sense that family life has its own momentum.

In Paul's living room there is a huge photograph of his three smiling daughters with their arms round each other at a family wedding. He says, 'That photo speaks volumes. One thing Toni and I are very proud of is that our girls are best friends. There are things that have gone on in their lives that we don't know, but they all know. They're there for each other. It's like they've formed their own family unit where we're just the doddery old parents!'

When siblings argue: should parents intervene?

It's so sad when somebody dies and their brother or sister refuses to go to the funeral. It's unusual, but siblings do fall out when they're adults, or simply lapse into indifference and stop communicating much beyond birthdays and Christmas. Ian has had little contact with his brother since they disagreed during their parents' divorce. Lindsey has had no contact with her siblings, apart from one brother, since a row in their fifties after their mother's death.

There are so many reasons why conflict can arise among adult siblings. The American psychologist Peter Goldenthal, who has worked with siblings on healing their broken relationships, says, 'Every difficult sibling relationship is difficult in its own way. Some start off fraught and get better, but there are many reasons why they get more fraught in adulthood: the way siblings handled the death of one parent, or fighting over an inheritance. Perhaps a sibling's spouse dislikes another sibling's spouse. Or one person has always found their sibling difficult, but now they're tired of accommodating their quirks. Sometimes siblings stop speaking to each other to avoid confrontation. They want to say something isn't right, but there's no way the other sibling will listen.'

If siblings fall out, parents need to judge carefully whether to let them sort things out for themselves or try to mediate. The risk is that intervention might make matters worse, particularly if one child feels their parent always sides with the other sibling, or thinks you've always liked them best. The last thing any parent wants is for their children to fall out permanently.

When he sensed tension between his three daughters, Paul decided to step in. 'I've always said to my girls, don't fight. If you've got the hump, take it out on me because you need each other, there's nothing closer than family,' he remembers. 'We don't want them to end up like my wife and her siblings, who don't get on. One night the girls were having a bit of an argument and I noticed there was an atmosphere. So I made each of them write down a promise to stay close and I told them to think about all the experiences they had been through together, good and bad.'

The family therapist Judith Lask is optimistic that sibling conflict can be resolved, as long as people are willing to see things from the other point of view. She says that the challenge for parents is to avoid doing something that could make the situation worse. She adds, 'It is often the case that parents get caught in the middle of disputes and prevent a possible resolution rather than helping. But there is always hope for getting things on a better foot, to repair what's happened so that you can move forward. Both sides need to understand why something happened and to feel they're not being blamed for it. It needs a level of recognition from everybody about the perceived hurt and about the experience of the others. It doesn't always mean everything is forgiven, and that siblings are going to be as close as they can be, but it is a workable relationship. Sometimes there will always be a bit of mistrust, but it works, it carries people forward.'

HOW TO ENCOURAGE HARMONY BETWEEN ADULT SIBLINGS

- Treat each child as an individual, don't make comparisons.
- Never complain about one child to another.
- Don't feel you've failed as a parent if your children don't get on, although that's not easy if your friend's kids share secrets and go on holiday together. There are so many different influences on sibling relationships that have little to do with their parents.
- Don't try too hard. Sometimes parents just have to accept that their kids don't have much in common, but the sibling bond will always be an enduring one.
- Remember that the relationship ebbs and flows as circumstances draw siblings closer, or apart, but usually it strengthens with age.
- Question labels and whether old assumptions about each child still hold water: look at the evidence in their behaviour now, not in the past.
- If there's a dispute, think carefully before stepping in. By intervening, parents could get in the way of a possible resolution.

KEEPING THE FAMILY CONNECTED

When children no longer live at home the family inevitably becomes a more abstract concept; it feels as if it could easily slip through your fingers. In fact, even though it's no longer in everyone's face, and there's no need to manage family dynamics on a daily basis, it continues to have a very real presence. It's somehow bigger than the sum of its parts, retaining an identity and cohesion even when individual members are scattered. It carries a sense of continuity, of looking back to previous generations as well as forward into the future.

But adult family life ebbs and flows. There are inevitably phases when siblings' lives go in opposite directions. In their twenties, for example, people often need a bit of distance between themselves and their parents, and perhaps their siblings too. There are times when they want to explore possibilities beyond their family's expectations and prejudices about them, but it's still good to know that the family is always there in the background. Ideally, it's a bit like ballast, something solid to be relied on that makes individual members feel supported and secure.

That may become even more important with emotional or physical distance, so it's good if parents can keep their children in touch with what's happening in each other's lives. Sensitivity is required: you don't want to sound as if you're more interested in the other sibling, or making comparisons. Putting pressure on children to make contact with each other can also be counterproductive. I used to get really irritated when I rang my mum and she'd say 'Your brother's here, would you like a word?' We're lucky that technology enables families to keep each other in the loop in more casual ways.

Staying connected: family gatherings

Family gatherings play a key role in keeping the family together. One of the essential factors for maintaining sibling closeness identified by researchers at the University of Cincinnati is the joint memories that build up a sense of family unity from childhood onwards. They concluded that family celebrations, rituals and reunions continue to be important throughout children's adult lives, because they create regular opportunities for sibling relationships to be renewed.

Annual celebrations and memorials also crystallise how things have changed. Milestones in the adult family calendar give it a sense of continuing connection and cohesion. Step-parenting expert Professor Lisa Doodson's advice is helpful for all families, not just blended families like her own. She says, 'I think it's your responsibility as a parent to allow sibling relationships to be maintained by creating opportunities for families to celebrate together – whether it's just regular barbecues and get-togethers, or birthdays and big events like weddings. If you don't give adult children these opportunities then it's completely down to them to keep in touch. It's important that everyone is invited and feels included: siblings, half-siblings and stepsiblings. It's about thinking positively about everybody, so if one sibling is not engaging, or if you know that one child doesn't get on well with another, it's your job as a parent not to let that breed. They may not all come to every event, but they all need the opportunity to be part of the family. It's important not to pressurise people: with adult children, it's ultimately up to them if they don't want to meet up. But by giving adult children opportunities to get together, you are allowing them to build their own new family memories.'

Studies have consistently found that it's women who take on the lion's share of 'kin-keeping' activities within adult families: mothers, primarily, but also daughters, organise family events and facilitate contact between siblings. One mother I interviewed emails her five children several weeks ahead of a gathering with the subject 'Family Matters' – the double meaning is intentional. Immy, who is in her mid-twenties, adds, 'There are these milestones Mum puts in the diary, like Easter, when we're all going to have dinner together. They're events we all look forward to, but it means the most to Mum.' It could be that women appreciate the importance of relationships more keenly than men and they know that they need thoughtful nurturing. But it's also habit: women have been organising their children's birthday parties and making Christmas special for years. Hopefully that will change and the responsibility will be more evenly shared; in some families it already is.

If gatherings are often tense or marred by bickering, children will only come to the next one out of duty – if at all. It helps if parents can stay relaxed and not try too hard to keep everyone happy. But that's a tall order. Family gatherings are notorious for bringing out the toddler in the best of us. They provide perfect conditions for families to slot neatly back into old patterns of behaviour, as unresolved conflicts and perceptions of parental favour explode on to the surface.

Jane, reflecting on her son's wedding day, says, 'Rituals are very delicate occasions. They bring things to the surface.' The family therapist Judith Lask adds, 'Patterns between siblings are always intensified when there's a visit to parents. The older bossy child makes the younger one feel they can't hold their own, and so on.'

Lindsey remembers how family dinners in her twenties often triggered tension: 'My mother expected all of us to come to family dinners once a week, either at her house or in the local Chinese. We felt we had to go. In a way it forced people to stay in their family roles. People got argumentative and sometimes they'd storm off. It felt like a big mistake to try to keep re-enacting family life in that way. We do things very differently with our daughters. We leave it up to them to come round or say when they want to come to supper. There's no expectation on our part. I've noticed recently that Amy, who is the youngest, asserts herself a bit more now. She's incredibly successful at work and intelligent and knowledgeable but they do treat her like baby Amy. And until recently she acted like the baby too!'

Staying connected: rituals and traditions

Some family gatherings have the status of rituals or traditions. They range from special occasions, like weddings and funerals, to religious festivals such as Eid or Diwali, and regular events, like Friday night dinner, Thanksgiving or Boxing Day football. Rituals can punctuate the family calendar in a positive way so long as they continue to have meaning as life changes and moves on. Sticking rigidly to a habit just because it's the way the family has always done things makes it more duty than joy. So while the essence of any tradition is its reassuring sameness and continuity, it should also have a degree of flexibility.

Dr Reenee Singh, Director of the London Intercultural Couples Centre, encourages families to reflect on what their own rituals mean to everyone involved, including in-laws and other outsiders. She says, 'Family rituals can be helpful or they can be constraining. It's all about whether they continue to have meaning. Families shouldn't be bound by a certain ritual without thinking about how or why it should happen. I often ask family members what they think of a particular ritual and what they would like to do differently, and how they want to influence it. Often adult children say it was fine when they were younger, but it's outlived its utility. Or someone will say it's great to have this opportunity of coming together as a family. With intercultural families, people also need to think about what it means to the outsider, particularly to the daughter- or son-in-law. Does it feel alienating or welcoming?'

Each family invents their own distinctive traditions. Just think of Christmas: one family always opens their presents after breakfast, another puts on a play they've been rehearsing for weeks, another plays poker and pop tunes into the wee small hours. It's wonderful if families continue to create new traditions when children are adults. Professor Doodson says this is particularly important with blended families: 'I often say to couples/parents, you've got to make your own memories and different traditions, whether it's what you do at Christmas or smaller things on a Friday night. Make those traditions that bind you, because that's what people remember – those things we did with our families.'

New traditions are often prompted by a change of circumstances: if one of the family can't come, for example, or when a new partner comes too, or when the arrival of grandchildren signals an end to late nights and boozy celebrations. Inviting an outsider or two is a surefire way of shaking up family patterns of behaviour and moving things forward.

COVID-19 forced us all to think outside the box about celebrating together when we're apart, from kitchen discos to virtual dinner parties and present-opening. Something that grows out of necessity often takes on the status of a new tradition.

FAMILY GATHERINGS

- Try not to get too hung up about the food and preparations, because what matters most is having a good time together. If one person – usually Mum – has to do all the cooking, she's usually too preoccupied to enjoy the moment. It also perpetuates family patterns that are past their sell-by date. Keep things simple: order a takeaway or ask everyone to bring a dish.
- Reflect on who the gathering is for and what it means to the people who come.

- Don't put pressure on people to attend. If they'd rather not, don't expect excuses, simply say they'll be missed. Afterwards, don't dwell on what a great time everyone had and what a shame it was that they weren't there.
- Don't keep up traditions purely for the sake of it. Rituals that have meaning bring the family together, but empty rituals may do the opposite.
- Inviting an outsider to join a gathering shakes up the dynamics and makes it easier for individual family members to be their new selves.
- If there's tension, think about doing things differently. Meet in a restaurant, go for a long walk together, do a quiz. If one child seems left out, ask them to suggest or organise the next gathering.

Staying connected: family holidays

Holidays with adult children have grown in popularity in recent years. A study commissioned by Virgin Holidays in 2019 found that an impressive seven in 10 families had taken multigenerational holidays. Taking the whole adult family away for a long weekend or a holiday is very different to going with just one adult child. You can see why parents like it: the family unit is recreated, albeit temporarily. There's none of the frustration of trying to please younger kids, or the anxiety and moods of holidays with teenagers. Adult kids like it because parents often contribute a fat wedge of the cost and if they have children, their doting grandparents will babysit and keep them entertained. But what both generations like most, according to the same study, is just being together.

The benefits are obvious. In a regular family gathering, catching up has to be crammed into a few hours and it might be hard for one sibling to get a word in edgeways. Family holidays give people more time to rub along together at their own pace. Over a weekend or several days people don't have to be together all the time, there are opportunities for siblings to spend quality one-on-one time going for walks or outings and not just sitting around talking. That's why a friend of mine rents a big house for her whole family – three sons, a daughter, a stepson and four grandchildren – to get together for a long weekend once a year: 'We all have busy lives so I think it's really valuable to have this rare chance to live alongside each other as a family again, to have time for proper conversations and be relaxed with each other.'

One possible downside, as with any family gathering, is that childhood family patterns are revived and dormant grievances get the kiss of life. One way to nudge the stuck needle out of its groove is by transplanting the family to a different environment, away from the nest. It's worth trying out the kind of place you never went to when the kids were young. Away from home territory, there's a better chance of individuals shedding the outworn skin of childhood roles – and for parents to relinquish domestic burdens. Many families find that being on holiday is very different to being together at home – you all feel like grown-ups together.

If parents can also take the lead by changing their own behaviour, the rest of the family should follow. I'm thinking of simple things, like making it clear you're not doing all the cooking and/or organising/driving, so that other people can step up. That also gives them more of a say in what happens. Roles might even be reversed: your formerly flaky son turns out to have a cool head when the car breaks down, your daughter speaks Portuguese and they're all better than you at finding interesting places to eat. If there's a range of different activities on offer locally, that can help too. Communication is as much about doing stuff together as sitting around a table talking. And that's what grown-up family holidays are all about: they are an opportunity to move relationships forward, because they prompt everyone to see each other with a fresh eye.

FAMILY HOLIDAYS

- Keep holidays short and sweet: a long weekend break or a week is quite enough.
- Don't try to recreate bygone family holidays. Choose an unfamiliar destination and different kinds of accommodation: a hotel if you always self-catered, a cottage rather than a campsite.
- Parents and adult children need their own private space to retreat to. One way to do this is by staying in different places that are within walking distance from each other, or in a hotel. It can be more relaxing than bundling into the same house together.
- Choose a destination with a variety of different activities on offer. It's easier to communicate when you do stuff together.
- Don't expect to do everything together; it can be an organisational nightmare, and it doesn't allow for one-to-one catch-ups.
- Don't put pressure on the whole family to come.
- Stop organising and start enjoying the moment.

10

When Your Child Finds a Long-term Partner

When a child finds a long-term partner, it alters the relationship with their parents, and indeed with the whole family, in so many different ways. You only have to think of the influence of Meghan Markle on Prince Harry's future to get a sense of how dramatically life can be changed by a marriage or long-term commitment. As well as shifts in the parent–child relationship, there's the new and lasting connection with another family, who may be relative strangers, that both parent and child have to take on board.

Deborah Merrill, Professor of Sociology at Clark University in Massachusetts, has studied how relationships between parents and children change when they marry. She believes that the impact of an adult child's marriage on the family has been generally overlooked, yet it has huge significance, not least by creating a separate family unit.

Intriguingly, Professor Merrill describes modern marriage as a 'greedy institution'. She believes that changing expectations of marriage in society, originating with the shift away from economic alliances and towards love-based unions, have had a huge impact on parents' relationships with their adult children. 'Once marriage became love-based the marriage became more important than the relationship between parent and child,' she says. 'More became expected of the couple relationship from a personal point of view. There has also been a more recent change, where we look to marriage for self-fulfilment much more than we have in the past, and it became less about parent and child as well. And that set up rivalry between parent and in-law. So to that extent marriage has become a greedier institution because we want more from the other person than we used to. And so each partner is giving more as well.

'The other factor is that the requirements of work have increased. So adult children now are really under the gun. They don't have as much time as they did in the past to meet the needs of everyone in the extended and the nuclear family. And more is expected of parenting. So there are some relationships that are getting short changed. And that may include the parent–adult child relationship.' What's more, the global trend towards delaying retirement means that the couple's parents may also have less time to spend with adult children and their partners. They may well still be working, or have other commitments, such as elderly parents of their own who need their help.

HOW PARENTS FEEL WHEN A CHILD FALLS IN LOVE

People have ambivalent feelings about even the happiest transitions. When your child falls in love, your feelings are likely to be a bit mixed, even if you approve wholeheartedly of the new person in their life. Of course you're happy for them, but at the same time anxious that they've made the right choice, worried that they could get hurt, nervous about how you'll get on with their partner and sad that your relationship will never be quite the same. This is a new phase for parent as well as child.

Steve, whose daughter married in her mid-twenties, remembers, 'Samantha had been away from home for a while then, and she and I both knew that our relationship had changed and that Brendan was now the man she had to focus on. I really felt that this was the next phase of her life and I was pleased about that.'

Your child's commitment to a partner puts the seal on changes in your relationship that are already happening. You are no longer the first person they turn to when they're upset or ill or they've got bad news. In many ways it's a relief to know they've got someone else to love and support them. But it's poignant too, because it signifies the end of an era.

Toni, whose three daughters are all married, remembers a turning point when her youngest daughter had been going out with her boyfriend for a few years: 'Leah had to come home early after a night out because she wasn't very well. Normally I would help her and sort her out, but her boyfriend told me to go to bed. He said, "Toni, this is my role – I'm there for her now. I'm going to be with Leah for the rest of our lives so I'd better get used to this." I went to bed and said to Paul, "She's my baby, but I'm not wanted any more." As a mother you always watch out for your kids when they're ill or anything. It did feel a bit hurtful; I felt like I'd been made redundant.'

THE WEDDING DAY

From now on your child's primary loyalty is to their partner, not to you. It's a shift of allegiance that started with the first boyfriend or girlfriend. Accepting that this is simply the way things ought to be doesn't make it any easier and inevitably it can create rivalry. Wedding day traditions encapsulate this shift of loyalties. Age-old rituals, such as the bride leaving for the ceremony from her parents' home and being given away by her father, still have profound meaning.

Now that so many couples leave home and live together before they marry, you might think these rituals have become purely symbolic, a rubber stamping of changes already underway. Yet there is still a strong association between marriage, independence and adulthood, even if couples have left home and become financially self-sufficient some time ago.

Emma, whose daughter recently announced her engagement, says, 'Being married is like a stage in growing up. I'm really pleased for Rebecca because I feel she's having a more grown-up life with Johnny. It feels like she's left home properly – although in fact she left home 10 years ago!'

Dr Reenee Singh, Director of the London Intercultural Couples Centre, adds, 'In many cultures getting married is a huge milestone – it's almost as if you're not treated as an adult until you're married, which seems so silly! In many traditional South Asian cultures, women attain adulthood by getting married and becoming part of her husband's family who would support her, so she would no longer be financially dependent on her own family.'

Some people think the old saying about losing your child when they marry is a load of nonsense but for many parents that's exactly how it feels and it's common to shed a tear on the big day. One distinguished family therapist even compared the loss to a kind of bereavement – although that's perhaps going a bit far. You haven't lost your child, but you do have to adjust to a different kind of relationship with them.

Paul, who is unashamedly traditional, remembers how he felt as his daughter's wedding day approached: 'I don't think I behaved well in the run-up to the wedding. I was dreading it. It was almost like I was going to the gallows! On the day we hired an old Routemaster bus to take the guests from our house to the church. Everyone had gone and it was just Kealy and me in the kitchen, waiting for the car. I looked at her and thought to myself, *This is it. This is the last day of me being a father for Kealy.* A big part of my life went when I walked her up the aisle.

'You're passing over your paternal role to another man. That man is now going to take care of your daughter. Toni and I are still her parents but that protective role has now passed on to someone else. That was very hard.

'After the wedding I felt terribly depressed. It was worse than when she first left home to go to university, because then I knew she would come home at weekends and she was still our girl.'

The wedding day itself crystallises the heady mix of ambivalent emotions that parents already feel. What's more, they have to hold it together in front of people they don't know well, but now have a long-term connection with; they may have to make a speech too. And if it's a big do, there's the build-up of emotion during the preparations. Disagreements over the guest list are par for the course and in some families they present serious dilemmas, even conflict. For divorced parents it means putting a brave face on meeting their ex, possibly with a new partner. Sometimes one parent has had little contact with a child for years, but they still expect to be invited.

Jane, a single parent, remembers her only son's wedding: 'I started off fine at the ceremony but then became very upset. My son was angry with me because he wanted it to be an enjoyable party and I was a gloomy presence, spoiling the occasion. Worse still, I think it could be said that I misbehaved by being rude to the best man's wife.

'Why did I react like this? Hard to say. Such a mixture. I don't think it was primarily to do with my son's marriage. People often say there's jealousy of the daughter-in-law, but I'm pleased that I don't think I've ever felt jealous, which is perhaps surprising, considering how close I was to my son. It was more a combination of irritation with my ex-husband and the best man's wife, who talked in a very clichéd and non-feminist way about marriage, and self-pity and loneliness as the occasion became more couple-focused. I think it would have been utterly different if there had been more friends and relatives from my side of the family. Afterwards I realised that my son would never cut me off, however "bad" my behaviour! In some way his love was unconditional. That may be why the bad aspects of the occasion have faded from my memory.'

AFTER THE WEDDING: LONG-TERM CHANGE

It's understandable if parents fear that the relationship with their child will change for the worse after they marry or move in with a partner, and that the precious closeness between them will be lost. It's hard to accept that from now on your child's partner will know them better than you do. One single mother said that she hadn't been prepared for being supplanted in her only daughter's affections.

Studies in the US and the Netherlands in 2008 suggest that marriage or cohabiting generally leads to less intense relations with parents and less frequent face-to-face meetings – although contact increases when grandchildren appear. This reflects Renate's experience: 'Now that Nathan is married, Nicole is the woman in his life and that's where his emotional life is now. He only calls me every two or three months and occasionally he'll invite me to an exhibition or something in London and we'll have a really good long talk. It's odd, because he was so up close when he was younger. But I find it fascinating that our relationship keeps changing. I can also see that if he has a child, it will change again.'

Both parent and child have to work out new ways to relate to each other. Renate points to the flexibility that parents need to cope with the way the bond will inevitably ebb and flow between closeness and distance in the years to come. It always helps to see the long view and remember that this is a lifelong relationship that will continue to develop and grow. It also helps to focus on the many good things that are intertwined with the loss. While the positives are obvious for the adult child, they are there for their parents too.

Seeing your child feeling good about themselves and embarking on a new chapter is wonderful, even if it is tinged with sadness. If it's taken a while to find the right person, and there have been broken hearts along the way, there's also relief. Theresa, whose two sons and two daughters are in their twenties and thirties, says, 'When your kids are young, you spend so much time wanting them to be successful, but when they get older, all you want is for them to meet somebody who loves them as much as you do, so that they'll be all right. That's when you feel they are totally independent, because they've recreated their bond with you with someone else.'

Now that your child has another source of support, your relationship can expand and become more equal. At the same time a son- or daughter-in-law can breathe new life into your relationship with your child, and indeed the family as a whole, as long as rivalry doesn't get in the way. They open up new conduits of communication; they might be chatty where your child is reticent and introduce new interests and new stuff to talk about. If they're interested in your life and don't just see you as a parent-in-law, it should prompt your child to see you through fresh eyes. You will no doubt see a new side to your child too.

Brenda says, 'I've always been very keen for my son to be better at relationships than I have been and I'm so pleased that he is. I've been delighted to see him being such a loving husband and nurturing father.'

The influence of a son- or daughter-in-law

At the same time, it can be disconcerting for parents to see how the influence of a partner changes the child they know so well: what they eat, the way they dress, their ambitions, where they want to live. They may curb their wild behaviour or encourage them to blow their savings on flashy kitchens or extravagant holidays. A partner's influence can create conflict, particularly if there are cultural, religious or political differences.

Dr Reenee Singh, Director of the London Intercultural Couples Centre, says, 'When a new partner comes on the scene, the adult child is exposed to the influences of another family. There is an added complication when they're from a different culture and there are completely different ways that things might be done so there are all sorts of levels of difficulties.'

A new partner may prompt your child to question what they think of you, the way your family does things and even the way you brought them up, and this is potentially painful territory. A newcomer also casts an outsider's gimlet eye on sibling relationships and family dynamics. They notice if the parents' spotlight shines too brightly on the eldest, or if the youngest always gets the most expensive presents.

'I can really empathise with my wife, because I know what it's like to have older siblings who think they're the most interesting thing and are used to being the centre of attention,' one daughter-in-law told me. This kind of validation can boost a child's confidence but it's decidedly unhelpful if partners are overly critical and don't recognise that it takes time to fully understand the subtleties of individual family relationships. It could make parents feel that they're being viewed – judged, even – through an unforgiving prism.

Seeing your child alone

Partners influence how often you see your child, either directly, if they organise their social life, or indirectly, because the couple are busy with their own preoccupations. This remains a particular concern for parents of sons, because women tend to be the ones who organise the family's social life. It can work in your favour, because daughters-in-law are often more thoughtful about remembering birthdays and keeping in touch. But if your child seems to prefer their partner's family, and spends more time with them, it can feel like rejection.

Professor Deborah Merrill explains, 'It's usually the son's wife who sets the social calendar for the couple and she naturally gravitates towards her side of the family because she's less comfortable with his parents than her own. So the son's family sees less of him as a result. However, I'm hopeful that that is changing.'

One inevitable difference is that parents see less of their child alone and that's something many parents say they really miss. Some kids are good at instigating one-to-one meetings, while others don't give it a second thought. Meanwhile, parents feel awkward about suggesting a solo outing for fear of offending a daughter- or son-in-law, or making them feel left out.

Theresa says, 'I've got a friend who wanted to celebrate a big birthday by having a day with her sons, without their partners or grandchildren. She told me she couldn't bear to mention it, because her daughters-in-law are lovely. So I decided to have a word with them and they organised it. She said it was the nicest thing she'd done in years, having time with her children on their own.'

One solution is to arrange separate solo outings not only with your child but with their partner too. If just the two of you can do something together it will help you get to know another side of them, as well as showing that you value them as an individual, not just as your child's spouse.

GETTING ON WITH YOUR CHILD'S PARTNER

In-law relationships are notoriously difficult and while there's no doubt that they are complicated and require sensitive handling, it's important to see the positives. Apart from anything else, from now on your relationship with your child depends on how well you get on with their partner. Even if parents don't admit it, the underlying fear is that you might lose your son or daughter, or they'll become more distant.

The issue is not just whether you like your child's partner or have similar views and values, although of course that's a big part of it. What sets in-law relationships apart is an intricate web of incomprehensible undercurrents, triggering irritation and frustration out of all proportion to an apparently innocent word or deed. I once overheard a group of women gossiping about their daughters-in-law as they pieced quilts during a crafting weekend. One mother was totally outraged that her son's wife always refused her offer of tea. It seemed such a small thing, but clearly there was much more than tea at stake!

While the focus is invariably on mothers-in-law, fathers have problems too, both with sons-in-law and daughters-in-law. But they're less openly discussed and more likely to be treated as a joke – think of Robert De Niro in *Meet the Fockers*. Of course, mother-in-law jokes are part of the public psyche too, but at the same time the relationship between women is treated as a bigger problem, the subject of academic analysis, advice columns and self-help books. Could it be that we have different expectations of father-in-law relationships because we don't know enough about them, because men are generally less forthcoming about their emotional difficulties?

I got an intriguing hint of this when I interviewed Charlie for my book *The Empty Nest*. He said, 'I've got one male friend whose daughters are also grown up and we often talk about what their boyfriends are like – that is a big thing for dads.' I have come across fathers who are much less tolerant of their sons-and daughters-in-law than their wives.

If we don't look for problems, are relationships less likely to be problematic? It certainly seems that stereotypes about mothers-in-law almost set the relationship up to fail: mutual suspicion is in the playbook. Professor Deborah Merrill's work supports this idea: 'I think stereotypes do a lot of damage. In the interviews I conducted for my research there were a lot of very good relationships between mothers-in-law and daughters-in-law. But the stereotypes are so strong that even in the good relationships the daughters-in-law almost felt obligated to find some problems in their relationship. They felt they had to fulfil that role of not getting on with their mother-in-law. So when I was setting up the interview they'd say, "Wait till you hear what I have to say" and then it really wasn't bad at all. I think they felt that was what was expected; that's how it's supposed to be.'

Intriguingly, Professor Merrill's research into the impact of same-sex marriages on relationships with parents suggests that gender does play a major role. For her book on gay and lesbian marriage, she interviewed parents who had one child in a gay marriage and one child in a heterosexual marriage, and found that relationships with in-laws of the opposite sex were less problematic.

'Mothers usually had better or as good relationships with their sons after they married another man,' she says. 'First of all, they're just so relieved that their son has found somebody, because it was always the case that they were worrying about that. They also said that it was easier to visit a son and his husband than a son and his wife because they didn't feel they were stepping on anybody's toes. With a son and his wife, it doesn't feel like their child's home, it feels like their daughter-in-law's home. They see their son's home as her domain.'

Getting off to a good start with your child's partner

Even if there's mutual affection between the parent and the child's partner, the relationship is still bound to get tense at times. If you can get things on a good footing early on, it will see you through inevitable phases of friction. This is particularly important before they have children, because that is a huge test as well as a unifying connection. Mutual respect is key: both parent and partner need to acknowledge the importance of the other person to their child/partner and that this new relationship demands – and deserves – effort and consideration. Above all, boundaries need to be respected.

The early days are critical, because they shape the relationship. This is often the hardest time, when parent and new partner are getting used to each other, and parent and child are working out new ways to relate to each other too. In a study by the Cambridge psychologist Dr Terri Apter, 68 per cent of mothers-in-law found the transition considerably more difficult than they expected. Parent, child and partner are all on unfamiliar territory and at times it can feel like a bit of a power struggle. A great deal depends on how secure you feel about your relationship with your child. Parents who know deep down that their child cares about them and enjoys their company are less likely to feel jealous or threatened than those who worry that the relationship is fragile. In my experience, this sense of security ebbs and flows: there are times when it feels like it's slipping away, others when it feels solid as a rock.

While your child's partner is working out how to get on with an unfamiliar family – yours! – your adult child is facing the same task with their partner's family. The newcomer probably feels more like a guest than part of the family. They're not privy to in-jokes and habits and expectations of how they should behave, so they just have to feel their way. In the previous chapter, the family therapist Dr Reenee Singh pointed out that it's important to think about what the family traditions and rituals we take for granted – whether competitive games or bracing country walks – mean to the son- or daughter-in-law: do they feel alienating or welcoming? It's easy for an outsider to cause offence by a reluctance to join in, or by treading on sensitive territory, simply because they've misread the signals. In theory, such misunderstandings should dissipate as people get to know each other better, as long as both sides are flexible, give the other the benefit of the doubt and try to understand their position. If grievances linger, they continue to make things fraught.

In-laws on both sides are often nervous of saying what they really mean, or talking about how they feel. They may want to avoid conflict at all costs, but that comes at a price, according to Dr Apter: 'Efforts to "get along" at the expense of genuine communication result in indirect aggression and self-silencing,' she writes in her helpful book on in-law relationships.

This chimes with Jane's experience with her daughter-in-law: 'She is not the type to have a standup shouting match or to go away and sob. Like most women, she's been brought up to be the good girl so she doesn't seek confrontation – probably much less than I might. I think in any other relationship she'd be more conciliatory than this one. This is probably the trickiest one of her life. Sometimes I feel she's become over-sensitive. So now even when I say something that I hope is OK, it's very hard for her to take it on board. I do see it as my fault and not hers. I sometimes feel I've blotted my copybook with her.'

Parents' expectations

A common stumbling block arises when parents' expectations and assumptions are disappointed. Even the most easy-going parents have surprisingly strong views about their in-laws doing things differently from the way *they* did things. Some parents I spoke to have set ideas about gender roles, particularly when it comes to domestic issues and childcare. That seems old-fashioned and the generation gap is narrowing in this respect. Mothers-in-law now are more likely to have combined work with child-rearing than their own mothers-in-law. This should lead to greater empathy and fewer pursed lips about un-ironed shirts and takeaways every night – in theory, at least.

Expectations of how in-laws should behave differ widely between cultures too. Erin's thinking has been deeply affected by living as a young married woman in India for 10 years. She says, 'I feel that a lot of men in England, unlike India, tend to go over to the side of the wife completely; that's considered the proper and appropriate thing. In India, by contrast, they are more likely to take the mother's side. Obviously now that my son is married, it's in my interests to adopt that Indian doctrine!'

Traditional ideas about behaviour are often ingrained and hard to shake off, even when parents think they are no longer an influence. As Director of the London Intercultural Couples Centre, Dr Reenee Singh works with families from many different cultures, including Italian, Jewish, Muslim and South Asian: 'I often work with parents whose adult children married out of the community, or who no longer conform to cultural or religious ideas about what their parents expected. That has created a rift. With a lot of intercultural couples I work with, their families struggle to understand their choice of partner and accept what that means, because culturally they're so different. The parents are upset because they can't imagine why their own children would make what are to their mind such bizarre choices. The younger generation just wish their parents would accept them for the choices they've made.

'Notions of respect and hierarchy are quite different in different cultures. The Western idea of being friends with our kids is not so common in other cultures, where families are often more hierarchical. In the Jewish families I work with, for example, there are strong ideas about the markers of what it means to be a good respectful family, such as attending Friday dinner together and who brings what and whose house it's at. That reminds me a lot of some of the South Asian rituals. If there is also the cultural idea that daughters-in-law are supposed to be subservient to their mothers-in-law, that can be terribly difficult.'

If there are differences of any kind, whether expressed or muttered behind closed doors, your child is caught in the middle. It's an unenviable position. Their loyalties are divided, but they are primarily with their new partner. When an argument throws the spotlight on this shift of allegiance it can be incredibly painful for parents – even if they accept it as a new fact of life.

Jane acknowledges, 'My son is in this difficult in-between situation. He is more prone to see things the way I did than his wife does, but he naturally cleaves to her. I would say she's won the battle! But it's not as bad as in some other families I've seen, where the son absolutely closes off to the mother.

'I think it would be fairly natural for any son to feel torn between his mother and his wife. In fact, I think it's odd if people *aren't* torn. I think there is nearly always a tension. But that awareness doesn't mean I'm any better at handling it! I am a thinker, which doesn't always mean I get my feelings right.'

IF YOU DON'T LIKE YOUR CHILD'S PARTNER...

Before they marry or move in together

When marriage or a big commitment is on the cards it makes the heart sink if you think your child is blinded by love and making a huge mistake. Even if they went out with the odd dodgy character in the past, you always hope they'll end up with someone you feel in tune with and it's a body blow if you don't. It's just as bad if they don't like you much!

Steve's response to his daughter's news that she'd met a new man within months of her divorce was decidedly lukewarm: 'When the new lad appeared on the scene, Samantha asked if I'd like to meet him and I had to tell her I wasn't ready yet. It took me a while to get my head round it, because there was a lot about her first husband that I liked and I found it quite sad that it all came to grief. Now she's pregnant and I'm thinking, I do hope this wheel isn't going to keep going round. I hope that this new lad is there for the long haul.'

Parents are caught between a rock and a hard place: if they say nothing, they'll never forgive themselves if it ends in misery. They know from experience how life-changing the choice of a long-term partner can be. But if they do have a quiet word in their child's ear – however tactfully – they risk stretching already divided loyalties and alienating them both. Anyone who has ever been in love will remember how resistant they were to the voice of reason – especially their parents' voice of reason.

I have interviewed parents who have spoken their mind, and although it's a risk, they didn't regret it. That could be because they had a strong inkling that their child was already having serious doubts themselves. After agonising for some time, Lindsey felt she had to talk to her daughter about her boyfriend: 'He was very controlling; her sisters were worried too,' she remembers. 'It all came to a head when Esther came home one weekend and she was getting very anxious about a big drive she had to do for work. I said it would be good for her to do it. Her boyfriend said that meant we didn't love her! That really worried me and I felt I had to say something. I was so relieved when she said she was already planning to split up with him.'

If you don't like your child's partner: the long view

Once the die is cast and their child is married or living with their partner, parents have little choice but to lump it and do all they can to make the relationship work. It may make you feel better to keep ranting on about the latest outrage, but it will bore your friends and won't get you very far. It's more constructive to try to work out the cause of the tension, including your part in it. If the bond with your child was particularly close, as is often the case with single parents and only children, for example, it's understandable to feel insecure and that the bond is threatened. Disagreements are often put down to jealousy. One mother I spoke to admitted to feeling a bit envious of her son's new wife, but on reflection she realised that what she really envied was the relationship, not the person, and that she longed to have a loving relationship of her own.

If there's disagreement, parents always have to be the grown-up and make the first move, rather than allow resentment to fester. When you feel calmer, try to see things from the other point of view: don't automatically assume they're wrong and you're right. Ask yourself how you would have felt if your mother- or father-in-law had behaved as you have. All parents have to take a close look at their assumptions and ask themselves searching questions: Are you harking back to a time when you had more influence or even control? Would anyone be good enough? Are you being any kind of snob? Did you prefer a previous boyfriend or girlfriend, and if so, why?

Brenda – a formidable intellectual – admits that for a long time she was inclined to share her parents' view that her son's fiancée was a bit lightweight: 'My parents, particularly my mum, made it clear that they weren't that keen on Christopher's fiancée, they wanted him to marry his previous girlfriend. They said things in front of them both that I wish they hadn't. My own opinion of Allison changed when she and I were sorting through some old papers together after her father died. We came across a piece of work for which she had won a prestigious award. When we talked about it, I think she felt for the first time I was taking her seriously. And I think she was right.'

HOW TO GET ON WITH YOUR CHILD'S PARTNER

- Don't go into the relationship expecting difficulties. But equally, don't assume you'll be best friends. Aim for a good enough relationship rather than a perfect one.

- Don't intervene in the couple's disagreements. If your child has a bit of a moan about their partner, be empathetic but try not to take sides.
- Don't expect things to carry on as before. Be ready to compromise on things like spending every Christmas together or speaking on the phone every day.
- Resist the temptation to talk to your son or daughter through their partner – even if he/she doesn't respond to your messages.
- Don't buy your son or daughter clothes: it feels like a statement of continuing influence.
- Be curious about what interests your child's partner; build a relationship that exists outside their relationship.
- Don't look for hidden meanings in what your in-law says or does. Equally, don't drop hints yourself! If you can't be direct – with sensitivity – it's probably best to keep quiet.
- Reflect on your relationship with *your* parents-in-law: what makes you love them and what drives you bonkers? Ask yourself honestly whether you're guilty of behaving in a similar way.
- If there's friction, talk to a sensible friend who will validate your feelings but help you to see the other point of view.

11

When Children Become Parents

For me the most extraordinary thing about having a grandchild was seeing my son – who was himself my baby not so very long ago – cradling his own newborn in his arms. It was literally mind-blowing. The artist Anne Truitt wrote in her final journal, *Prospect*, 'However commonplace, it is an odd feeling to have borne babies who have grown up and had babies themselves.' Or as Rolling Stone Keith Richards once said in a documentary: 'When you see offspring of offspring, something else hits home.' So this chapter is not just about being a grandparent, but about how the relationship with a son or daughter – and with their partner – changes when they have children of their own.

Before you become a grandparent, people love saying how wonderful you'll feel and how utterly amazing it is. There's not much room for ambivalence. Yet the birth of a grandchild stirs up a complicated mixture of emotions as well as overwhelming love.

In the first few weeks after my granddaughter and grandson were born within a month of each other, I felt tearful and emotional a lot of the time. Perhaps there was a twinge of longing to turn back the clock, to be where my sons were now, in the intense, joy-drenched, all-absorbing bubble of life with a new baby. But that wasn't entirely it. There was a sliver of foreboding too. I couldn't understand it until I picked up a copy of Salley Vickers' novel *Grandmothers*. In it, a grandmother stands in front of that very familiar Leonardo da Vinci painting of St Anne with her daughter, the Virgin Mary, and her baby grandson Jesus, and it's described as 'an image for the love of all grandmothers, everywhere'. In St Anne's proud grandmother's smile, the character Blanche sees 'the harrowing foreknowledge of all that lay ahead for this pair, in all the world closest to her heart, her dearest and most precious flesh and blood'.

For me, that perfectly captures the essence of being a grandmother. The future for Jesus, his mother and grandmother was unbearable. But all grandparents know, in a way that new parents can't begin to imagine, the pain and anxiety of bringing up children as well as the untold joy and fulfilment. It's hard to know that your adult child, who you still feel such tender protectiveness towards, will have to go through all the endless anxieties about health, all the accidents and trips to A&E, all the angst about schools, friendships and teenagers veering off the rails. The magic of a new life is tempered by a grandparent's wisdom and experience.

But it is still magic. In his book on life transitions, the psychologist Dr Oliver Robinson refers to a study in which 90 per cent of grandparents described grandparenting as very rewarding. Other research is equally positive: another study found it brought new meaning and motivation, plus the sense of immortality that comes from knowing that the family will live on after one's own death. Grandchildren help grandparents to make sense of their personal past, because they inspire them to reflect on their own childhoods, as well as the things they did with their children when they were young. Grandchildren can also strengthen their grandparents' couple relationship by creating a new bond between them, as well as prompting them to look back over their shared history as parents.

Being a grandparent has changed dramatically over the past 40-odd years. There are three main reasons. Adult children start families later than in the past, so when grandchildren finally arrive, many grandparents – who may well have worried that it might never happen – are well up for it. The increase in life expectancy means that on average the grandparenting role lasts for about a third of people's lives and the relationship passes through several distinct phases, from the grandchild's baby years right through to adolescence and into adulthood. But the change that has had the most significant impact on the parent-adult child relationship is the rise in grandchildcare and the new expectation that grandparents will step up and do their bit. Two-fifths of the nation's grandparents – a staggering 5 million – have provided regular childcare for their grandchildren, according to a YouGov poll for Age UK in 2017 (for more on grandchildcare, see pages 226–230).

HOW A GRANDCHILD CHANGES THE RELATIONSHIP WITH YOUR CHILD

When your child becomes a parent, you see them in a whole new light. It puts the final seal on adulthood: you're both parents now and that brings a new understanding, a new equality and hopefully, a new bond. Elizabeth Hamlin, a couple psychoanalytic psychotherapist at Tavistock Relationships, says, 'When you have children, you have to grow up in a very particular way. Children are such a formative part of life.' The relationship between grandparent and adult child takes a big leap forward as the new parent and, to a lesser degree, the new grandparent go through a huge, parallel transition. Both have to adjust to new responsibilities, a new sense of self and their place in the world. Parent and adult child are adjusting to a new way of relating to each other, not only in the heady days after the baby's birth but in the years ahead. It becomes even more important for grandparents to maintain a good relationship with their child's partner, who is now the mother or father of their grandchildren, because more than ever before, the new parents are a team. As the grandchildren grow, the relationship between their parents and grandparents continues to develop and change.

It is usually a positive change: a baby brings adult children closer to their parents. They see more of each other – geography permitting – and adult children often ask their parents for help and advice in a way they haven't for years. The generations are united in adoration of the child, with no risk of the other person's eyes glazing over as they marvel over the latest milestone.

Tru, whose twins are now 14, says, 'When you have kids it gives you a very different perspective on your mother. I'm aware my mum appreciates how I feel about my kids and the kind of thoughts I have. She is a big-time worrier, that's her job. I can appreciate that a little bit now because I'm a bit like that with Stanley and Mabel.'

There is greater empathy too. As new parents discover for themselves the anxieties as well as the joys of being a parent they're prompted to reflect on what their parents went through. It can be quite gratifying when a son who used to roll his eyes at his mother's worrying suddenly gets what parental anxiety is all about. Many adult children discover a new respect for their parents.

Renate, who has a two-year-old granddaughter, says, 'My daughter often says she really respects what I did as a parent. Since she had Libby, she understands the challenges of having just one child and the challenges I faced with working and looking after three children. I feel I've earned her respect and what's great is that it's mutual. She used to make decisions and then tell me – she didn't want a discussion. That's changed. Now she will explore things in relation to parenthood with me.'

At the same time, the parent sees a whole new side to their son or daughter. The self-interest of adolescence and young adulthood gives way to a new selflessness and awareness of wider responsibilities.

Reconciliation after conflict

If there has been conflict between parent and child in the past, the arrival of a new baby can thaw the ice. Ian, who hadn't spoken to his mother since his parents' divorce, was prompted to make contact when his daughter was a toddler: 'Being a dad really opened my eyes to the fact that my mum wasn't just this woman who had divorced my dad, she was also this woman who had changed my nappies and stayed up all night when I was ill and had done all kinds of really lovely things for me as well. I realised I needed to look at my mother again.'

In her clinical practice, the family therapist Judith Lask has found that adult children's attitudes to their parents often soften when they have children themselves. She says, 'A trigger for reconciliation I've found quite frequently is that an adult child realises that their parent is quite a good grandparent. At first they might feel jealous of that, if they feel that they didn't treat them in the same way when they were younger. But it can also be a bridge into another relationship in which they appreciate their parent more as a grandparent. They may also be aware of the struggles and dilemmas of parenthood. Parents and children can build on that and go forward.'

THE DIFFERENCE BETWEEN SONS AND DAUGHTERS

There's a natural assumption that it is the relationship between mother and daughter, rather than between parent and son, that changes most dramatically. From my own experience I'd say the new closeness with sons is pretty dramatic too: it's the icing on the cake, perhaps because it's more unexpected.

Daughters

But it's undeniably true that there is a special bond between mothers and daughters, simply because they both go through the intense physical experience of pregnancy, childbirth and breastfeeding. Broadcaster and author Janet Ellis wrote in *Saga* magazine, 'I hadn't realised how much being a grandmother would deepen my relationship with my daughter. It was amazing to see her love, nurture and play with her baby son, then catch her eye, mother to mother.'

It's not for no reason that the maternal grandmother is traditionally seen as 'top granny', an idea brilliantly explored by Joanna Trollope in her novel *Daughters-in-Law*. As the mother of two sons, I don't like the idea of a granny hierarchy one bit, but I have to concede that there's a nugget of truth. As the paternal grandparent you're at one remove, in the early days at least. You're less involved in the pregnancy: a son might forward scan images or give factual updates, but that's about it. A new mother is naturally more likely to want her own mother around to help, or even stay, after the birth. Brenda, who has a son and two grandsons, is sanguine: 'It's different if you're the mother of a son. There are occasions when Allison wants her mum and that's totally understandable.'

Daughters naturally talk to their mothers about infertility treatment, pregnancy, miscarriages and birth in a way that sons don't. Tru, whose mother supported her through three rounds of fertility treatment, remembers, 'My mum was there for me emotionally when I was going through the IVF, and then through all the complications of my pregnancy. She was always there on the end of the phone, and I do think it made us closer. The twins are teenagers now, but we still speak every day.'

Tru's mother was even at the hospital when the twins were born and that sealed the already special bond between them. Nisha was also with her daughter when her first child was born: 'It wasn't intentional. Stella's husband had had to leave the hospital for some reason and he came back just in time for the birth. If we'd discussed it beforehand, I don't think she would have wanted me there, but as it turned out, I think she was grateful that I was. She had to be induced, and I was holding her hand and mopping her brow. Honestly, words can't describe how I felt... it was amazing. Because I was there, I feel a complete bond with her and with my granddaughter.'

Sons

The bond that grows between parents and sons when they become fathers may be different to the new closeness with daughters, but it's just as special. Many parents find that their sons open up emotionally and are more affectionate, that it establishes a deeper kind of connection. New fathers often say they now 'get' their fathers in a way they didn't before; they may even see them as role models. This feels really wonderful, particularly if parents have felt a bit distant from an adult son's emotional life. It gives the relationship new energy and a new depth.

It's partly that things have changed for the younger generation of fathers. Men now get as involved as they can with pregnancy, birth and babycare; they go to antenatal classes and step up to help with night feeds. At the same time, grandfathers take on more grandchildcare, which opens up the possibility of a closer emotional bond between father and son. And while childbirth is not physically painful for men, it's still a totally life-changing – and in some cases traumatic – experience. When difficulties arise during labour, the expectant father is often more aware of what's going on than his wife.

Brenda remembers, 'My son rang me to say his wife's waters had broken in a shop and she had been rushed into hospital for an emergency caesarean. I heard pain and real profound panic in his voice when he told me he feared he was going to lose them both.

For the first time I realised how deeply he loved her, and his terror of losing her.'

So, while it's true that during the pregnancy sons tend to involve their parents less, and paternal grandparents often feel a bit left out as a result, that changes after the baby is born and again as the child gets older. There is something incredibly moving about seeing your adult child as a new parent, totally absorbed in an unfamiliar nurturing role. I think that's especially true for parents of sons, who tend to be more hands-on than their own fathers were – you can't help feeling that you got something right.

Brenda, a single parent since her only son was a toddler, adds, 'I saw a side of my son I hadn't seen before, and I was delighted to see him being a nurturing father, changing nappies and feeding bottles of expressed milk. My respect for him grew, and our relationship was changed profoundly, and was in many ways rebuilt.'

THE PARALLEL TRANSITION THAT NEW PARENTS AND GRANDPARENTS GO THROUGH

It's important that new grandparents make allowances for the huge change that their adult child and partner are going through. Emotions are all over the place. Overnight, the new parents' couple relationship undergoes a dramatic upheaval as they adjust to a new person in their lives. As a parental double act with responsibility for another life, rather than a couple with free time and only themselves to think about, they have to explore new ways of relating to each other. Sleepless nights, a disconcerting lack of control and a new sense of responsibility that at times feels overwhelming makes new parents vulnerable and hypersensitive to the merest hint of criticism. They need looking after themselves, but they also need their own space. Grandparents can support their adult children through this huge upheaval by remembering how it was for them and thinking about the support that genuinely helped.

Meanwhile, grandparents are themselves going through a significant transition. Ambivalent feelings about becoming a grandparent are natural; friends often ask how it feels as if you're entering another dimension, which in some ways you are. Certainly, you're moving on to another level. Grandparents today look younger and behave very differently to our own grandparents, and that's mostly positive, but a bit bewildering too. Grandchildren are wonderful: they give grandparents new purpose and energy as well as endless opportunities for personal growth. But grandparents have to face the fact that in effect they are passing the baton on to the next generation. They are stepping out of the family driving seat and that might feel like an uncomfortable loss of control. Many grandparents complain about not having a say, whether it's about how often they see their grandchild or the treats they're allowed to bestow. From now on they have to concede that their own views on child-rearing carry less weight than their adult child's. That can make people feel redundant, out of date, displaced and irritated. They may feel that the way they brought up their children is being viewed through newly critical eyes, both by their own child and their son- or daughter-in-law.

At the same time, they're adjusting to a new label, whether it's 'Granny', 'Grandpa' or 'Nanny', and an altered image of themselves, both in the world's eyes and in their own. That's palatable for people who had good relationships with their own grandparents and have a positive view of ageing, but the rest of us only have the Werther's Original grandpa to go on. Grandchildren force you to face up to getting a bit long in the tooth. The huge compensation is that they help you to see the point of getting older. Call me shallow, but I take heart from what the English actress Kristin Scott Thomas told *Vogue* about being a grandmother: 'I refuse to be bullied into thinking it's not cool. It is super-cool. Absolutely thrilling.'

In time most grandparents ease into their new role, and find that it can be incredibly fulfilling and enjoyable in a rather different way than parenting was. But it has to be said that once you get past the heady weeks and months following a new arrival, relations with adult children can become strained as opposing views on bedtimes and feeding, childcare and schooling emerge. Even parents who get on well with their adult children can be disconcerted by a slight distance that opens up, as the adult child and partner assert their own way of parenting. Issues that seem trivial to an outsider cut to the quick because what one generation does or advises can feel like a rejection or a criticism of the other. So, while grandparents automatically refer back to the way they potty-trained or juggled work, that kind of well-meaning advice could make the new parent feel undermined. It works both ways: the new parent's choices might feel like a condemnation of the way the grandparent did things. And of course, grandparents always have to accede to the son- or daughter-in-law's views.

HOW THE RELATIONSHIP WITH A DAUGHTER-IN-LAW OR SON-IN-LAW CHANGES

From the moment the pregnancy is announced, the relationship with your son- or daughter-in-law moves on to another level. As the father or mother of your grandchild, he or she gains new and permanent standing in the family. Getting on well matters more than it ever did before, not just now but in the future. In-law relationships are already delicately balanced and grandchildren raise the stakes and introduce new layers of complication.

Jane remembers, 'My daughter-in-law is a really nice woman, and I didn't have any problems with her when my son was first married, although that did feel like a very different stage in my relationship with him. The problem now is that she and I differ in our approach to bringing up children. I think this is very common in my age group, because I hear it from lots of people. I'm not saying it's just my daughter-in-law, it's my son too, but I have been more conscious of it being different with her. That has been quite a struggle, and I'm sure it's not been easy for her either.'

I'm focusing on grandmothers and daughters-in-law here because the female relationship takes centre stage when parents become grandparents. It is still overwhelmingly mothers who deal with the daily details of bringing up children, even though fathers have become more involved. The arrival of children creates a lasting bond but it also opens up new areas of potential conflict. Traditionally, mothers-in-law cast a beady eye over the way daughters-in-law bring up the grandchildren and how they treat their precious sons. And of course it's reciprocal. A daughter-in-law may be privately critical of your views on childcare, perhaps even the way you brought up your son.

Jane says, 'My son has reinterpreted his upbringing, as is natural since he's become a parent. That is probably partly through his wife's eyes. From my friends I gather this kind of reassessment is common. One friend told me that her daughter never complained when she was growing up, but now that she's a mother, she makes it sound as if she was a total monster. That's a larger cultural change in society, I think, but it is a bit painful.'

In many cultures it's the other way round: there is an expectation that the daughter-in-law will spend more time with her husband's family and that she will bend to her mother-in-law's opinions on child-rearing. When husband and wife come from different cultures it can add layers of stress to the already highly charged in-law relationship.

As Director of the London Intercultural Couples Centre, Dr Reenee Singh helps families work through the conflict this can create. She says, 'All grandmothers can feel terribly disrespected, or just dissed, as if their opinions aren't being taken into account. But if there is also the cultural idea that daughters-in-law are supposed to be subservient to their mothers-in-law, as there is in some South Asian families for example, that is terribly difficult for everyone. Cultural differences add another layer of complication because of the completely different ways that things might be done. The older generation just can't imagine why their own children would make what are to their mind bizarre choices, about going back to work, for example, or sending a child to nursery when the grandparents could be looking after them. The poor son who is caught in the middle tells his mother that they're the parents, they have the right to make these choices.'

Paternal grandparents are often taken aback when they find that they don't get to see their grandchildren as much as they expected and it can be a shock to realise how little say they have in all kinds of things. Jane says, 'I feel the lack of control. I want to be able to control things and I can't. That is my big problem: my difficulty in accepting my loss of control. And theirs, probably.'

New grandparents want to visit but feel hesitant about intruding or staying too long; they want to help but they don't want to interfere. Lurking in the background is the fear of what could happen if the couple separated in the future and the unimaginably painful possibility that the child's mother could stop them seeing their grandchildren. It's estimated that there are about a million grandchildren in the UK who have no contact with their grandparents. Professor Janet Reibstein says, 'It's tragic for everybody if there is a cut off after a divorce. If it happens, grandparents have to maintain a good relationship with the ex. That needs to be explicitly faced.'

WHY GRANDCHILDREN CAN CREATE TENSION BETWEEN MOTHER-IN-LAW AND DAUGHTER-IN-LAW

It is clearly in everyone's interests – especially the grandchild's – that grandparents have a good relationship with their son- or daughter-in-law. But everyone knows it's not always easy. There has been a huge amount of research and discussion exploring the underlying reasons why in-law relationships become more challenging when children arrive. Feelings of irritation or annoyance bubble up out of nowhere, out of all proportion to the apparent trigger. Understanding what underpins such emotional gut responses is a step towards working out how to handle the relationship well.

There is a new pressure to get on, simply because you see more of each other. A difference of opinion, even about something minor, can cause greater and more lasting irritation with a daughter-in-law than it would with your own child. It carries such weight, somehow. In-laws don't have the same instinctive understanding of each other's moods, sensitivities and sore points. With a daughter or son your shared history acts as a kind of ballast when you disagree – you've made up after arguments in the past and you know the bottom line is that you love each other unconditionally and mean well. But that's not a given with in-laws. It takes effort and thoughtfulness to build a relationship of love and trust and to find ways of making peace.

Mother-in-law stereotypes don't help and they are hard to ignore. They're so ingrained that they create an expectation of problems where none exists. Yet they often contain a kernel of truth. There is a natural rivalry, whether acknowledged or not, between mothers of different generations. Competition for the son's/partner's affections is superseded by rivalry about being a good mother. On top of this are new cultural and peer pressures on both generations of women, not only to be the perfect mother, but to be the perfect grandmother.

Meanwhile, both daughter-in-law and grandmother are ultra sensitive and prone to interpret a well-meaning suggestion as criticism or rejection. Grandmothers naturally feel a need to pass on their experience, but advice, however well-intentioned, can undermine a new mother's confidence and get in the way of her working things out for herself.

If grandparents are worried about the child, they often agonise about whether or not to voice their concerns. When I asked Jane whether she offered her daughter-in-law advice, she admitted, 'I offered worse than advice – there's no doubt I'd be classed as terrible on that front! It's not that I think I was a wonderful parent myself, not at all. But I can see a real problem in the way my older grandson has been treated since his younger brother was born and that really upsets me. These two very devoted and conscientious parents seemed to me to have a complete lack of imagination about the experience of their eldest child. I feel powerless. The trouble is that since then my daughter-in-law has become highly sensitive to anything I say.'

HOW TO MAKE THE RELATIONSHIP WITH A DAUGHTER-IN-LAW WORK

The perfect time to build a stronger connection, and even heal old wounds, is when a baby first arrives. If the relationship has been a bit strained in the past, a baby heralds a new softening. A growing child is a unifying force. There's so much love in the air, as well as so much to talk about, and so many opportunities to be helpful. The ideal is to establish a relationship that also exists in its own right, outside the grandchildren and your son/her partner. Both sides need to see the other as a whole person and not just a mother or grandmother. This means finding common ground to talk about as well as the child you both adore: a television series, exercise, hobbies, books.

Professor Deborah Merrill says, 'If you have a good relationship with your daughter-in-law, it's easier to discuss things and for her to realise, this is my husband's mother, they still have a relationship despite the fact that I've swooped in. And that I need to be mindful of that and give their relationship room to grow and to continue.'

But perhaps the best way to build a strong relationship is to be genuinely supportive and avoid being judgemental – as well as offering to babysit and thinking empathetically about ways to make your daughter-in-law's life easier. It is useful to recall how it felt to be a vulnerable young mother yourself and the things that really helped. This should point to different ways of framing advice: as suggestions, not diktats. It's good to think about what your daughter-in-law hears when you talk about the way you did things: does it come across as disapproving or laying down the law? Sometimes it's better to keep your views to yourself. But if you're worried about something – a child's eyesight or hearing, for example – it's often best to just say it in a gentle way that won't cause panic.

In some situations it's fine to make suggestions or offer advice to sons, but if you go behind the daughter-in-law's back, or if it smacks of divide and rule, it will only cause trouble. And if there is friction, it's tough on sons too. He is stuck in the middle, loyal to his partner but not wanting to upset his mother. You can hardly blame sons for wishing that the women in their lives would sort things out between themselves. But that's not good enough!

Professor Deborah Merrill says, 'I think part of the problem up until now is that sons weren't playing a role, they weren't saying anything to their mothers or their wives. They wanted them to work it out and not involve them. In fact, sons can play a role – for example, in representing to their wives that they need time with their mothers. There is a lot of room to work this out at an individual level. I don't think problems are a given.'

HOW TO GET ON WITH YOUR SON- OR DAUGHTER-IN-LAW

- Respect boundaries. Don't expect to drop in without agreeing on a convenient time first.

- It's helpful to give a rough idea of how long you'd like to stay – whether it's a couple of hours or a couple of days – and stick to it.
- Don't make loaded remarks and never use your grandchild as a way of getting your message across.
- Resist the temptation to refer back to the way you did things, unless you're asked.
- Don't go behind your in-law's back by expressing concerns to your son or daughter.
- Avoid interfering with decisions about going back to work or childcare.
- Don't only buy presents for your grandchild – daughters-in-law need treats even more, and not just when they are new mothers.

HOW TO BE REALLY HELPFUL

- When the baby is new, take food: cakes, meals, soup, fruit. My mum used to arrive with a stack of sarnies when I was breastfeeding, which was what I needed most.
- Don't expect to be made a cup of tea or coffee – or given food – when you visit. Make your own drink and make them one too.
- Avoid making assumptions about what would be helpful: too much cleaning and cupboard-sorting can feel like you're taking over, or a criticism of domestic standards. And never clean the loo! Having said that, I absolutely loved it when my mum stormed in and sorted out the mess.
- New parents need treats and thoughtful care, but they also need space.

- Stay curious about your child's whole life, rather than seeing them as a parent and gatekeeper to your grandchildren. That goes for your son- or daughter-in-law too.
- Don't forget to say they're doing a good job, without sounding patronising! Steve says, 'My nine-year-old grandson is very gentle and considerate and sharing. That makes me think, my daughter is a really good mum, she's bringing her child up with all the right values. I have to make sure I tell her that.'
- With older babies and children, offer to look after the child overnight so that the parents can go away or just have a lie-in together. It's invaluable for the couple's relationship.
- It's fine to say 'no' occasionally when asked to babysit. In fact, it makes the parents feel more comfortable about asking.

GRANDCHILDCARE

Grandchildcare is a new norm. These days grandparents are almost expected to look after the grandchildren some of the time while their parents go out to work. Grandparents are an obvious childcare choice: they adore the child, have loads of experience and their care is free. And they get a lot out of it too. Research points to the considerable emotional and psychological benefits, both for grandparents and their grandchildren. Some report a positive effect on grandparents' brain function and one study, in the journal *Evolution and Human Behavior*, suggested that grandparenting might even lead to a longer life.

Yet many grandparents have mixed feelings about committing to the role of childminder. The family therapist Judith Lask says, 'Quite a lot of conflict comes up around expectations of grandparents to be part of regular childcare. Most women are very happy to be a grandparent but they don't want to stay in the mother role because their lives have moved on and they have other commitments. Some adult children see that as real treachery. They say things like, "You say you love me but when I really need you…'"

It's not that these grandparents don't love spending time with their grandchildren and want to see them often – they do. Most grandparents are more than happy to babysit and have the grandchildren to stay, and make it clear that they would drop everything in an emergency – which offers the reassurance parents really need.

Steve is fairly typical. He says, 'My grandson and I have a very close relationship but long before he was born, I told my daughter that I wasn't going to be a childminder, because I've got my own life. I dip into my grandson's life every two or three weeks and I take him camping every year. We sit on the beach and build castles and dig pits.'

What many grandparents find uncomfortable is the idea of a regular, formal commitment. A lot of grandparents are still working; many grandmothers relish no longer having to have to juggle work with bringing up children. Grandparents want to pursue interests they had to give up when their own families were growing up. They want to be spontaneous, to make the most of every opportunity before it's too late.

Renate remembers how she felt when her daughter asked if she and her husband would look after their granddaughter one day a week each. In the end they compromised on one day: 'At first I was like *No*! We've got our own lives and we need to make our own living. But I feel torn, and when I'm looking after Libby, I totally adore it and I want to do it full-time. In fact, it takes all my willpower to stop the words coming out of my mouth, offering to do just that. Not least because I can see the impact on my daughter and son-in-law of having to struggle.

'But I know I would feel ambivalent about not giving myself the chance to focus on my work now, because I gave a lot to the kids when they were growing up. Every week, I feel I could really do with another day of work. I try not to do things that I feel ambivalent about, because then there's room for resentment, and I don't want to feel resentful so I try to make clear decisions about what works for me and for them.'

Committing to regular grandchildcare

Despite all this, the rewards of grandchildcare are huge and they're different to informal babysitting. A regular commitment, even one day a week, takes things to another level. Many grandparents welcome a second chance to look after children without all the struggles and uncertainty they went through as young parents themselves. Without the distractions of full-time parenting it's possible to totally throw yourself into the moment. Spending time with children without their parents is one of the best ways to get to know them and to build an independent, lasting bond. Noticing how they change every week is a privilege. Besides, it's incredibly flattering to be asked: my husband said it made him prouder than being made a professor.

Equally importantly, it injects new life into the relationship with your adult child. Seeing them regularly means you're more involved with the ups and downs of their daily lives than you have been for years. You hear about things they might not bother mentioning if you saw them less regularly, whether it's problems with a jobshare or the sunshade that didn't get delivered. There are more opportunities for the casual chats that offer a way into deeper communication.

But it can get tricky too. Grandchildcare may be a labour of love, not money, but adult children have to be able to rely on the arrangement in the same way they would rely on professional childcare. After her divorce, Tania's parents moved house so that they could look after her daughter at least one day a week and she remembers, 'There was a bit of tension because my mum would say that's fine as long as we're not on holiday. And I'd be like, this is either childcare or it's not; I need it to be 100 per cent guaranteed. But that worked itself out and my daughter has an extremely close relationship with my mum and dad as a result.'

There are many stories of grandparents who feel they are being taken for granted, that adult children expect them to be too flexible and don't reckon on how tired they might get; it doesn't help that grandparents don't want to admit it either. For grandparents without a partner, childcare can be particularly challenging and exhausting; even if married grandparents look after children on their own, there's someone to cook them dinner when they get home. Some grandparents are so desperate to be fair that they give up more time than they would like because they stretch their energies equally between different sets of grandchildren.

One way to pre-empt these problems that has been discussed by the Grandparents' Association is the introduction of childcare agreements. The idea is taking time to catch on, perhaps because a formal agreement with adult children seems a bit heavy-handed. But there is a lot to be said for laying down informal ground rules from the start so that everyone knows where they stand: it might prevent disappointed expectations and resentment further down the line. It works best if both sides can discuss days, times, holidays and whether the child will be looked after at theirs or yours. Both sides should agree to give plenty of notice of holidays and days off. As long as they give ample warning, grandparents should never feel they have to justify why they want time to themselves.

Tension also arises from disagreements about childcare, particularly knotty issues like diet and discipline. Again, grandparents are treading the fine line between indulgent grandparents and professional childcarers. They have to follow the simple rule that grandparents ought to do things the way the parents want them done. Of course there'll be times when grandparents disapprove or disagree, but they just have to accept that they no longer know best – it's consistency with the parents' view that counts.

MAKING GRANDCHILDCARE WORK FOR EVERYONE

- Come to an informal agreement about days and times and stick to it.
- Discuss the different activities the parents would like you to do with their child.
- Talk about how much tidying and laundry (if any) you're prepared to do and what's expected. I've heard of grandmothers cooking dinner for working parents, but that sounds like making a rod for your own back.
- Always follow the parents' rules, even if you don't agree with them. It's easier if you understand the rationale.
- Whenever possible, give plenty of warning when you can't make it so that they have time to make an alternative arrangement. The same goes for holidays.
- Be flexible about staying late as long as the parents text with a revised ETA rather than assume you're happy to stay. If it happens too often, establish your own deadlines, like meeting a friend or going to a class.
- Make sure you maintain your own interests and activities so that you won't be lost if they move to a different area.
- If your child is expecting another baby, think realistically about whether you want to look after more children. If you do, plan ways of making it work for both of you.

THE OTHER GRANDPARENTS

The idea that there might be tension, or even rivalry, between different sets of grandparents is little talked about. When I bring up the subject, people look a bit taken aback and laugh it off, but after a while they warm to the theme and say how they really feel. So I think it's worth a mention because even if people don't admit to it – and that's understandable – it's still a thing and it makes life much easier for the whole family if grandparents are on friendly terms with each other. And that's more likely if potential tension is acknowledged.

The first tussle is about whether you want to be called Grandma or Nanny, Grandpa or Grandad. Anne-Marie, who is one of the easiest-going women I've ever met, was anything but before her first grandson was born. She remembers, 'My daughter-in-law asked what I wanted to be called and I thought, right, I'm in for a battle. I wanted to be Grandma, like my mum and my grandma. I really didn't want to be Nan or Granny and I wasn't going to be bullied into giving up Grandma. It was pure luck that my son's mother-in-law wanted to be Granny.'

The traditional idea of the maternal grandmother as 'top granny' sets up a hierarchy before the baby is even born. It's a bit old-fashioned, because it ignores wider changes in family life as men become increasingly involved with their children. Nevertheless, it primes the number two grandparents to look out for reasons to feel slighted: the grandchild spends less time with them, has Christmas with the other family, there are fewer photos of them on the wall and so on. As always, it's the older generation who have to be grown-up, try not to be over-sensitive and cultivate a generous spirit. It helps if you can get to know the other grandparents when children and grandchildren aren't around and I've heard of many people who make a point of doing this. One sensible new grandmother I know invited her opposite number for a walk and their friendship grew from there. Adult children can help too, by involving both sets of grandparents, perhaps in different ways, and making sure they all feel welcome. It starts in pregnancy, with keeping both sets of grandparents in the loop about hospital appointments and scans and the onset of labour.

Circumstances and geography have a big influence too. For example, if one grandparent is still working full-time, they won't have time to offer childcare. If one grandparent lives far away, they'll see less of the family. The growing trend towards multigenerational households gives one set of grandparents the advantage of daily contact. During the pandemic, many new parents formed a bubble with one set of grandparents, which must have been bliss, but I felt for the ones left outside the bubble, who couldn't see the new baby at all. Even if the arrangement is temporary, as it is for Anne-Marie's grandsons, it still has an impact. She says, 'It's an interesting relationship between the two sets of grandparents, because you're kind of joint, but at the same time you can definitely compete! My two grandsons have been living with the other granny for over a year. It's hard for me when they run up to her and throw their arms round her. I am not jealous but I do want to retain a place in their affections.

'I decided I had to find my own role as spoily Grandma who does the treats, because I can't replace the day-to-day contact the boys get with Connie's parents. It also makes a difference that I'm the son's mother and not the daughter's. But the good thing about not being the constant carer is that I don't have to be sensible. I hide chocolate animals in the garden and they go wild with excitement.'

The potential for hurt is even greater if one grandparent has remarried and introduced a new step-grandparent on to the scene, particularly if the divorce is relatively recent and was precipitated by the new partner. One divorced woman told me how she tried to avoid family occasions if it meant meeting her former husband and his new partner. I imagine she must have felt so sad and even a bit envious when the baby spent time with his step-grandmother, not least because it's a continual reminder of the loss of an anticipated joint future. Even when ex-partners have kept things on an amicable footing for the children's sake, as Theresa has, it can give them a pang. She and her first husband have both remarried, but their connection continues through their four children and two grandsons. She admits, 'I get a little bit jealous when my ex-husband and his wife look after the children on Fridays. Obviously, I don't let my daughter know! Her partner has no contact with his mother at all, so there isn't another grandma in the picture. But it is hard.'

Professor Lisa Doodson, an expert on stepfamilies, acknowledges the potential for rivalry and resentment between step-grandparents and biological grandparents. She says, 'A lovely step-grandma recently said to me, "I don't know my place, I don't know what I should be called – I'm just *her*." It was so sad, because she had such a lot of love for the children. My advice was to try not to get hung up about not being the biological grandparent and just enjoy the children. Find the things you enjoy doing best with them, because that's what children want. Be the granny who bakes cakes with them or grows flowers. Find your thing and they'll love you for it.'

That's sound advice for all grandparents. Every grandparent and step-grandparent has something special to bring to the party; their different skills and interests balance and complement each other. As grandparents develop their own bond with their grandchild, the significance of whether you're number one or two grandparent fades. The more people a grandchild has to love them the better, and that becomes more obvious as they grow older, and when younger siblings are born. With a second or third child, grandparents' help is invaluable, because they can provide the continuity and love that the older children need when their parents have tunnel vision about the new baby.

And if there's a crisis, it's all hands on deck. Brenda felt pretty lukewarm about her son's mother-in-law until a series of crises beset her son's family: 'We got to know each other better through the crises, because we were both supporting our child through a difficult time. There's no time for silly games, you just focus on what's important. I started developing a much better relationship with Allison's mother over that period. We've formed a good double act.'

12

....

Adult Children Who Need More Support

When I started interviewing parents and experts for this chapter, it soon struck me how helpful their insights are for all families and not only those whose children need more support. While it's true that the challenges they face loom larger and are more complex, they echo the dilemmas all parents have to work through, particularly when it comes to nurturing independence and having faith that adult children will find their own way. They have to work hard on themselves and continually question their own behaviour; they have to listen carefully and respond with empathy. Jenny Langley, who works with parents of adult children with depression and eating disorders, says, 'It really comes down to empathy and stepping into the ill person's shoes. This is a life skill for everyone, not just parents of children with problems. We should all be seeking to apply empathy all the time.'

There are endless different reasons why some adult children need more support than others. Some young people find the transition to adulthood much harder and fraught with more stumbling blocks than their peers. At some stage most adult children go through a difficult phase with clear external triggers: they're out of work or they get divorced, or they have a crisis of purpose and direction. They may struggle with adjusting to life with a new baby, or suffer from postnatal depression. Parents are often the first port of call in such crises, which are hopefully relatively short-lived – they are covered in Chapter 6.

This chapter deals with long-term health issues and special needs. Some children are born with a disability, such as autism or Down's syndrome, while others develop physical or mental health issues while growing up, or when they are fully adult. Either way, this has a profound and enduring impact on the relationship between parent and child, and indeed siblings too. Independence is thwarted by the need for continuing care and involvement. Fears and anxieties for a child's well-being are writ larger and colour the relationship for longer than would be the case otherwise. Some adult children will never be fully independent; some will never move out of their parents' home.

Meanwhile, parents aren't getting any younger. While their peers face empty nests and an end to hands-on parenting, they have to soldier on. Anna Karin Kingston, whose 29-year-old son has autism, longs for an empty nest: 'When your child is younger, there is still hope that they might fulfil their potential. But when they reach 19 or 20, what you have is what's going to stay. It's more about adjusting to the reality. The older you get, the less energy you have, the more tired and drained you get.'

Parents of children who are born with special needs have to adjust to different expectations about their future from the word go. They need to acknowledge that their child may never be fully self-sufficient and aim instead for the highest possible level of independence. Liz and her daughter Laura, 34, who has Down's syndrome, have always worked towards this aim. Laura went to the same state schools as her three siblings and then on to a residential college for adults with learning disabilities. Since then, she's led an independent life with minimal support.

'Laura is very capable, but she's still a child, really,' Liz says. 'In most situations she wouldn't want to hold my hand because that would be really uncool, but when we were crossing the road this morning she automatically took my hand. There's always that contrast.'

It's very different if problems emerge in adulthood. After years of looking forward to the familiar milestones of adult life, parents are forced to get their heads round a future that looks nothing like what they imagined. It's a massive adjustment and there is a sense that life has been put on hold.

Leonie's 35-year-old son was doing well in his career as a sports psychologist until, out of the blue, at the age of 28, he had the first of several psychotic episodes. Leonie says, 'Before Matt became unwell, I was expecting him to just carry on with his own independent life. And now he's not, he's back living with me and he hasn't got a proper job. His mental health has had a huge impact on both our lives.'

Karen, whose daughter became anorexic in her early twenties, describes a similar sense of life stalling. She's now 32 and has been in and out of hospital over the past 10 years for several months at a time. Karen says, 'As a parent, you have all these future milestones ahead in your mind. You expect certain things to happen. And then it all stops. I was just getting used to Maisie being gone and the whole empty nest thing. She used to ring up, so excited to be in charge of her life and enjoying her independence. Then everything suddenly collapsed. It changed the family dynamic; it changed everything.'

MENTAL ILLNESS

Parents have good reason to be concerned about the mental health of their adult children. Alarming statistics about the rise in mental ill health across the population, and particularly among young adults, are borne out by the anecdotal tales we hear all the time: of sons who are too depressed to leave their rooms, of daughters who have panic attacks on the way to work. According to the National Institute for Health and Care Excellence (NICE), the average age that the first episode of a major depression occurs is during the mid-twenties. Other common mental health problems, such as obsessive compulsive disorder (OCD), social anxiety and panic attacks, often begin in early adulthood. According to the Royal College of Psychiatrists, around one in 10 young people will self-harm at some point. Suicide is now the biggest killer of people under 35 in the UK.

Various causes have been suggested for the rise in mental ill health in young people: uncertainty in the job market, student debt, difficulty finding an affordable place to live, social media. The uncertainty and isolation created by COVID-19 has piled on the pressure. In the UK population as a whole, rates of depression almost doubled during the pandemic, according to the Office for National Statistics in 2020; adults under the age of 39 were more likely to be affected, with one in three experiencing moderate to severe depressive symptoms.

Parents are understandably resistant to the possibility that their child is mentally ill. It doesn't help that the generation who grew up in the 1960s and 1970s retains a more doom-laden view of mental ill health than their adult children. As a child, I remember overhearing the mysterious phrase 'nervous breakdown', whispered in appalled tones. Mental illness was never discussed in my family, even though my father suffered from chronic depression. The popular movie of Ken Kesey's sixties' novel *One Flew Over the Cuckoo's Nest*, released in 1975, set the seal on the nightmare image of mental healthcare.

Thankfully, mental ill health is no longer a secret scourge or seen as an incurable life sentence, as more people in the public eye open up about their experiences and high-profile campaigns hammer home 'It's OK not to be OK' messages. Optimism is growing that mental health problems can be prevented, or at least managed successfully with the right treatment and support. It's reassuring to know that, according to Mental Health First Aid England, up to 90 per cent of young people recover from depression in the first year. And while it's distressing that young people are 'flocking to therapy', according to the website wellbeing.com, it is also a hopeful sign that they are increasingly clued-up about ways to prevent and treat mental ill health.

Mental illness varies widely in severity and responsiveness to treatment. Earlier, Lindsey talked about her daughter Esther's panic attacks at work and Liam described his struggles with mental health in the years after leaving university (Chapters 6 and 2 respectively). They both found ways of managing their symptoms with the right treatment and support – not least from their parents.

But some mental health problems become more entrenched and interfere with both adult children's and their parents' lives for much longer. Some kids first experience problems in their teens, which leave them vulnerable into adulthood.

Lucy's son Duncan had a breakdown when he was 16; he's now 29 and has lived at home for most of his twenties. Lucy says, 'If you'd said to me 10 years ago that Duncan would have a good career one day I wouldn't have believed you. He was off the wall at times. He started unravelling when he was 16 and that went on until he was about 23. He went away to university but after a term he just couldn't take it. He came home and transferred to another university and finished his degree living at home. He's doing remarkably well now and he's about to move out. Therapy has made all the difference, but that's not to detract from his own achievements.'

According to NICE, incomplete recovery from depression and relapse are common. The NICE clinical guideline on mental disorders refers to a World Health Organization report that said 50 per cent of sufferers still had a diagnosis of depression a year later. As a result, some young adults have to delay leaving home, perhaps for years, until they're well enough to cope on their own. Others become ill after they've been living independently. The years after university are a particularly vulnerable time.

The Charlie Waller Trust was set up in memory of a young man who had a successful career in advertising, good friends and a loving family, yet suffered from depression and died by suicide at the age of 28. The trust in his name focuses on the mental health of young people at key transitions, particularly between university and work.

Spotting the warning signs

It's not surprising that parents worry about missing the warning signs when they don't see their child every day. It is difficult to distinguish behaviour that doesn't seem quite right from a serious problem that needs attention. If there is a history of mental ill health in the family, you can't help but be watchful. But at the same time, fear and denial muddy the waters. This is brilliantly described in *The Boy Between*, a memoir in which the novelist Amanda Prowse and her son Josiah Hartley, now in his mid-twenties, give their own accounts of his depression and plan to take his own life. What's uniquely illuminating are the insights into a mother and son's very different thoughts and reactions: Josh's irritation with his mum's 'pretend happy' smiling; Amanda's doubts that perhaps she should just tell him to get out of bed and snap out of it. But perhaps the most helpful thing of all is Josh's testimony to what depression feels like; what's going on inside the head of a young man whose world is his oyster, yet who sees life as an endless series of exhausting processes and one day gets scarily close to ending it.

Warning signs are inevitably harder to spot when you're no longer living under the same roof. Parents always hope for the best, even when they know in their sinking hearts that something is badly amiss. They probably have doubts about whether tough love is what's required and whether they're making things worse by tolerating odd behaviour and a reluctance to conform.

I spoke to one mother whose 30-year-old son had never left home or found regular work because of his struggle with drugs and mental health issues; she worried that living with her held him back because he knew she was always on hand to sort things out for him. She felt torn: she wanted him to find work, yet she still paid him to do odd jobs when he needed cash. In this situation it only adds to the confusion if friends or relatives make thoughtless comments like, 'If he was my son I'd make him get a job/find his own place/get out of bed…' And it's worse if mothers and fathers disagree with each other about how best to help.

Identifying the problem is not straightforward. Parent and child then face coming to terms with what the diagnosis means to their lives and what on earth happens next. Parents invariably feel they're to blame. They sift through the past with a fine toothcomb, wondering what they did wrong when their child was growing up, as well as in more recent years. Amanda Prowse told an interviewer that Josh's illness made her question her parenting and whether there were warning signs she had missed. Parents have to accept that the future they dreamed of for their child might never materialise. They know that their own lives can never get back on track until their child gets better and that can feel like a long and uncertain road. They feel the truth of the old adage, 'You are only ever as happy as your unhappiest child'.

Supporting an adult child with mental health issues

The next hurdle is to work out how best to support an adult child. How can parents persuade an independent child to seek help? We know that mental health issues are easier to treat if dealt with earlier rather than later. Should parents get involved with finding the best treatment? Would moving back home help?

Leonie has struggled with these dilemmas over the past seven years, since her son Matt had his first psychotic episode. Psychosis usually emerges for the first time between the ages of 15 and 30; it can signal an underlying illness, such as bipolar disorder or schizophrenia, and it is often hard to pinpoint the cause. Matt's illness seemed to come out of nowhere, although Leonie believes its roots lie in deep anxiety: 'Certainly the first episode happened during a very anxious time. He came home for the weekend and said he needed to sleep but he couldn't, and then he had what I can only describe as a breakdown. He was in a terrible state, crying and very paranoid. I took him to A&E and they gave him some medication, which he was very suspicious of. I managed him at home, alone, and finally took him to see a psychiatrist privately, as the NHS didn't offer. He had two or three appointments and seemed much improved and went back to Liverpool. He managed for a while and then one day I had a call from him and his girlfriend, who was very concerned as Matt was behaving extremely bizarrely. We managed to persuade him to go to the hospital and I got straight into my car and drove two hours up the motorway to meet them in the hospital car park. He was very paranoid; thankfully he was sectioned under the Mental Health Act.

'That was the first section. Since then he's had about two episodes a year and he has been sectioned several times – you lose track of how many. And each time, after three days on medication, he's fine, he's asking for a lawyer and talking about his human rights. When Matt takes his medication, he is the most lovely person. When he doesn't, he goes back into psychosis and paranoia and all that.'

Parents often feel confused about how far they should get involved and their child's responses often add to the confusion. In her wise book *The Myth of Maturity*, the psychologist Dr Terri Apter points to evidence that parents often withdraw emotional support from depressed young adults because it appears to be what their child wants. Parents misinterpret a lack of communication or a sullen response as an indication that their adult child doesn't want anything to do with them when, in fact, Dr Apter insists, 'A parent's responsiveness and affection remain crucial supports for self-esteem'.

Yet parents have little choice but to stand back because they have frustratingly little influence and no control when it comes to treatment and medication. Legally it's up to the adult child and the medics, but a parent's instinct urges intervention – they're desperate to march in to battle to get the best possible care. What makes it even more painful is that they know their child better than anyone and pick up warning signs that others might miss.

Leonie says, 'I'm aware of small, very subtle changes that happen within a few days of Matt stopping his medication. I get a bit panicky about any little nuance. When Matt was living in Liverpool, I'd get the odd call and he'd say, "I'm not great, Mum," and I knew he was on the verge of another psychotic episode. Now that he's living at home, I'm desperate to ask if he's taking his medication, but I don't because it pisses him off and I don't want a row.

'Last year he had another terrible episode. Police and paramedics were involved and he was sectioned again. It was the first time I had really witnessed how bad it could get and it was truly distressing for me – and obviously for him in his acute paranoia. It was the first section in about four years, because I had always managed to intervene in time by reminding him that stopping the meds could result in hospitalisation; that was usually enough to get him back on them. But this time we had argued and he'd gone off to London without the medication and when he returned five days later, he was too far gone.'

Even when parents are beside themselves with concern about their child's health, they know they risk crossing a line already blurred by mental ill health and the dependence that comes with it. Questions about medication or eating habits or sleep patterns or alcohol are like a red rag to a bull. The young adult is either beyond caring or thinks they know best; at the same time, they may have conflicting feelings about the pros and cons of medication and they certainly know better than anyone what the side effects feel like.

Jenny Langley, who works with parents of young people with mental health issues, says, 'Part of what we talk about in our workshops is how to get the balance between being aware of medical risk and caring for your adult child, but at the same time letting them be independent and take responsibility and not be hovering over them the whole time. This is something parents struggle with and it affects the relationship if the young person feels they're not being respected or treated as an adult.

'Our advice is to give more attention to the behaviours you like and less attention to the behaviours you don't like. This doesn't mean you ignore the illness, it just means you're not obsessing about it all the time. That's what parents find so hard, because often they're just so scared. Whether it's depression, anxiety or self-harm, they're scared their loved one might die.'

Living with an adult child with mental health issues

Many adult children with mental health issues live at home. Some young adults have never managed to move out into a place of their own. Others have lived independently, perhaps for years, until mental illness precipitates a move back with parents. It is often the only option for someone who is ill, out of work, can't afford rent and needs support, whether they acknowledge it or not. But even if both sides agree that living together is the best solution, it's not easy for either parent or adult child, who both have to sacrifice a degree of independence.

Living with anyone with a mental illness stretches people to their limits, but with an adult child the reluctant return to dependence adds another layer of difficulty for both sides. The adult child may see moving home as an added failure to add to already low self-esteem. And while it's reassuring for parents to be on hand in case of a crisis, and to be able to check that their child is OK, their problems and lifestyle are in parents' faces every day, with no respite.

'And of course it's hard not to slot straight back into full parenting mode, even with a 35-year-old son who has lived independently for several years,' Leonie says. 'When Matt asked to live with me two years ago I thought great, he'll have some stability, maybe get some counselling and get his life together. But it's been two steps forward, one step back. It's difficult to accept that even though Matt is living with me he doesn't need his mother. Generally, I treat him as the adult he is, I give him privacy, I don't cook for him. I don't try to control anything and I do my best to give him his independence as much as possible. Sometimes that means we don't even talk, because he'll come home from work and go straight up to his room. Is that to do with his mental health or just because he's sick of living with his mum? I don't know.

'It's not easy for him either. He is so keen to get his own place and his life sorted. The last episode seems to have given him a bit of a wake-up call; he has been very proactive in finding work and I hope it's a turning point. The consultant psychiatrist told me that it takes about seven years before a patient will take full responsibility and accept the situation.'

Mental health issues make people highly sensitive and irritable. Parents' hyper-vigilance and false enthusiasm can be deeply irritating and often they know it but can't help themselves. At the same time, they are nervous of making their child feel worse by broaching a difficult subject, or making a suggestion, whether it's about therapy, having a wash or what time their child gets up in the morning.

Lucy has found her way through this minefield by doing her best to see things from her son's point of view – the empathetic approach that experts like Jenny Langley talk about. Lucy's son Duncan, 29, has lived at home for most of his twenties and it provided the stability he needed as a young adult. Having coped successfully with a stressful first year in a new job, he is about to move out, although it's been a happy arrangement for the whole family: he pays rent and leads a totally independent life. Lucy does her best to listen carefully, questions her own motives and thinks carefully about her responses. She says, 'Duncan is his own man, completely. Occasionally if I ask him a question that he doesn't like he'll back off, or just say "I'm not going to tell you." He's quick to let us know if we're being in any way invasive. He's got very clear lines, and that's fine. So you have to think, hang on, am I asking a question that's going to really piss him off? Why am I asking this question? Is it driven by my anxiety and it's actually got nothing to do with his well-being? And if the answer is probably yes, I shut up! Anyone who has had teenage children does that all the time.'

Parents need to curb the instinctive urge to jump in with solutions to problems and casual suggestions about treatment or courses or jobs. But if an adult child seems stuck, parents naturally want to give a gentle nudge. Leonie says, 'I worry a lot about my son's future and him not getting a job, but I try not to suggest too much because it annoys him. Recently he mentioned going back to university and I thought, just *do* it! And of course being me, the mother, I went straight on to the local university website and then stupidly had that conversation with him: "Have you seen the new course they're doing..." I've got to stop doing that, because although he's living with me he's an adult and he doesn't need his mother. But it's difficult *not* being the mother.'

Learning not to 'be the mother' is about allowing the child to work things out rather than fixing things for them. This kind of support requires patience and it goes against the grain if you're a natural fixer, but it's the best way to nurture self-sufficiency and resilience. Even when adult children ask for advice, what they are usually after is someone to listen, to allow them space to say how they feel or discuss a problem.

Jenny Langley says, 'It's about realising you can't fix your child, but you can create a better environment for them to fix themselves. Also, parents have to learn to tolerate their own distress, rather than being frozen with it, by taking a step back and looking after themselves. It's a skill that you can learn. And it helps the young adult to see that it's OK to have distress and tolerate it. It's a big part of resilience.'

The impact on parents' independence

In order to create the kind of healing environment that Jenny Langley describes, parents need to maintain their own interests as much as possible. For one thing, if they can keep up with friendships and activities they enjoy, parents are modelling healthy behaviour and that's a powerful positive influence on the adult child. It is also essential for their own health and well-being. Yet it seems wrong to parents who blame themselves. And it feels counterintuitive to parents who have good reason to be anxious, who are terrified of what might go wrong if they take their eye off the ball for an evening out or a weekend away.

Jenny Langley says, 'A lot of parents stop doing things for themselves, like having a night out or going to a yoga class, because they're so busy caring and they get stuck in a vicious circle. And parents of adult children with mental health issues are often struggling themselves, so role modelling that they're going to the GP or to see a counsellor can be really powerful.'

If you're living under the same roof it's even harder to have your own life. Leonie and Matt have shared a two-bedroom flat for the past two years; before that, they had been living apart for several years, since Matt first went away to university.

Leonie says, 'I feel I've lost my independence. Matt's not very sociable anyway and he goes to bed early because of his mental health issues, so the idea of me chatting downstairs with my friends would not be on. It doesn't stop me completely but I don't do it as much as I'd like to. I definitely factor him in to my plans, and a lot of that is to do with his mental health, because it wouldn't be the same with my daughter. Recently, Matt went to stay with his dad and it was a huge relief, knowing I had a week off, and that I could wake up and didn't have to think about him. Isn't that awful?'

EATING DISORDERS

Eating disorders are thought of as primarily adolescent illnesses, yet adults suffer too. In her book, Professor Janet Treasure, a psychiatrist who specialises in the research and treatment of eating disorders, points out that anorexia nervosa can develop at any crisis point in life. Bulimia nervosa mainly affects women between the ages of 16 and 40, and recent studies suggest that 8 per cent of women have the condition at some stage in life. An eating disorder that started in the teenage years can continue or recur in adulthood: according to Mental Health First Aid England, 20 per cent of anorexia patients and 23 per cent of bulimia sufferers stay chronically ill.

It's also worth mentioning the kind of disordered eating that hovers on the borderline of becoming an entrenched problem. Weight is one of those things parents worry about, and sometimes needlessly, long after their children have left home. They worry that weight gain is a sign of depression or unhappiness, and that weight loss might go too far – even if there's never been a problem in the past. If there has, parents are painfully alert to signs of a recurrence, such as frequent trips to the bathroom, overenthusiastic exercising, or a baggy jumper disguising weight loss.

Eating disorders are terrifying for parents, whatever their son or daughter's age. Anorexia has the highest mortality rate of all psychiatric disorders, according to research by Evelyn Attia, Director of the Center for Eating Disorders at New York-Presbyterian Hospital. It can cause long-term damage to internal organs, infertility and osteoporosis. Eating disorders are notoriously difficult for parents to handle; one of the worst phases must be before the illness is acknowledged and diagnosed. It's clear that there is a problem, but parents fear saying something that could make matters worse to a child who may be in denial, yet they're haunted by the consequences of not intervening. Then comes the difficult business of getting treatment and that can be a struggle, with long waiting lists for therapy and a shortage of beds. Life has stalled and independence seems impossible.

Karen, whose 32-year-old daughter first became ill when she was 20, says, 'Your child is stuck and you're stuck. Maisie's illness stopped her in her tracks at a time when her friends – and eventually her siblings – were starting to explore their own independence.'

Starvation affects the part of the brain that deals with managing relationships. Sufferers often become isolated and less able to make and keep friends, and that is exacerbated if the illness has excluded them from the process of learning how to build and maintain relationships. As a result, the bond with a parent takes on an exaggerated importance. Emotions are heightened on both sides. Stress, anxiety and fear make it difficult for parents to step back and react in a calm and considered way.

Karen remembers, 'When I was frightened I'd revert to the way I now know you're *not* supposed to behave. When Maisie first became seriously ill it was panic stations. Everything was skewed because we were so scared. She was on the brink of organ failure and we were just totally focused on getting her into hospital. But there's so much pressure on specialist services that sufferers often don't get the help they need until the illness is entrenched. It's even worse now.' Karen first noticed her daughter's dramatic weight loss when she visited her at university. Within weeks her weight had plummeted to a point where she had to abandon her studies and move back home. Since then she has been in and out of hospital several times.

People with eating disorders are often depressed, irrational and unreasonable. Communication is further complicated by a tendency to interpret what other people say in a negative way, while kindness and positive emotions are ignored. For 20 years, Gill Todd, a psychiatric nurse, ran workshops for parents at the Maudsley Hospital in London, a centre of excellence for the treatment of eating disorders. She advises parents, 'You can't expect your child to hear what you say in the way you want them to hear it, because they will always fall on the negative side of whatever you say, even if you haven't meant it. They don't have any self-compassion when they make mistakes and they don't get compassion from relationships with other people. So, parents have to be very thoughtful because this is not normal communication.'

Living with an eating disorder sufferer

It's very common for adult sufferers to live at home. A recent study of Gill Todd's Maudsley patients who were over 18 found that more than 70 per cent lived with their parents. She explains why: 'Their whole development has been arrested. They haven't been able to finish university, they haven't done the things adult children need to do to separate themselves. They are often frightened of leaving home.'

Eating disorder sufferers lag behind their peers in learning how to look after themselves, both emotionally and practically, to feel OK on their own and manage relationships. It's a big challenge for parents to nudge them towards acquiring these skills as they recover, so that they can eventually move out and into a place of their own. Gill Todd believes it helps to plan progress to full self-sufficiency in gradual steps, like cooking for themselves and doing their own washing. That way when the move actually happens, it is much easier for the parent to believe that their child can manage alone. This is important with all adult children and it doesn't mean paying their bills and popping round every five minutes.

Yet when a child is ill, parents' protective instincts go into overdrive and that hampers progress towards confidence building and independence. It can be particularly hard for mothers to avoid being overprotective, according to Jenny Langley, whose son suffered from anorexia as a teenager, 'because the mums are the ones who are really caught up in that emotional web'.

Jenny works with Gill Todd and they both agree that it is incredibly hard for parents to get the balance between being protective and encouraging the change of behaviour that is essential. Rather than offering advice, it's better to ask permission to make suggestions and then offer a few options to choose from.

Gill Todd says, 'Parents often say things like "I won't be here to look after you…" That's the fear talking, and it's just going to push that person's self-confidence down. If you want someone to be independent, you have to let go. You've got to give them some personal space and allow them to make mistakes. It's all about raising their self-esteem and helping them to have self-belief. If you're intrusive in somebody's life, you give the message that they can never learn to look after themselves. You have to steel yourself and believe that they can. Because they have got to do this without you.'

Be more dolphin

I first heard about Gill Todd's workshops for parents from Karen, who, like many parents, went through a steep learning curve while struggling with her daughter's anorexia. Gill worked for many years with Professor Janet Treasure, who is head of the eating disorders unit at the Maudsley Hospital. They have both written excellent, easily accessible books on the subject (details in the Resources and Further Reading section at the end of this book). I was particularly taken by the animal metaphors used for the six different caring styles that parents adopt. It struck me that they're useful for all parents, whether or not their children are ill.

The same goes for so much of Gill's advice about relationships with adult children: the need for empathy and to really listen, for parents to step out of their comfort zone and question how they do things. She explains, 'We want all parents to be self-reflective about their own personality biases. Some people are more rhino-like – they want to fix things and tell you what to do – while others are more ostrich-like, they manage their lives by avoiding conflict. If you're a kangaroo, overprotective and always wanting to be involved, you have to learn to stand back a bit.

'There isn't a wrong way – there are no good or bad animals! – but we need to look at our individual strengths and be flexible enough to switch different modes on and off. You do the thing that's necessary at the time. For example, when you're trying to get your child treatment, you need to get your rhino hat on and then maybe step back a bit. This kind of self-reflection can also help mothers and fathers complement each other more, rather than go in polar opposites and sit in their own silos, which happens when you're under stress.'

Despite what Gill says about there being no good or bad animals, everyone loves dolphins! It sounds like an ideal all parents would aspire to: a gentle guide who swims alongside, nudging a member of the pod if they're swimming towards a danger zone, but who generally takes a hands-off approach. This signals trust and confidence in a child's ability to work things out for themselves, albeit with gentle guidance. If parents step in with a solution, it won't boost self-esteem or move things forward. There is no learning curve.

Yet parents love fixing things, because it's quicker, easier and makes them feel better. The only alternative is to learn to tolerate their own distress and that's a tough call if your daughter rings for reassurance several times a day, as Karen's daughter used to. She says, 'I have always talked to Maisie on the phone a lot more than is normal. Even now I am conscious of how to give a helpful response and how not to. I'm still capable of wanting to close down an issue or concern by fixing it, whereas what she really needs is for me to just sit with it, to let her say how she feels. I've learnt not to judge her by the way other people behave, but to try and understand what's going on for her. And that being inside her head is distressing a lot of the time.'

Gill calls this 'a reassurance trap. When an adult child rings, they feel better for five minutes or an hour, but then they have to ring you again. They're not learning to self-soothe, just like babies have to do, and to sit with their own anxiety. So they're not making a permanent shift. If a parent still wants to answer all the calls, they could try shortening them to a couple of minutes and end on a positive note. It's about chipping away at habits and changing bit by bit.'

Parents' well-being matters too

A big challenge for parents is looking after their own well-being. It's important for their own health: nearly a third of the parents who attend Gill Todd's workshops have clinical levels of anxiety and depression. But it's equally important for an adult child to see parents taking care of their own health and appearance, showing self-compassion, valuing relationships and interests. Yet many parents are resistant to thinking about their own needs – they feel they have to give up everything to look after their child. That's partly because, perhaps even more than any other mental health issue, parents tend to blame themselves and question what they did wrong. It doesn't help that anorexia, unlike bulimia, is so painfully public and strangers' stares increase feelings of shame.

Gill Todd believes that blame is not just misplaced, it gets in the way of progress: 'There is a lot of shame and guilt involved,' she says, 'and that definitely affects the parent's ability to think about changing their responses because they get stuck in a loop where everybody just does the same thing. You have to be able to acknowledge and role model that you can be different. And if you can role model that you can be different, then that is a hopeful message for your child.

'We all need to learn a bigger repertoire of behaviours we can use to deal with problems and difficult emotions. We all get into habits to help us cope, like having a glass of wine, and we don't ask ourselves, is this really working for me? It's true of people without an eating disorder too, but the eating disorder makes it worse because what people resort to every time is either not eating or bingeing, and this becomes a habitual way of dealing with emotional stress of any kind. We need a model that doesn't make families feel they're the problem, a model that is more solution-focused.'

SPECIAL NEEDS: DOWN'S SYNDROME AND AUTISM

Most of us don't have to think about what will happen to our adult children when we die. Our kids will mourn us, and hopefully miss us, but they will manage just fine without us. However, it's a major concern for parents of adult children with special needs.

Dr Anna Karin Kingston, whose 29-year-old son has autism, mild intellectual disabilities and epilepsy, has studied other parents whose adult children have Down's syndrome or autism. She says, 'I don't know any parent of an adult with special needs who isn't worrying about what will happen when they die and who will take over then. Many see themselves mothering indefinitely. My son says, "You're going to live to 110 and then I'll mind you." But the stark reality is that we cannot die, basically. I do worry about my daughter too, but it's different because Alex is vulnerable and will always be vulnerable.'

Most parents want their children to be as independent as their special needs allow, for their own sake. That's a very individual judgement but it also depends on the outside support available, as well as their own and their family's efforts. Support services vary enormously. Dr Kingston compares the patchy services in Ireland, where she lives, with her native Sweden, where she says no one is expected to have a child over 18 living at home, regardless of whether or not they have a disability.

Liz, whose daughter Laura has Down's syndrome, has always encouraged her to be as independent as possible and they now live in different parts of the country. Laura, 34, lives in a shared flat with support from carers. In the morning, she and her flatmate catch the minibus to work and in the evening, the carers pop in for a few hours to help with cooking and washing.

When Laura left home at 19 to go to a residential Camphill college for adults with learning disabilities, it was a painful but necessary wrench for both mother and daughter. Looking back, Liz says, 'At the time I hadn't realised that Laura had been getting much more emotionally dependent on me, because her friends from school were getting boyfriends and doing their own thing, so going off to college was really marvellous.'

Liz and I met in the early months of the COVID-19 pandemic, when she and Laura had just spent nine weeks locked down on their own. COVID was a sudden reminder that, despite her relative independence, Laura is still vulnerable in many ways and there are times when she needs her mum. As Liz says, 'In some ways Laura isn't really grown-up, she's still a little girl. When I kiss her goodnight she automatically puts her arms round me.' When the threat of lockdown was imminent, and fear of COVID mounted, Liz had an overwhelming urge to get to Laura and make sure she stayed safe. She left her husband at home, sped 200 miles down the motorway and got there in the nick of time: 'Having this time together has been lovely, but I was really pleased the other day when Laura said that she would quite like to go back to her flat. I thought it was really nice that she was wanting to go home and that she enjoys her independent life.'

Stretching boundaries

Of course, independence carries extra risks if an adult child is vulnerable. There are alarming stories of people being conned out of money or taken advantage of in other ways, even being abused, so there are finely balanced judgements for parents to make throughout their children's lives and the temptation to wrap them up in cotton wool is understandable. But Liz has always wanted to stretch her daughter's boundaries: as a teenager, she was allowed to do things like go to town on her own.

'You have to take a bit of a risk, although there have been difficult consequences sometimes,' she says. 'Because Laura is quite capable she probably does more than some parents would let their children do. She has a friend who is also in his thirties who has never done anything on his own and has always lived at home, although he's quite able. It will be very hard for him if anything happens to his parents, because that's the only life he's ever known.'

For Anna Karin Kingston, one of the most worrying risks is the internet. Her son, like many adults with high-functioning autism and mild intellectual disabilities, finds it difficult to befriend able-bodied peers and socialise face to face in pubs or other places. Instead, he socialises on the internet. Dr Kingston has even thought about joining some of her son's social media groups under a pseudonym to keep an eye on what's going on. She explains, 'Because Alex lives relatively independently, in a separate building on our farm, it leaves him vulnerable to the life on social media. This is scary territory, because as a parent you have no clue what's going on. Many get into trouble for posting inappropriate stuff. And because Alex is gullible, he often loses money through scams. I have to monitor his budget, otherwise he would be permanently broke. Inevitably it causes arguments when I say he can't have any more money this week.'

Dr Kingston would love Alex to be more independent, but it has been a struggle at times, not least because of the lack of support available in her area and because they live on a remote farm in rural Ireland. Alex's epilepsy means he can't drive, so he's dependent on his parents for lifts. And it's not easy for him to find work because he finds conforming to the 9–5 so difficult; he currently has a part-time job in a pallet business on the family farm. Although he has his own apartment, Alex is dependent on his mother for meals, lifts and emotional support. She has to nag him about tooth brushing, bedtime, eating habits and to go off social media at night time.

'Nagging may be fine when kids are teenagers but when they're approaching 30, it's really no fun,' she says wearily. 'As a mother you would gladly step back if you knew that someone else was monitoring the risks and providing the support when it was needed. But to actively work on independence you need the right support.'

A recurring theme of Dr Kingston's research at University College Cork in Ireland is the emotional dependence that adult children naturally develop after years of intensive parenting. It can make it hard for parents to step back, and for kids to separate, and that often creates tension. Her own son is deeply frustrated by his reliance on her: 'Alex sometimes says, "I need someone who understands me like you do." He is aware that we need to break away from each other. He needs a place outside his family home, where he can get away from parental nagging and control. He wants more choice in daily life. He wants sex.'

The intensity and closeness that continues into adulthood gives parents a special insight into a child's sensitivities, what they're capable of, what upsets them and what makes them laugh. This level of inside understanding usually dissipates in adulthood, but if a child has special needs, their life remains closely intertwined with a parent's. Alex acknowledges this when he says he needs someone who understands him as well as his mother does. And it's clear that Liz understands her daughter Laura like no one else, and can make sense of the world for her in a way that no one else can. She says, 'The older Laura gets, the more accepting she is. But there is always that contrast between not understanding some things but in other ways being really capable.'

Conclusion

How did the toddler who was inconsolable when you left for work and over the moon when you came home become the adult who rarely picks up the phone and who snaps 'I'm not a child, Mum!' in response to a helpful suggestion? You can't help wondering, how did that happen? We all know it's a gradual, developmental process, but it's still both disconcerting and marvellous to see in your adult child the five-year-old who loved My Little Pony and the teenager who gave you so much grief. What makes the relationship between parents and adult children so complicated, and so special, are these stratifications of joint experience and interaction that have built up over the years to make the relationship what it is now. What's confusing is that there are times when the toddler re-emerges. There are moments when we all want our mum, no matter how old we are. And there are times when parents find it hard to resist going back to being the mum or dad they used to be.

I wrote this book because I was looking for clues to the puzzle of parenting adult children. Few other adult relationships have such layers of complexity; friendships and even marriages are arguably more straightforward. But then few other relationships last as long: several decades in many families.

There were so many lightbulb moments during my conversations with other parents and experts. A key revelation came when one mother described how her children made her feel a confusing mixture of emotions, often simultaneously. She was torn, too: she wanted to support them, but she also longed to get on with her own life and felt a bit miffed when they brushed her needs aside. Similar feelings of ambivalence came up in interviews with other parents, as well as psychologists and family therapists. It's an indication of how complex intergenerational bonds are. And they're becoming more complicated, now that adult children are more likely to need their parents' support well into their twenties and again when they have children of their own. Meanwhile, research indicates that relationships between parents and adult children are strengthening and becoming more important to people and that all the hype about generational conflict really doesn't hold water.

Closeness and conflict often go hand in hand. Even parents and adult children who have a tight-knit bond get on each other's nerves. Adult children can make their parents deliriously happy and proud, but they can also make them feel hurt, past it or even disapproved of. It's often hard to understand why you're feeling infuriated, or what you've done that's so irritating to your adult child, never mind work out how to stop doing it! The parents and adult children in this book offer helpful clues. It's impossible to generalise about family relationships, because personalities and situations are unique. But hearing other people's stories about how they dealt with particular issues is one of the best ways to work things out for yourself.

The bond between parent and adult child is unique in so many ways, because at its heart lies the protective, unconditional love you feel from the moment they're born. When my mother died I was very conscious that I could no longer rely on the unconditional love I had taken for granted my whole life. Parents are the people a child can safely let off steam with, whether that's a toddler throwing a tantrum or a young woman frustrated by the world. They're the people who are interested in hearing about the dull details of life as well as the triumphs. Whatever their age, a child should feel able to sink back comfortably and be themselves with their parents.

So while it's true that a parent's job is never done, that's a good thing, because it keeps us alive, learning and growing. Adult children are life-enhancing, even when things are problematic. And as time goes by, they support their parents as much as the other way round, and the relationship settles into a new equilibrium. The day will almost certainly come when parents need more of their children's support, a prospect that no one relishes, but in the meantime the feeling of being there for each other, as equals, is to be treasured. As one father put it, 'When you raise your kids it's all one way; they are dependent and you have to support them. Now that they're in their thirties and in the prime of life it's tipped the other way. It's not that they have to support me, it's more that I feel they are good people to have on my team. They give me a sense of security; I trust in them.'

Resources

EMERGING ADULTHOOD

Society for the Study of Emerging Adulthood (SSEA)

A multidisciplinary, international organisation with a focus on theory and research related to emerging adulthood, which includes the age range of approximately 18–29 years.

www.ssea.org

FAMILY AND RELATIONSHIPS

Happy Steps

Professor Lisa Doodson's website provides information and support for stepfamilies, including workshops, coaching and meditation, both for couples and to improve relationships with adult children.

www.happysteps.co.uk

Ian Argent

Psychotherapist and counsellor

www.ian-argent.co.uk

Kinship (formerly Grandparents Plus)

Supports people who raise children when parents are unable to. About half of kinship carers are grandparents.

www.kinship.org.uk

The London Intercultural Couples Centre at the Child
and Family Practice

Offers couples therapy, family therapy and family mediation for intercultural couples and dual heritage families.

www.tcfp.org.uk

Stand Alone

Supports adults who are estranged from their family or children.
www.standalone.org.uk

Tavistock Relationships

An internationally renowned charity for practice, training and research to support couples and families.
www.tavistockrelationships.org

ILLNESS AND BEREAVEMENT

Cancer Research UK

Offers information and support, including a Cancer Chat forum.
www.cancerresearchuk.org

Cruse Bereavement Care

The leading national charity that supports bereaved people in England, Wales and Northern Ireland. It publishes a series of helpful booklets on grief, free to download, including *After the Death of Someone Very Close* and *When Your Parent Dies: Insights for Adults*.
www.cruse.org.uk
Helpline: 0808 8081677

INFERTILITY

The British Fertility Society

The BFS has a series of Quick Guides to fertility issues and treatment to download from its website.
www.britishfertilitysociety.org.uk

Human Fertilisation and Embryology Authority (HFEA)

The UK government fertility regulator provides information about IVF, clinics and other treatment.
www.hfea.gov.uk

MENTAL HEALTH

The Charlie Waller Trust

Focuses on young people's mental health, particularly at key transitions, such as the early years of their working lives. It was founded in memory of Charlie Waller, a successful and much-loved young man who took his own life when he was 28.

www.charliewaller.org

Mental Health First Aid England

Runs courses to help people to support others' well-being.

www.mhfaengland.org

The Mental Health Foundation

Publishes several helpful booklets, which are free to download and can also be purchased as hard copies.

www.mentalhealth.org.uk

Papyrus

Offers advice and support from qualified professionals about suicide and self-harm in people under 35. Its helpline – *Hopeline UK* (0800 068 41 41) – offers confidential suicide prevention advice to young people and anyone concerned about them.

www.papyrus-uk.org

The Royal College of Psychiatrists

Offers a range of information on mental health issues and treatments.

www.rcpsych.ac.uk

Sane

Offers support and information to anyone affected by mental illness, including family and carers.

www.sane.org.uk

Welldoing

Website with a comprehensive range of articles and resources on mental health and well-being. It is also a therapist-matching service for both online and in person therapy.

www.welldoing.org

EATING DISORDERS

Beat

Provides information and support to people suffering from eating disorders and to their parents, carers and families.

www.beateatingdisorders.org.uk

New Maudsley Carers, Kent

Offers workshops, worksheets and videos for parents and carers of people with eating disorders.

www.newmaudsleycarers-kent.co.uk

Further Reading and Viewing

GENERAL

'The Ascension of Parent-offspring ties', Karen Fingerman, *The Psychologist*, February 2016, Vol 29, pp. 114–117

The Aviva Family Finances Report, August 2012

The Bank of Mum and Dad, 2020, Legal & General, August 2020

'Child-parent Attachment Relationships: A Life-Span Phenomenon', German Posada and Ting Lu, Chapter 4 in *The Handbook of Life-Span Development*, edited by Karen Fingerman et al., Springer

'The Clark University Poll of Emerging Adults: thriving, struggling, and hopeful', Arnett and Schwab, 2012, Clark University

'Clinical Work with Intercultural Couples', Singh et al., in *The Handbook of Systemic Family Therapy*, edited by Karen Wampler and Leonore McWey, Wiley Blackwell

Dancing to an Indian Tune: an Education in India, Mary Searle-Chatterjee, Matador

Development through Adulthood, Oliver Robinson, Red Globe Press

'Death and the Family', Uhlenberg, *Journal of Family History*, 1980, 5, 313–320.

Don't Bite Your Tongue: How to Foster Rewarding Relationships with Your Adult Children, Ruth Nemzoff, Palgrave Macmillan

'Explaining Mothers' Ambivalence Toward Their Adult Children', Karl Pillemer and J. Jill Suitor, *Journal of Marriage and Family*, Vol 64, Part 3 (2002) pp. 602–13

The Empty Nest: Your Changing Family, Your New Direction, Celia Dodd, Piatkus

'The Family Lifecycle – The Learner Years', *Sainsbury's Bank's Second Family Finance Report*, 2016, www.sainsburysbank.co.uk

The Financial Journey of Modern Parenting: Joy, Complexity and Sacrifice, Merrill Lynch and Age Wave

Generations: Does when you're born shape who you are? Bobby Duffy, Atlantic Books

Getting to 30: A Parent's Guide to the 20-something Years, Jeffrey Jensen Arnett and Elizabeth Fishel, Workman Publishing

The Intercultural Exeter Couples Model, Janet Reibstein and Reenee Singh, Wiley

Intergenerational Financial Giving and Inequality: Give and Take in 21st-Century Families, Karen Rowlingson, Ricky Joseph and Louise Overton, Palgrave Macmillan

'Longitudinal changes and historic differences in narcissism from adolescence to older adulthood', William Chopik and Kevin Grimm, *Psychology and Aging*, 2019, Vol 34, No 8, 1109–1123

The Marriage Book, Nicky and Sila Lee, Alpha International

Mothers of Adult Children, edited by Marguerite Guzman Bouvard, Lexington Books

The Myth of Maturity, Terri Apter, Norton

'Out of the woods? Young people's mental health and labour market status as the economy reopens', Rukmen Sehmi, Resolution Foundation, July 2021

The Oxford Handbook of Emerging Adulthood, Jeffrey Jensen Arnett, OUP, USA

'Parent-child Relations in later life: trends and gaps in past research', Grunhild O. Hagestad; and 'Parenting, Grandparenting, and Intergenerational Continuity', Vern L. Bengston; both in *Parenting Across the Lifespan: Biosocial Dimensions*, edited by Jeanne Altmann et al, Aldine Transaction

'Parent and Adult-child Interactions: Empirical Evidence from Britain', John Ermisch, *Institute for Social and Economic Research Working Paper Series,* 2004–02, University of Essex

'Parent-child relations over the lifespan: a cross-cultural perspective', Gisela Trommsdorff, in *Parenting beliefs, behaviors, and parent-child relations: a cross-cultural perspective,* edited by Kenneth H. Rubin and Ock Boon Chung, Psychology Press

'Parenting adult children: a project combining narrative, clinical and empirical methodologies', Myrna Gower, Emilia Dowling and I. Gersch, in *Narrative Therapies with Children and Their Families,* edited by Arlene Vetere and Emilia Dowling, Routledge

'Parenting adult children – invisible ties that bind?', Myrna Gower and Emilia Dowling, 2008, *Journal of Family Therapy,* 30: pp. 425–437

Prospect: The Journal of an Artist, Anne Truitt, Prentice Hall

'Relationships between young adults and their parents', Fingerman, Cheng, Tighe et al, 2012, in *Early Adulthood in a family context,* Booth, Brown et al (eds), pp. 59–85, New York: Springer

'Second Phase Parenting: narratives of parenting when children become adults', Myrna Gower and Emilia Dowling, in *Narrative Therapies with Children and their Families,* edited by Arlene Vetere and Emilia Dowling, Routledge

Shane, Sheba and Sky, Paul Viner, Fursaken Tails Publishing

Sharing Lives: Adult Children and Parents, Marc Szydlik, Routledge

Student Mental Health and Wellbeing in Higher Education: A Practical Guide, edited by Nicola Barden and Ruth Caleb, SAGE

The Things You Can See Only When You Slow Down, Haemin Sunim, Penguin Life

'The Ties That Bind: Midlife Parents' Daily Experiences With Grown Children', Karen Fingerman et al., *Journal of Marriage and Family,* Vol 78, number 2 (2016), pp. 431–450

ADULT CHILDREN LIVING WITH PARENTS

Boom(erang)Time: An analysis of younger adults living with their parents, Maja Gustafsson, Resolution Foundation, June 2021

'The experience of co-residence: young adults returning to the parental home after graduation in England', Jane Lewis, Anne West, Philip Noden and Jonathan Roberts, in *Families, Relationships and Societies*, April 2015

Families and Households in the UK: 2019 Office for National Statistics

'Helicopter Parenting' and 'Boomerang Children': How Parents Support and Relate to Their Student and Co-resident Graduate Children, Anne West and Jane Lewis, Routledge

Home Truths: Young adults living with their parents in low to middle income families, Katherine Hill, Donald Hirsch, Juliet Stone and Ruth Webber at the Centre for Research in Social Policy, Loughborough University and the Standard Life Foundation, September 2020

'Marriage, parenthood and social network: Subjective well-being and mental health in old age', Christoph Becker, Isadora Kirchmaier, Stefan Trautmann, *PLOS ONE* 2019

'Returns home by children and changes in parents' well-being in Europe', Marco Tosi and Emily Grundy, *Social Science & Medicine* 200 (2018) pp. 99–106

'Young Adult Graduates Living in the Parental Home: expectations, negotiations and parental financial support', Anne West, Jane Lewis, Jonathan Roberts, Philip Noden, SAGE, 2016

ILLNESS AND BEREAVEMENT

Bereavement: Studies of Grief in Adult Life, Colin Murray Parkes, Penguin

'Communicating Cancer to Adult Children', Paula K. Waller,
www.patientpower.info
The Orphaned Adult: Understanding and Coping with Grief and
Change After the Death of a Parent, Alexander Levy, Da Capo Press
Talking with Bereaved People: An Approach for Structured and
Sensitive Communication, Dodie Graves, Jessica Kingsley
When Parents Die: Learning to Live with the Loss of a Parent,
Rebecca Abrams, Routledge

INFERTILITY

The *British Fertility Society* has a series of Quick Guides to fertility
issues and treatment to download from its website. www.british
fertilitysociety.org.uk/public-resources
Childbearing for women born in different years, England and Wales:
2019 Office for National Statistics
Conceivable: The Insider's Guide to IVF, Jheni Osman, Green Tree
Fertility treatment 2019: trends and figures, Human Fertilisation and
Embryo Authority, May 2021
European Society of Human Reproduction and Embryology, data for
2014 quoted by British Fertility Society www.eshre.eu
Human Fertilisation and Embryology Authority (HFEA)
The UK government fertility regulator provides information about
IVF, clinics and other treatment. www.hfea.gov.uk
NICE Guidance: Fertility Problems, 2014, www.nice.org.uk
Twin Stars and a Mother from Mars: Heartache and Joy in an IVF
World, Tru Spencer, Silverwood Books

DIVORCE

The Family Through Divorce: How You Can Limit the Damage, Janet
Reibstein and Roger Bamber, Thorsons

Home Will Never Be the Same Again: A Guide for Adult Children of Gray Divorce, Carol R. Hughes and Bruce R. Fredenburg, Rowman & Littlefield

Rafa: My Story, Rafael Nadal and John Carlin, Sphere

'Support across two generations: Children's closeness to grandparents following parental divorce and remarriage', Lussier, Deater-Deckard, Dunn and Davies, *Journal of Family Psychology*, 2002, Vol 16, Part 3, 363–375

'Understanding Children's Family Worlds: Family Transitions and Children's Outcome', Judy Dunn, *Merrill-Palmer Quarterly* Vol 50, No. 3, July 2004, pp. 224–235, Wayne State University Press

The Way They Were: Dealing With Your Parents' Divorce After a Lifetime of Marriage, Brooke Lea Foster, Three Rivers Press

'Your parents' divorce is always painful', Ian Argent, www.welldoing.org, October 2016

CONFLICT

Hidden Voices: Family estrangement in Adulthood, the Centre for Family Research at the University of Cambridge and Stand Alone (www.standalone.org.uk)

Reconnecting With Your Estranged Adult Child, Tina Gilbertson, New World Library

When Parents Hurt: Compassionate Strategies When You and Your Grown Child Don't Get Along, Joshua Coleman, William Morrow

ADULT SIBLINGS

Adult Sibling Relationships, Geoffrey Greif and Michael Woolley, Columbia University Press

'Important Variables in Adult Sibling Relationships: a qualitative study', Helgola Ross and Joel Milgram; 'Sibling Influence

Throughout the Lifespan', Victor Cicirelli; and 'Similarities and Differences Among Siblings', Sandra Scarr and Susan Grajek; all in *Sibling Relationships: Their Nature and Significance Across the Lifespan*, edited by Michael E. Lamb and Brian Sutton-Smith, Psychology Press

'Interpersonal relationships of siblings in the middle part of the lifespan', Victor Cicirelli, research presented at the Biennial Meeting of the Society for Research in Child Development, April 1981

'The Role of Perceived Maternal Favoritism in Sibling Relations in Midlife', J. Jill Suitor, Karl Pillemer et al, *Journal of Marriage and Family*, 2009; 71(4): 1026–1038

Separate Lives: Why Siblings are so Different, Judy Dunn and Robert Plomin, Basic Books

Siblings: Love, Envy and Understanding, Judy Dunn and Carol Kendrick (Harvard University Press)

Sibling Relationships Across the Life Span, Victor Cicirelli, Springer

Sibling Rivalry, Sibling Love, Jan Parker and Jan Stimpson, Hodder

Siblings, Linda Blair, Crimson Publishing

The Sister Knot, Terri Apter, Norton

'State of the Art: Siblings, the illuminating perspectives offered by the study of what are, for most people, their longest-lasting relationships', Judy Dunn, *The Psychologist* Vol 13, Part 5, 2000, pp. 244–249

Why Can't We Get Along? Healing Adult Sibling Relationships, Peter Goldenthal, Wiley

WHEN YOUR CHILD FINDS A LONG-TERM PARTNER

Don't Roll Your Eyes: Making In-laws into Family, Ruth Nemzoff, Palgrave Macmillan

'Mother-in-Law and Daughter-in-Law: Friendship at an Impasse', Terri Apter, paper presented at the *British Psychological Society London Conference*, December 1999

Mothers-in-Law and Daughters-in-Law: Understanding the Relationship and What Makes Them Friends or Foe, Deborah M. Merrill, Praeger

What Do You Want From Me? Learning to Get Along With In-laws, Terri Apter, Norton

When Your Children Marry: How Marriage Changes Relationships with Sons and Daughters, Deborah M. Merrill, Rowman & Littlefield

When Your Gay or Lesbian Child Marries: A Guide for Parents, Deborah M. Merrill, Rowman & Littlefield

WHEN CHILDREN BECOME PARENTS

'Caregiving within and beyond the family is associated with lower mortality for the caregiver: A prospective study', Sonja Hilbrand et al, *Evolution and Human Behavior*, 2017, 38:3, 397–403

Celebrating Grandmothers, Ann Richardson, Glenmore Press

'Does Grandparenting Pay Off? The effect of child care on grandparents' cognitive functioning', Arpino and Bordone, *Journal of Marriage and Family*, 2014, 76:2, 337–351

'Five million grandparents take on childcare responsibilities', YouGov poll for Age UK

The Good Granny Guide, Jane Fearnley-Whittingstall, Short Books

Grandparenting in Britain, Dench, G, and Ogg, J, 2002, Institute of Community Studies, London

'Role of grandparenting in postmenopausal women's cognitive health', K. Burn et al, *Menopause*, 2014, 21:10, 1069–1074

ADULT CHILDREN WHO NEED MORE SUPPORT

'Adult Siblings of Individuals with Intellectual Disability/Autistic Spectrum Disorder: Relationships, Roles & Support Needs', Leane, Kingston, Edwards, December 2016, School of Applied

Social Studies, University College Cork, for the National
Disability Authority, Ireland

'Anorexia Nervosa: Current Status and Future Directions', Attia,
2010, *Annual Review of Medicine*, 61, 425-435

*The Boy Between: A Mother and Son's Journey From a World Gone
Grey*, Amanda Prowse and Josiah Hartley, Little A

*Boys Get Anorexia Too: Coping with Male Eating Disorders in the
Family*, Jenny Langley, Paul Chapman Publishing

*Caring for a Loved One with an Eating Disorder: The New Maudsley
Skills-based Training Manual*, Jenny Langley, Gill Todd and Janet
Treasure, Routledge

'Common Mental Disorders: Identification and pathways to care:
National Clinical Guideline Number 123', NICE, May 2011

Mothering Special Needs: A Different Maternal Journey, Anna Karin
Kingston, Jessica Kingsley

'Understanding cross-national differences in depression prevalence',
Simon et al, *Psychological Medicine*, 2002, Vol 32, Part 4,
585–594

Work is the biggest cause of stress in people's lives, Mind, 2013

STEPFAMILIES

How to be a Happy Stepmum, Lisa Doodson, Vermilion

*Understanding Stepfamilies: A Practical Guide for Professionals Working
with Blended Families*, Lisa Doodson, Oxford University Press

FICTION

Relationships between parents and adult children are an important
theme in so many novels, movies and drama that it seems inadequate
to single out such a small selection here. These are the ones that
have particularly struck me since I started work on this book and

have increased my understanding in all kinds of unexpected ways; there are, of course, many more.

All Adults Here, Emma Straub, Penguin
Beautiful World, Where Are You, and *Normal People*, Sally Rooney, Faber
Relationships between parents and adult children may not be the main focus of Sally Rooney's writing, yet her novels offer helpful insights into parent-adult child relationships, and the way adult siblings get on, from the younger generation's perspective. They also offer a vision of the way the world is for young people now.
Daughters-in-Law, Joanna Trollope, Black Swan
Grandmothers, Salley Vickers, Penguin
Little Fires Everywhere, Celeste Ng, Abacus
Sweet Caress, William Boyd, Bloomsbury
The final chapters explore a mother's guilt and ambivalence about living her own life since her daughters became adults, and her estrangement from one of them.
The Fortnight in September, R.C. Sherriff, Persephone Books
The Most Fun We Ever Had, Claire Lombardo, Weidenfeld & Nicolson

MOVIES

Hope Gap. Based on the director William Nicholson's experience of his parents' separation when he was 29, this film looks at divorce from each parent's perspective, and crucially, the adult son's.
Keith Richards: under the influence. Morgan Neville's 2015 documentary features the Rolling Stone guitarist talking about reuniting with his father and being a grandfather.
Meet the Parents and *Meet the Fockers*. Comedies that hit a nerve.

Tokyo Story. Made in 1953 by the Japanese director Yasujiro Ozu, this is a moving, meditative film about a couple visiting their adult children.

DRAMA (TV & STAGE)

There is so much drama that centres on dilemmas and difficulties between parents, adult children and siblings, from soaps like *EastEnders* and *The Archers*, a daily staple on BBC Radio 4 since 1951, to eighties' classics like *Dynasty* (recently resurrected), and more recently *Succession*. By nature they're often over the top, yet the adult family issues they explore are universal.

Comedy dramas on UK television touch a nerve too:

Fleabag by Phoebe Waller-Bridge, BBC. Sibling and brother-in-law tension and an unforgettable stepmother.

Friday Night Dinner, All 4, created by Robert Popper, apparently inspired by his own family.

Last Tango in Halifax by Sally Wainwright, BBC, explores a wide range of familiar issues.

Mum by Stefan Golaszewski, BBC. Lesley Manville stars as a widow negotiating relationships with her adult son and his partner while trying to carve a new life for herself.

The Royle Family, BBC. First shown in the late 1990s, it's got the lot: adult sibling rivalry; kids living at home; daughter's marriage; relationship with son-in-law, women as kin-keepers.

Snowflake (NHB Modern Plays), Mike Bartlett, Nick Hern Books, 2018. A poignant story of a reunion between an estranged daughter and her father.

Love love love, Mike Bartlett, Bloomsbury Methuen Drama, 2015. Charts the changes in one couple's life from the 1960s to the present day. A brilliant exploration of intergenerational tension.

Acknowledgements

I'm very grateful to all the parents and adult children who talked to me about their relationships so honestly and thoughtfully; this book would be nothing without their insights and experiences. A big thank you also to the psychotherapists, psychologists and the experts on young adult mental health and eating disorders, who gave up so much time to share their knowledge and wisdom with me. Their contribution is invaluable. Thank you also to Aggie MacKenzie for her thoughtful reading of the manuscript. And while this book is not about my own children, my experiences as a parent inevitably inform my work and I'm grateful to them, and to my daughters-in-law, for their support and understanding.

A massive thank you to all the team at Bloomsbury, especially my brilliant and incisive editors, Charlotte Croft and Holly Jarrald, the copy editor Jane Donovan and the proofreader Jenni Davis, and to my agent, Laura Longrigg. Finally, thank you to the staff of the British Library for creating a great environment to work in.

Index